INTERPERSONAL
RELATIONS

About the Author

Genevieve Burton, now a private practitioner in family and marriage counseling in Havertown, Pennsylvania, as well as counselor in a similar capacity to the Livengrin Foundation, Inc., is a member of the faculty at the Summer School of Alcohol Studies at Rutgers University, New Brunswick. Formerly, she was a professor in the School of Nursing, University of Pennsylvania, where she simultaneously had a faculty appointment in the Department of Psychiatry, of the University's School of Medicine. A graduate of the Germantown Hospital School of Nursing, with a degree of M.P.H. from the University of North Carolina and an Ed.D. from Teachers College, Columbia University, Dr. Burton has published numerous articles in professional journals on the subjects of nursing and alcoholism. Earlier editions of her present book, eminently successful in this country, have also been translated into German, Japanese, and Swedish.

FOURTH EDITION

INTERPERSONAL RELATIONS

A Guide for Nurses

GENEVIEVE BURTON, R.N., Ed.D.

SPRINGER PUBLISHING COMPANY, NEW YORK

Springer Publishing Company, Inc.
200 Park Avenue South
New York, N.Y. 10003

77 78 79 80 81 / 10 9 8 7 6 5 4 3 2 1

Library of Congress Cataloging in Publication Data

Burton, Genevieve.
    Interpersonal relations.

    First-3d ed. published under title: Personal,
impersonal,and interpersonal relations.
    Bibliography: p.
    Includes index.
    1. Nursing—Psychological aspects. 2. Nurse and
patient. I. Title.
RT86.B8 1977   610.73′069   77-2948
ISBN 0-8261-0294-8

Printed in the United States of America

CONTENTS

Preface to the Fourth Edition

During the years since the first edition of this book was published, the basic tenets upon which it is based have changed very little. Previous revisions provided additional material in two areas. Broadened nursing responsibilities and functions had made it necessary to include more counseling information. In response to requests for "how to" counseling techniques, the number of case studies was increased, providing in-depth information about talking to and counseling patients. The other area, that of drug dependence, including alcoholism, was given a full chapter, since this major health problem had grown at an alarming rate, while the preparation needed by nurses to cope with the problem had lagged. Therefore a chapter on this topic seemed essential. This chapter is now enlarged and updated for the fourth edition.

This edition also contains two new chapters that deal with topics of considerable current interest. The first of these topics is communication. In all activities, particularly nursing activities, good communication is the key to successful interpersonal relations. In this new chapter, stress is placed on nurse-patient relationships, although all of the nurse's professional relationships are discussed.

Second, recent changes in nursing practice have been in the direction of a broadened scope of nursing, inherent in which are rapidly increasing opportunities and responsibilities for the nurse in the community setting. These changes, which include changes even in nurses themselves, provide the focus of a chapter on the nurse in the community, in which the principles considered earlier in the book are made applicable to community nursing.

For their help in updating my knowledge of current nursing practice, I should like to thank Mrs. Jackie Rudolph, R.N., and Mrs. Pauline Horner, R.N. Additional thanks go to Dr. Ursula Springer and Mrs. Helen D. Behnke for their invaluable

editorial help. I appreciate not only the specific contributions
of these four people, but also their continued emotional support
during the writing.

GENEVIEVE BURTON

March, 1977

Preface to the First Edition

Although this book is primarily a guide for the young nurse with yet little experience, the writing of it was motivated by the expressed needs of practicing nurses, some of them professionally active for years. Many of the graduate nurses who have been my students in an interviewing and counseling course have expressed regret that in the early part of their basic education they could not have had concrete help in developing interpersonal skills. Even in classes of new basic students, still ignorant of most of their educational needs, there have been frequent requests for discussions that will teach them "how to talk to patients."

The major goal of the book is to increase insight and understanding on the part of nurses which will lead to improved interpersonal relations in whatever situation a nurse may find herself. Patients frequently ask a nurse for help with their personal problems. In many situations the nurse *could* help if she had the necessary knowledge and understanding of the way in which problems develop, of the needs of the person who turns to her for help, and of simple counseling skills. In addition, the nurse needs an understanding of her own motivations and emotions, sensitivity to the feelings of others, a knowledge of the dynamic interaction between herself and those she is trying to help, and, finally, the willingness to give of herself in helping others. Admittedly, these abilities cannot be developed through a book alone. But if this book creates an interest and desire in developing them, it will serve its purpose.

In the human relations field, there exist a number of books addressed to the nursing profession and designed to orient the nurse in the psychodynamics of human behavior and allied subjects; for a nurse with a background of nursing experience they are distinctly valuable. The student nurse and the young graduate, however, have a limited frame of reference for utilizing theoretical concepts and principles. This new book, therefore, has been deliberately kept simple. It attempts to make the theories behind psychodynamics, interpersonal relations and counseling technics meaningful through the extensive use of case material, so that the nurse will be able to relate theories and concepts to her work and her own life. It discusses how nurses may utilize their knowledge of personality development and family influences to gain insight into their own motivations and behavior and to increase their skill in working with their co-workers and in helping their patients. The patients you meet in these pages are mainly people like you and me who are essentially "normal," but who in times of stress, such as illness, deviate from their usual behavior—in need to be understood by the nurse and helped by her skills in handling interpersonal relations.

It was with some guilt feeling that I consistently referred to the nurse with a feminine pronoun. With this admission, I wish to make an apology to the male nurses who may use this book.

To all those who have contributed to the completion of this book I wish to express my thanks: to Miss Sarah Binder and my niece, Miss Edith May Harbison, for their clerical help in preparing the manuscript, to Miss Charlotte E. Bentley, R.N., for support with case material, suggestions and proofreading, and to my husband, W. Laurence Casebeer, for his forbearance and, beyond that, for supplying the layman's view. There are hundreds of others who, unknowingly perhaps, have contributed to the book—co-workers in a variety of professional experiences, patients, people who have tried to help me, people whom I have tried to help, and particularly, my students who, over the years, have taught me far more than they can realize. To all of these people I am grateful. For it was in my contacts with them that the thoughts presented here had their roots, were nurtured and, finally, matured.

GENEVIEVE BURTON

1

Human Relations in Nursing

Practically all of life on a human level involves relationships with other people. We have to say "practically all" because there may be rare, very rare, instances in which a human being has cut himself off from all contacts with other humans. But for most of us life consists from birth until death of relating to other people. Sometimes these relationships are highly personal and very precious. Sometimes they are quite casual and impersonal, not having much influence on us or significance for us at all. Whether a relationship with someone else is very meaningful and important to us, or whether it is a taken-for-granted, unimportant relationship, it is composed of an interaction between two people, it is an *interpersonal* relationship.

Reactions and interactions

Not long ago I went to a large department store to buy a small gift for a relative. Not only was the store crowded, but the counter where I shopped to make my purchase was crowded, and I had to wait. When the saleswoman got to me I was feeling neither warm toward her nor was I feeling particularly "put out." I was "neutral"—just waiting my turn like everyone else. The saleslady herself was warm, vibrant and friendly. She may have been this way, in spite of all the hard work, milling crowds and tired feet, because of a pleasant interaction *she* had had with someone else. At any rate, marked pleasantness was the behavior she presented to me. I reacted to her behavior by being equally pleasant because she made me feel good. Perhaps she made me feel important. But I was pleasant right back to her. She *reacted* to my *reaction* by re-

1

maining pleasant and friendly. I left there with a warm comfortable glow of well-being. Here was an example of a relatively
insignificant impersonal relationship between two human
beings, consisting of a simple interaction of feeling between
two strangers. Beyond making my day momentarily more pleasant, this brief impersonal relationship with another human
being had little influence on my life.

As contrasted to this, the interaction in a more personal
relationship may have a great deal of influence. Suppose you
leave the nurses home for a date with your current boy friend.
You are not yet sure how much he means to you, but you are
fond of him and you anticipate seeing him. Your feeling of
anticipation and pleasure reaches him, and he reacts in kind
by showing pleasure at seeing you. This makes you feel good
and *you* react to *his* reaction of your initial feeling by continuing to let him know that you are enjoying being with him.
This is a much more *personal* relationship than the one described before, and because it is very personal it may, of course,
lead to something quite meaningful and desirable in your life.

Both of these illustrations might have been presented just
as well from a negative point of view. For instance, even
though this boy meant a great deal to you it is possible that
you, because of other events of the day, might have greeted
him in a very disgruntled, unhappy way. Assuming that he
had been anticipating seeing you, in spite of his anticipated
pleasure he might have reacted to your depressed state of mind
with irritability. You, in turn, might have reacted to his irritability with annoyance of your own. Then, unless one of you
consciously tried to stop this build-up by seeing what was
happening in this interpersonal relationship, it could have
progressed into a real fight which might become equally meaningful in your life, but possibly quite undesirable.

Between these two extremes in interpersonal relationhips,
the one impersonal and unimportant and the other very personal and quite important, lie hundreds or thousands of others.
While everyone's life centers around interpersonal relationships,

there are some occupations or ways of life in which relationships with others have paramount importance in terms of success and happiness. Nursing is one profession in which satisfaction, happiness and success are dependent to a great extent on the skills a nurse has developed in promoting good interpersonal relations. The day-by-day routine of a nurse's work, whether she does bedside nursing in a hospital, or public health nursing in the community, whether she is an operating room supervisor or an instructor or a nurse in industry, consists of a series of interpersonal relationships. In any type of nursing she is interacting in a variety of situations with many different kinds of people. The success she experiences in her chosen field in her efforts to help other people will depend upon her ability to interact with them in a positive way. It will depend upon the interpersonal relationships she experiences and upon how she *uses* herself in these relationships.

People are different

Because of the diversity of personality and background among the people she meets, it is almost misleading to talk about a nurse's "day-by-day routine." Routine there may be in the kind of physical care she gives to patients or in the teaching she is required to do or in many of her functions. But in relating to people, whether patients or doctors or co-workers, there can be no routine, because all of these relationships involve two people. They are dependent upon the other person as well as upon the nurse herself.

Reading a thermometer, quite desirably, becomes a routinized part of a larger routine. The thermometer is always the same. It is always scaled in the same way. The numbers on it do not change. The little arrow denoting a "normal" temperature is always at the same point. Given certain conditions (heat or fever of a specified amount) the mercury rises to a certain point until shaken down into the bulb again. Unless the thermometer is dropped and broken, the well-behaved, predictable mercury stays in the tube and bulb where it belongs. People are not like this. They are not the same. They are not predictable. They are not all built alike, they do not think alike, they do not react alike. Given certain specific conditions, there is no way of predicting how two different people are going to react. The interpersonal part of nursing can never, and should never, be considered "routine." The nurse who attempts to make her interpersonal relationships as routine as her other work will deprive herself of much of the satisfaction she should be experiencing in nursing. In addition she will not be making the wholehearted contribution to others which, for her as a nurse, is a professional responsibility.

No two patients will react in exactly the same way to the stress of illness. No two nurses will react in exactly the same way to one particular patient. This is impossible because of the presence of *inter*action. Your own unique personality causes you to react in a certain way to the unique personality of someone else. Even though *your* personality remains the same, you cannot react to B in the same way you react to A because their personalities and behavior are *inter*acting with yours in different ways.

To put this in very simple terms, let us consider three familiar articles of food: flour, milk, eggs. If you mix flour and milk, the unique properties of both the flour and milk combine to produce something different from either individual item. If you mix flour with eggs, the combination is different from the first mixture, and yet, the flour you used in each instance was the same. Similarly, if you mix eggs with milk, the unique individual properties of each of these items are the same as when you mixed each of them with flour, but the mixture again is quite different. So it is with reactions and interpersonal relations. Each individual will behave in a way which will call forth one reaction in one person and a different reaction in a second person. The individual will then interact with another individual according to the reactions which have been aroused.

Whether interpersonal relations are to be constructive or destructive depends upon the way in which personalities interact with each other. A consideration of this necessarily takes us back a step further to what produces personalities. How do they develop?

Understanding self and others

The ability of a nurse to recognize emotional needs and to satisfy them in others is based on her understanding of how individuals develop, what methods they use in their efforts to adapt to life, what responses they produce in their struggle with conflicts, and on insight into her own role in interpersonal relations.

Behavior of others must be understood in the light of self-understanding. Most nurses consider themselves to be fairly insightful people; they usually have, or believe they have, an acute sense of social consciousness, a vital interest in understanding and helping others. This is all to the good, but it stops short of the equally desirable goal of exploring and analyzing some of the factors that produce a "difficult" individual or a problem situation. For instance, given an undesirable working situation or a difficult person with whom to relate, a nurse may conscientiously go on about her work, deploring the conditions, determined not to make them more complex or unhappy, consciously doing her "best," but at the same time maintaining a certain self-protective remoteness. However, if a nurse is to make her optimum contribution to herself and to her patients she needs to do more than this. There are questions she may raise in order to promote real understanding: Why does this person act in this way? or How did this situation develop? These questions should not be confused with similar ones that one frequently hears: Now why does he have to be like *that?* or Why did I ever let myself in for a situation like this? Rather, the meaning of the questions one may ask is what went into making this person behave in this particular negative way. What does he feel he is gaining emotionally by acting in this way? What were the factors operating to bring about this difficult situation? Following this, one needs to ask: Is there anything I can do to help him want to act in a more desirable way? Is there any way in which I can improve this situation? These are good analytical questions, but they still explore only one half of the problem, whether the problem involves an individual or a total situation. Unfortunately, too many people stop here, forgetting the other half, which is oneself.

A nurse, particularly, needs to be sensitive to the kind of reaction she calls forth in others. We need to ask ourselves: What is there in me which produces this kind of behavior in him? What is there in me which contributes to the development of problem situations involving difficult interpersonal relations? Why do I react this way? Why does someone or something annoy or frighten me, fill me with worry or anxiety, make me angry or irritable? Is there any way in which I can change myself so that I will react differently to what he does, or will behave differently in such situations? Do I really want to change, to react differently? What emotional need in *me* is *my* behavior in this situation attempting to meet? Answers to these questions lie largely in one's own family background and early experiences within one's family life. Attempting to find the answers can make our work with other people a dynamic, living experience which eventually will make a difference in each of us, in the satisfaction we find in life and in our relations with others.

The developing personality

It has already been stated that one's ability to relate to others in a constructive way is dependent upon one's personality development. How does a personality develop? What has made *you* the person you are today? What kind of personality were you when you were born? Has your personality changed any since then? What influenced it to change? When you kicked your way out of your uterine home and gasped for

your first breath of delivery room air you probably didn't
have much personality. That is, your personality at that time
was not developed enough to be noticeably different from the
personalities of other newborn babies. The beginning of your
personality was there, however, in the undeveloped physical
and mental attributes which had been handed down to you
from both your mother's and father's families. These were the
contributions heredity made to your personality. Also present
at birth were tremendous emotional forces associated largely
with the will to live. These forces made you cry out demanding
food and other physical comforts. The rest of your personality
(your unique combination of character traits, your way of
reacting to people and to situations, your particular hopes
and wishes and fears, the person you and the world recognize
as *you*) developed through the influence of your early environment. The term "environment" refers not only to the place
in which you live, and the physical comforts and advantages
you had; far more important, it includes all the people who
were associated with you. These interpersonal relations of your
early childhood had a tremendous influence on the kind of
personality you developed. Personality, in other words, is the
result of environmental forces acting upon the attributes,
physical and mental, with which one is born.

For another illustration of how personality develops,
picture a rocky coast with the sea beating upon it day after
day. Each rock formation is composed of certain elements.
These may be considered analogous to the mental and physical
traits human beings receive through heredity. Because of the
constant beating of the ocean, the rock formations may change
in time. Some are exposed to the full force of the water's
strength; others lie in sheltered areas where they may be worn
smooth by the flow of water, but not broken by it. Some,
unable to withstand the pressure of the ocean waves, will gradually wear down. Others will take unto themselves plants and
shells with a resultant change in appearance. But, basically,
the elements comprising the rocks remain the same. Thus,

also the elements of which we are composed, the gifts of heredity, essentially remain.

There is a complicating force in a human being with which the rocks do not have to contend. These are the internal emotional forces, our feelings and desires. Frequently they are pushing us in one direction while society pushes in another, and there is conflict between what we want emotionally and what society demands of us. Life is full of conflicts of this kind, and part of each unique personality grows out of the patterns we develop for resolving or living with, or adapting to these conflicts. We have to adapt in order to survive, just as the new-born infant needs to adapt to a new way of breathing and taking nourishment if he is to survive. Later on, when a small child's will comes in conflict with the will of his parent, the child has to adapt because he is dependent on his parent for survival. And so on, throughout our lives, we have to adapt, to conform to the pressures of society, if we want to live comfortably and happily. This pattern of adapting to the environment's demands on us instead of being able to achieve all of our emotional desires continues throughout life. The methods a person chooses to achieve satisfactory adaptation, the pattern developed by his particular ways of reacting, contribute to the creation of a unique, individual personality.

Our personalities, within the limits set by our hereditary traits, will be determined largely by our environments. The pattern of unique responses which constitutes an individual's personality develops by means of all the experiences of a lifetime, but primarily through the experiences of an interpersonal nature—through one's associations with others. Since the average, so-called "normal" individual continues having interpersonal experiences as long as he lives, it might be expected that his personality structure will continue to grow, change, develop. To a limited degree this is true. There may or can be some personality modification, even in adult life. But the *basic* personality structure is developed in the environment of our earliest years, the most influential part of this environment being the interpersonal relationships within the family group, or whatever substitute there may be for a family group (institutions, foster homes, etc.). Thus, no two individuals can react or behave in exactly the same way in any given situation. They will behave differently because they will have *learned,* in their associations with others, in their early years, that certain ways of reacting will bring certain emotional satisfaction. Without the individual actually knowing why he behaves in a particular way, he goes through life using the same kind of response, the same reaction pattern, that was comfortable for him and emotionally satisfying to him in childhood. In adult life his way of adapting, of resolving conflict, his reaction pattern and his emotional responses, in conjunction with his mental and physical traits, will become identified as his unique personality.

Differences in perception

The nurse who is most skillful in her relations with others and who has a high degree of inner satisfaction in relating to others is the nurse who recognizes and understands that differences in personality are going to result in differences in behavior and reaction patterns. She understands at least some of her own emotions and behavior and recognizes when her own feelings are responsible for interpersonal difficulties. If other people see things differently from the way in which she sees them, or react differently from the way she reacts, the good nurse is not condemning. She recognizes that such differences are inevitable, and she believes in the right of other people to be different from her. In constructive interpersonal relations the attitude described above is of paramount importance. It has to do with the concept of perception.

Perception may be defined as an awareness of something through sensory impulses. One hears something, that is, one perceives something through the ears; one sees something, or perceives it through the eyes, and the thing heard or seen makes an impression on the mind. But no two people have

the same impression or perception of any one object. Our
definition that perception is awareness of something through
our various senses is correct, but it is also limited because it
fails to take into consideration our emotions. The interpretation of what we see and hear—or even smell and taste—is
based on past experience. A telephone bell may be a comforting sound to one person whose past experience associates
the bell with anticipatory feelings of pleasure. To another,
the same sound may bring feelings of irritation or fear because
past experience has made the sound of the bell indicate unpleasant interruptions or unfortunate news. Accident cases
have proven many times that two witnesses who have seen
the same accident happen have not perceived it in the same
way because of their own past experiences and their emotions
related to those experiences. The woman who is terrified of
being alone in the house at night, regardless of the reason for
her fear, may hear noises which do not exist in reality. She
perceives something which is not there. This is faulty perception based on past experience.

   In the interpersonal relations with which nurses are concerned differences in perception are very important. No two
patients perceive impending surgery in the same way. Therefore in attempting to help two patients to be emotionally
prepared for an operation the nurse must be astute enough
to observe the difference between the perceptions these two
people have of surgery. Only then is she able to give them
the comfort and reassurance they need. No two nurses perceive
a patient in the same way. One nurse may perceive an elderly,
fussy woman as a demanding, cantankerous, mean old woman.
The perception another nurse may have of the same patient is
a lonely, helpless, pitiful old lady. No two student nurses
perceive an instructor or a head nurse, or a supervisor, or even
one of their classmates, in exactly the same way. A supervisor
may be perceived by one student to be a kind, just, understanding person. Another student may see the same supervisor
as a tyrant who is incompetent and unfair. Although in reality

one or more of these adjectives may describe the supervisor, the difference in these two perceptions lies at least partly within the feelings of the two student nurses doing the perceiving. It is quite possible that the first student is sure of herself; having a strong belief in her own worth and capabilities she is free of the need to compete. She does not need to tear others down in order to make herself seem important. Feeling secure in her own competence she is free to look for the best in others, and she finds it. It is equally possible that the other student is unsure of herself, both as a person and as a professional woman with a contribution to make. Feeling inadequate and unworthy herself, she is driven by a need to compete with others, by a need to belittle others so that she may be made to appear more important, if only to herself. Not feeling competent or secure, she cannot bear to find these qualities in others. When she looks at others she is blinded by the reflection of her own feelings of inadequacy and unworthiness.

Just as two individuals have different perceptions of a third, so two individuals will perceive things and situations differently. For instance, no two nurses perceive their responsibilities in the same way. If a dozen nurses were asked to write a paper on the most important phase of their lives and work when they were students, there would be a dozen different opinions as to what was most important. This is necessarily so because the perception of each nurse would depend upon her feelings about her work. Her feelings about it, in turn, would be dependent upon the unique personality she had developed through all the experiences of her lifetime.

When faulty perception is carried to an extreme point, it can contain elements of danger. An example of this is the mental patient who, because of his own feelings of fear, anxiety, hostility and resentment, misinterprets the actions, comments and even the thoughts of others. For instance, the cook who prepares the food for a mentally ill patient may be perceived as a dangerous enemy who is trying to poison the patient. The friendly attendant who walks with the patient may be perceived as a spy who is trying to trap the patient in some imagined wrongdoing. Less extreme are dozens of examples in the lives of everyone. If we are able to recognize and to accept differences in perception, interpersonal relations will be improved; if we fail to understand and to accept the perception of others, interpersonal relations will be damaged.

Pre-conceived ideas

Perception is influenced by one's own pre-conceived ideas of what a situation or person will be. Related to the pre-conceived ideas are our prejudices and bias, learned from others early in life, and gradually incorporated into our own thinking and behavior. Our pre-conceived ideas of what something will be, determine to a great extent the way in which we will perceive it. For instance, the person who, in childhood, has been taught a mistrust of people whose religious faith differs from his own, will as an adult be either disdainful of other faiths or, perhaps, even afraid of their power. The child who has been frightened by a mustached, red-headed doctor may be uncomfortable as an adult upon meeting a mustached red-headed man before he knows what kind of person the man really is and without knowing why he feels this way. Similarly we perceive a patient, a fellow student, a supervisor, a doctor, to be a certain kind of person, based on the feelings our pre-conceived ideas have given us rather than on the reality situation.

Thus, among other things, our families provide us with pre-conceived ideas which have tremendous bearing on our role in interpersonal relations. Acceptance breeds acceptance, acceptance makes possible understanding, understanding promotes cooperation, without which nurses cannot function effectively. Applied to patient care this concept is of vital importance. Theoretically we are interested in the whole patient. The health of each patient consists of far more than its physical aspects. Good health means total well-being and this includes mental, emotional, social and spiritual aspects in addition to the physical. And yet, if we fail to consider his pre-conceived ideas and the way in which they are operating in his illness we are not taking care of the whole patient. For example, to the nurse a simple appendectomy arouses no fear or apprehension. She is familiar with the procedure, she knows what the operating room looks like, she understands the use of the various pieces of equipment, she knows that the surgeon is competent and that he will have adequate assistance in the event of any emergency. (She may know all these things and still be apprehensive if her *own* appendix is involved, but we are now assuming that this is someone else's operation.) The patient, on the other hand, may never have been in a hospital, let alone in an operating room. When he is about to undergo surgery, his experiential background may give him no help at all and he is afraid. In the name of good human relations, as well as of good mental health, these fears and *the right of the patient to have them* must be recognized.

The struggle with fear

If we were to set down in order of importance the diverse feelings of our patients, fear would lead them all. Fear, perhaps the most powerful of all the emotions, can give rise to behavior over which patients have little or no control. We need to recognize fear as it is felt toward the hospital experience itself, and not consider, at this time, the many ramifications that fear engenders. To us, as nurses, hospitalization can become a rather commonplace experience; we have become imbued with its routines and used to its functions. This is not true of the newly hospitalized patient. To the patient the routine is not commonplace, the hospital functions are not known. In many instances treatment is interpreted by the patient as an assault against the patient's self, against which he has no power to defend himself. Fear is particularly pronounced in the surgical patient, for obvious reasons. Fear begins to crystallize in the surgical patient long before hospitalization. Fear begins with the surgeon's recommendation of hospitalization; it begins with the keenest of all fears—fear of an unknown which may possibly lead to death.

In the hospitalized child, fear is more often manifested in a recognizable form than in an adult patient. It is true that many of our pediatric patients are unable to express their fear openly, but usually children are not devious in their expression. They scream, they cry outwardly, they slap, they run from us; fear here is obvious and direct. But how does fear manifest itself in the adult patient? Much of the answer to this question depends on the personality of the patient, on the pattern of reactions which has grown out of his experiences. The reaction, however, may be entirely different than we expect, and still rest within the framework of the particular personality of the patient. An important part of nursing care is recognizing the manifestations of fear. Fear, alleviated as far as possible—or at least acknowledged as permissible—by the conscious efforts of the nurse will go far in bringing about a quicker and less complicated recovery for the patient. Following are two cases which illustrate the fear reaction a patient may have to surgery. The first case illustrates also how a nurse may help to alleviate the fear.

TALK THE FEAR OUT

It had been only twenty minutes since the weary young nurse had been in room 301, reassuring and comforting the frightened pre-operative patient. Now Mrs. Callen's light was on again. As Miss Benton went into the room, the patient was sitting up in bed. Hesitatingly she asked the nurse if it was all right for her to drink all the water she wanted. Patiently, Miss Benton replied that it was all right, then added, "But wouldn't it be better if you tried to sleep now?" The ensuing conversation went something like this.

"But I can't sleep. I've tried. I don't know what's the matter with me. I don't think I'm afraid. As you said, there's nothing to this operation at all, but—I don't know—I . . ."

"Why don't you just put the operation out of your mind? Don't worry about it tonight. You need your sleep to be ready for it. Why don't you just close your eyes and try to sleep?"

Then, maintaining her manner of kind reassurance, Miss Benton asked, "Is there anything I can get for you before I leave?" The patient lay down, shaking her head in the negative. Miss Benton said cheerily, "Good night, then. Sleep well. I'll see you tomorrow afternoon."

A little later, in giving her report to the night nurse, Miss Benton spoke kindly of Mrs. Callen's fears and nervousness. She added, "I just came from there; she'll be all right now."

In a few minutes Miss Terry, the night nurse, was going quietly down the hall, in and out of rooms, making her first rounds for the night. As she silently opened the door of 301 she was surprised to hear the sound of muffled sobs. Moving quickly over to Mrs. Callen's bed, Miss Terry laid her hand gently on the patient's shoulder, saying nothing. Gradually the sobs lessened, and Miss Terry asked if she could help Mrs. Callen. "Nobody can help me, I guess. I just can't sleep. I had my medicine ages ago, but it isn't working." The nurse said nothing, but patted the patient's shoulder soothingly. The patient continued, "I don't know what's the matter with me, I'm sure I'm not afraid. Everyone says this operation is nothing to be afraid of, but . . ." For a moment the nurse did not answer, then she said, "No matter what people say, an operation is frightening anyway, isn't it? I mean, the person having the operation can't help being a little bit scared, don't you think?" "Maybe I am a little scared, even though I try not to be." "You try not to be?" "Well, I don't want people to know I'm afraid." "It sounds to me as though you think other people aren't afraid when they have operations." "Well, I've had friends who have had operations, and to hear them tell about it, I wouldn't think they were afraid." "Maybe *they* try to keep others from knowing how they feel, too. Sometimes it's better to let your feelings out if you want to."

The patient did not answer this immediately and Miss

Terry said, "Why don't you lie down and let me rub your back for a minute or two. That sometimes helps people to relax." Then, as Miss Terry gently rubbed Mrs. Callen's back, she said quietly, "You know, I think perhaps you are a little bit afraid." Questioningly she added, "Maybe you are afraid that you won't be able to take care of your family as well as you used to? You have three children, haven't you?" Mrs. Callen, with this kind of encouragement from Miss Terry, talked a little bit about her family. This was the first time she had been separated from her children and she was worried about how they would get along. She brought out also that she didn't want to worry her husband, particularly by letting him know how fearful she was because he had too much on his mind anyway. In addition to his work, he now had the financial worry of her illness and concern about the care of the children. For a few minutes the patient talked about her fear, what this operation meant to her, to her family. The nurse listened, occasionally saying something which would encourage Mrs. Callen to go on talking. The patient's crying had stopped, and she seemed more relaxed. She said, "You know, I believe that pill is beginning to work. I'm getting sleepy." Softly, Miss Terry said, "That's fine. I'll say good night now and let you go to sleep." The patient murmured a drowsy "good night", and Miss Terry left the room, quietly closing the door.

MEN, TOO, HAVE FEAR

The second case reveals to us a different way of expressing fear, a man's way, which might not be recognized as fear by an unobservant nurse. This particular nurse did recognize it, and we shall let her tell about the case in her own words.

"Mr. B. was my patient on a busy private floor of a large busy hospital. I read his admission sheet and mentally recorded two facts. 1) Mastoidectomies are rather rare in this age of antibiotics; 2) My patient was born in Scotland—an interesting variation in my work-a-day world. Mr. B. was admitted into a semi-private room about ten o'clock in the morning. He was not 'sick,' yet, and so demanded very little attention, and frankly, I forgot all about him until that afternoon when it was time to prepare his head for the impending operation.

"I entered his room. Mr. B. lay on top of the bed wearing crisp new pajamas and an initialed bathrobe. He was smoking. He was also fingering a popular magazine. I introduced myself, and told him I was going to shave part of his head. Obediently, Mr. B. crushed his cigarette and put aside his magazine. He swung his feet over the side of the bed and said 'What do you want me to do?' I positioned him and told him the few things I wanted him to do. Mr. B., 'cooperating' all the way, laughed and said, 'While you're at it, you can shave my face, too—I'll need it for the morning!'"

And there it was, observable to the nurse who was trained in observation, an overt expression of apprehension, shaded and tempered as became a man. Now, the question is, what can you do with this kind of remark? The answer is a matter of training and professional philosophy. We shall discuss techniques of counseling in a later chapter. Suffice it to say that the nurse's reaction to a man's fear is an important facet of the interview, and is a "feeling-tone" that the patient is quick to be aware of.

Look for emotional signs

Essential in the art of "devoting ourselves to the welfare of those committed to our care" is the skill in accurately observing and understanding the manifestations of our patient's symptoms, as the nurse in this last illustration observed covered-up fear. The clinical observations of the astute nurse have long been valuable to the physician in planning the treatment for his patients, for it is the nurse who, hour by hour, is in the key position to become acquainted with the physical as well as the emotional behavior of her patients. We cannot assume that the nurse, by virtue of her title, automatically possesses the skill of observing a patient's behavior, any more than we can assume that she knows how to recognize the manifestations of an inflammation on the day she enters training. Learning emotional symptoms is as complex as learning physical symptoms, if not more so.

Which of us, as nurses, have not categorized a ward full of sick people into "good" patients and "bad" patients. To the average nurse, what constitutes a "good" patient? Undeniably, the good patient is the patient who does not give us "any trouble." The good patient is cooperative, readily submitting to Rx. The good patient cooperatively gags on the Levin tube as it passes his uvula; he patiently extends his arm for the intravenous therapy; he obediently exposes an already over-perforated upper outer quadrant; he may grouse, but he submissively partakes of the prescribed 200 mg. salt luncheon, as though it had not lost its savor. This then is the good patient—he cooperates.

But what is a bad patient? Bad (adult) patients are demanding; they frequently want more than their normal quota of getting on bedpans, if, indeed, they wait that long. Bad patients pretend to take pills, and some have been known for the multi-colored collections of pills found by supervisors in bedside cabinets. (And what of the bad nurse who didn't administer the medication according to the accepted procedure?) Bad patients are prone to say such things as, "Nurse, what's in this pill?" or "You can take this tray right back again. I'm sick and tired of rice;" or "Raise the shade an inch or two. That's right, no a little more. No. There. No, nurse, I said an inch or two. Oh, if I could only get out of this bed!" There, then, are the bad patients. We have all known them, we can't escape them—and we classify them according to the degree that they interfere with our nursing routine. "Bad" patients, however, are sometimes better than "good" patients, if we only have eyes to recognize some of the emotions behind the behavior of the so-called good patient.

In discussing the personality differences among patients

and the resultant reaction differences, we have found, in brief: All patients do not openly show apprehension and anxiety before surgery or when they become ill. Some patients joke about it; others become irritable and complaining; others are quiet and withdrawn. Some patients battle with the doctors and nurses, rejecting treatment, refusing to accept suggestions, exhibiting behavior which professional people smugly term "unwillingness to cooperate." Others placidly act upon all suggestions, accept all treatment without a murmur of complaint.

We have seen the differences in the reactions of nurses also. In the first illustration, two nurses had the opportunity to comfort an apprehensive, frightened patient. Both young women were sincere in their efforts to want to help the patient. Both nurses realized that the success of Mrs. Callen's surgery and her speed of recovery were dependent, in part, on her being relatively free of anxiety and the muscular tension it generates. But only one of the nurses was successful in relieving Mrs. Callen's tensions and fear to the extent that she could sleep. Part of Miss Terry's superior ability to relieve her patient's tensions grew out of the kind of person Miss Terry was, and the sort of personality she had developed. But part of it, also, was her recognition of what the patient wanted and needed at that moment, and being able to give it to her.

The emotions play a part in any illness, not only as a causative factor but also in regard to outcome. An emotional disturbance can easily upset the therapeutic measures being used, so that nursing skills must be combined with an understanding of the patient as a whole, including the way in which he reacts to being sick. How does a patient react to his diagnosis? What is his attitude about the medical care involved? What is the dynamic meaning of the diagnosis in relation to his personal life? These considerations are vitally important. Too often patients are treated as though they were, during illness, separated from the rest of their lives. When they enter the hospital they bring with them not only a physical condition needing care and treatment, but also their resentments, their fears, their anxiety, their love, their hatred, their economic, social and marital problems.

Understanding and accepting pre-conceived ideas, attempting to understand how others perceive things, accepting the right and the necessity of other people to have perceptions different from our own are all basic to the promotion of good human relations. They are basic to nursing at its best—a kind of nursing that makes demands on nurses that are difficult to meet. Patients are not reassured, comforted and cured only by the words and actions of doctors and nurses but just as much by the unconscious attitudes of acceptance which speak much louder than words and deeds.

When perception was discussed, another important concept, that of reality, was introduced. The ability to face reality, to face life situations in a realistic way, is another factor in interpersonal relations that is learned, or not, in the early years within the family group. The degree of happiness or the state of mental health each individual will be able to achieve is directly related to the reality of his expectations. The more realistic an individual's expectations, of himself, of others, of his environment, the less likely is he to be faced with frustration. Too often nurses are frustrated and unhappy in their working situations because they expect too much from their co-workers, their supervisors, their patients, and even from themselves. They are hurt, disappointed, angry when other people fail to live up to the standards they have unrealistically established for them. In any of these situations the frustration grows in proportion to the lack of reality in an individual's expectations.

Unless a nurse realizes that she cannot judge the behavior and decisions of her patients and their families by her own standards, she will frequently be disturbed by people failing to do what she expects of them. This is not only disturbing to the nurse but it is upsetting to the other person, resulting sometimes in what the nurse loosely calls "lack of cooperation." To avoid this the nurse needs to understand the feelings lying behind the actions of others, and to allow others their own particular standards or expectations.

EXPECTING TOO MUCH TOO SOON

Mrs. Lang, an experienced public health nurse, knew after her interview with Mrs. Anderson that she had done something wrong because she had left the woman distraught and upset. The visit had been made in behalf of Mark, a fourteen-year-old boy with a serious congenital cardiac anomaly. His mother had died in a state tuberculosis sanatorium when Mark was four. When his father remarried and moved away, Mark was separated from his family and went to live with Mrs. Anderson, a childless family friend who was as anxious to have Mark as Mark was to go to her. She and her husband wanted to adopt Mark but his father would not consent to it.

Because the boy was apparently enjoying a happy normal life within his physical limitations, Mrs. Anderson did not take him back to the cardiac clinic as had been recommended. After two years during which the other members of Mark's family had been seen in the chest clinic, Mrs. Lang, armed with the family physician's approval, decided to visit Mrs. Anderson. During the interview, Mrs. Anderson berated Mark's father for his lack of interest in the boy. Mrs. Lang made her first error by reminding Mrs. Anderson that the boy's father was still his legal guardian and the ultimate decision about Mark's medical care was his, not Mrs. Anderson's. When Mrs. Anderson said that she didn't like the clinic doctor, the nurse's response was shocked surprise followed by a long explanation about what an important doctor he was. Mrs. Lang was expecting Mrs. Anderson to see the situation as Mrs. Lang saw it. There was no understanding of what a threat to Mrs. Anderson these two men, Mark's father and the cardiologist, were. Either one could remove the boy who had become the sun around which her little world revolved.

Mrs. Lang left the house angry and frustrated because what she had expected of the visit had not happened. Mrs.

Anderson, too, was angry and frustrated because she was terrified she might lose the boy who meant so much to her. Until now she had been able to shut the truth of Mark's physical condition out of her mind. Like many people in times of stress, Mrs. Anderson had closed her eyes to the situation hoping it would go away. Instead, along came the public health nurse, pointing up the seriousness of Mark's condition and reminding Mrs. Anderson that the father was the legal guardian and could have the child taken from her. Not once had Mrs. Lang offered emotional support to Mrs. Anderson or shown understanding of her point of view.

As Mrs. Lang thought further about her visit, she realized she was angry because Mrs. Anderson had rejected good medical help that was free of charge. Mrs. Lang also remembered how emotionally involved Mrs. Anderson was with Mark and how threatened she was by the thought of losing him, either through cardiac surgery or to Mark's father. With these feelings in her mind Mrs. Anderson could not possibly live up to the nurse's expectations of what should be done for Mark.

It is always difficult to accept the letdown feeling we have when someone does not live up to our expectations for him. When the other person is one with whom we are emotionally involved, the mutual frustration is even greater. It happens in the life of any nurse to be called upon to care for someone she loves. Unfortunately, this is usually a trying experience. Possibly the nurse's own unrealistic expectations create the most difficulty in these nursing situations. We expect the patient to behave like husband or mother or son or friend. Instead he acts like any other patient, sometimes frightened, sometimes belligerent, sometimes uncooperative.

MY MOTHER OR MY PATIENT?

Mrs. Hunt had been going to an internist for treatment of hypertension. After six months in which she did not respond to medication Mrs. Hunt was advised by the doctor to enter the hospital for a series of tests. Carol Hunt, a registered nurse, was with her mother in the doctor's office. She noted the look of helplessness on her mother's face when the doctor asked if they had any questions. Carol felt her first twinge of irritation when her mother said that she did not want to have an operation. Nothing had been said about an operation. Why did her mother need to embarrass her by making such a foolish comment?

Carol lived in the city near the hospital in which she worked while her mother lived in a small town a few miles away. For six weeks there were almost daily phone calls in which Mrs. Hunt questioned her daughter about the need for hospitalization. The pros and cons of hospitalization were gone over and over. Had this been any other patient, Carol might have been able to accept the behavior, but this was her *mother*. Carol expected her mother to act like the mature adult she had always been—stable, able to think for herself, capable of making decisions. When Carol could not cope with her frustration any more, she lost her temper, and her mother agreed to enter the hospital. This was the goal, of course, but reaching it this way meant that Mrs. Hunt entered the hospital feeling hurt and rejected in addition to being fearful and worried. Carol was left with feelings of guilt complicating her feelings of concern for her mother.

Carol's brother drove Mrs. Hunt to the hospital where Carol met them. She could see that her mother had been crying, but she expected that her mother would feel better now because she, Carol, was there. Carol's expectations that her mother would soon realize there was nothing to fear, was an effort to reassure herself. (We want to be able to expect certain behavior from people because it will relieve our own anxiety.) After the intern had examined Mrs. Hunt, Carol returned to the room to find her mother in tears. Here is the situation, in Carol's own words, as she looked back upon it later.

"I could not understand what was wrong. I did not want her to be like other patients because she was my *mother*. What would people at the hospital say if she was so afraid? They'd probably wonder what was wrong with me for not being able to put her at ease. I know what was wrong with me. I was just as scared as she was, but I didn't dare show it, instead I hid behind my being a professional nurse. As she sobbed and asked more questions I told her I wanted her to stop crying because she was getting me upset. I was ashamed of my reactions and couldn't understand them at the time. Once, right after she was admitted, I looked at the chart. The doctor had written three impressions of what might be causing mother's symptoms; the last was anxiety-depressive reaction. I could feel myself becoming tense: 'How dare she embarrass me this way, and at my own hospital?'

"That first day I stayed with her for several hours explaining the tests and procedures she would be undergoing and answering the same questions she had asked before. This continued all the time mother was in the hospital, and I was hurt because she didn't seem to believe what I said.

"As I look back on the situation, I can see how my own feelings got in the way of helping my mother. Sometimes I think my parents are about perfect, and I want everyone to feel that way. I expected her to act like my mother; instead she acted like a patient. If I had remembered that she was primarily a patient, I would not have expected so much of her and both of us would have adjusted better to her hospitalization."

Work with nurses in the past indicates that frequently they have a theoretical acquaintance with many of the principles involved in constructive interpersonal relations. They have an understanding of family life factors and their influence on human lives. They know something about personality development and they recognize and accept differences in people. But all such knowledge and understanding is limited, if it is not put to daily use. Unless it makes a difference in the way in which each nurse looks at herself, in the degree of her acceptance of other people, it is merely an addition to her store of academic information rather than a living satisfying experience.

One of the steps leading to the satisfaction of good interpersonal relations is to know oneself. The principles and concepts to which we are exposed in theory must be used to do some intensive exploratory work on our *own* attitudes, and in discovering the effects we have on other people.

Nurses come in contact with all kinds of people. In order to work with these people, the nurse must really accept them emotionally as well as intellectually, accept them with all their neurotic tendencies, their differences of background, their differing philosophies of life. The individual who from childhood has grown up feeling unloved, unwanted, unworthy may look upon others in that same light. He will find other people unloving, unworthy, undesirable. The methods he uses to adapt to life will protect him from seeing himself as he really is, but the person he really is will still be there underneath. It is these unconscious forces, in herself and in others, that the astute nurse must learn to discover, in an effort to control them in herself and to understand their influence on the behavior of others. Only in this way will nurses be able to make their maximum contribution toward improving interpersonal relations.

2

Emotional Development
and Illness

The start toward maturity

One of the ways in which we can improve our skills in interpersonal relations is by learning something about the ways in which human beings develop emotionally and socially. We have already looked at personality development as the result of environmental pressure on each individual. We know that the most important part of the environment in personality development is the people with whom an individual is associated in early childhood. The influential part of these early associations is the feeling which predominates. To explore our own selves, to uncover the unconscious forces which motivate us and other people, to learn how to understand and to accept others, we need first to understand the development of these early feelings.

Regardless of the fact that each individual has his own unique personality which makes him unlike anyone else in the world, each human being goes through definite stages of growth emotionally and socially just as he does physically. For instance, we know that an average three-year-old child shows certain physical characteristics and has certain physical abilities which are different from the physical characteristics and abilities of the average six-year-old child. Interestingly enough, in spite of personality differences, the average three-year-old child will differ emotionally in characteristic ways from the average six-year-old. In order for a child to develop "normally" in a physical sense, certain conditions need to be present. A developing child needs rest, sleep, fresh air, activity and a well-balanced diet. Without these things he will not be as strong, robust and healthy as he is potentially capable of being. In order to keep him strong and healthy emotionally certain other conditions are required. It is from the viewpoint of these needs that we will talk about emotional development.

Sometimes instead of emotional development the term "psychosexual development" is used. The inference behind the use of this term is that a human being's psychological development and sexual development are related. The term sexual is applied in a very broad sense, not in the narrow sense of referring only to genital sexuality. It doesn't matter which term one uses; we will call the development we are discussing emotional and social. It is emotional because it deals with feelings, and it is social because it deals with one's developing relationships with other people. But it is wise to be familiar with the term psychosexual, because it is used by psychiatrists and social workers to refer to emotional development.

Meeting emotional needs

As one grows and develops, moving toward emotional maturity, one attempts to satisfy two basic emotional needs, needs which are present in every human being from birth until death. One is a need for love and security. The other is a need for satisfaction or pleasure. Consciously or unconsciously, all human beings have as a goal the meeting of these needs. You may hear or read of other emotional needs, but if you study them carefully you will find that all emotional needs basically come under either one of these headings. Ideally one finds security by being sure that one is loved and wanted. Sometimes, particularly in adult life where love may not be present, attempts are made to satisfy the need for security by substituting for love other kinds of attention, such as recognition of achievement or respect. A hard-driving business man, a research scientist, or even a criminal may be struggling, fundamentally, to achieve something which will add to his status and prestige. But people like these will rarely find the security of loving and being loved through such efforts; they do find substitutes that help to give them a measure of security. Early in life the need for satisfaction and pleasure is related largely to physical comfort. Later on the areas are greatly expanded, although they still include the pleasure of physical satisfaction. The new-born infant in nursing achieves not only the satisfaction of appeasing hunger but also the physical pleasure of sucking. And how many of us are not familiar with the genuine physical pleasure of having a substantial meal when we have been very hungry, or the real physical relief and pleasure of going to the toilet when we have had to wait too long? Much of the physical pleasure and satisfaction we achieve in a lifetime is related to sexual activity. This is true in infancy and childhood just as it is in adult life. The infant's physical pleasure involved in sucking or eating or voiding or moving the bowels is believed by many psychiatrists to be akin to sexual pleasure.

When needs are not met

In the early years of life it is the family which provides an individual with love and satisfaction, or which produces frustration because it fails to provide them. When these needs have not been met in early childhood, an individual goes through life in what frequently is an endless search for love and satisfaction. Not knowing or understanding what is motivating his behavior and feelings, too often his insatiable demands result in his defeating his own purposes. We see this very often in nursing. There are patients who feel they are not receiving enough attention, no matter how much is done for them. This is true not only of patients, but of our friends and co-workers, and even of ourselves, sometimes. We have friends or relations to whom we give a great deal of time and interest, but it is never quite enough, they keep asking for more from us. There are doctors who seek a tremendous amount of "waiting upon" and respect from nurses and everyone else. And the more the nurses wait upon them, the more service do these doctors demand. There are supervisors and instructors who want constantly to receive the appreciation and adulation of their students but whose desires to be liked and appreciated are never satiated. All of these people are attempting to satisfy their own emotional need for love or security at the expense of other people. This is true of everyone to a limited degree; to a larger degree of people whose needs were not adequately met in early childhood.

Unmet needs are like a snowball which grows and grows. For example, the newborn infant for several months of his life needs to feel especially the warm touch of a mother figure who shows her love for the baby by fondling, and caressing him as well as by giving him physical care. If the baby is unwanted and unloved he passes on to the next stage in his emotional development with a nucleus of unmet needs. As a preschool child, if he is still unloved and unwanted, he does not have the opportunity to develop a feeling of belonging, a feeling that he is an important and worthy individual in his own right. These needs for love and recognition are added to those he already has, and his "snowball" of unmet needs continues to grow. If when he reaches elementary school age he is not accepted by his peer group, the youngsters of his own age, his needs become even greater. By the time this individual, who has been emotionally deprived all of his life, reaches adulthood, he may have what seems to be an insatiable need to be loved, to be reassured of his worth and to be praised. As a contrast to this unfortunate person, the infant who is cuddled and made sure of his mother's love moves on to the next period of his life with few left-over unsatisfied needs. If his needs in the next stages of life are met with equal satisfaction, he reaches adult life with a feeling of individual worth and assurance. Of course, still, he attempts to meet his normal needs for love and satisfaction, but he is sure enough of himself that he does not have to demand attention in abnormal or undesirable ways.

The importance of love

It should be clear now that the most important factor in the emotional climate is love. When we talk about love in emotional development, we are using the word in its broadest sense. To many people the word love has a romantic meaning, and this kind of love certainly should not be underestimated. But in considering the emotional environment, the love that is important is a warm, unselfish, outgoing interest in other people; it may have romantic elements or it may be the love between parents and child or between friends. Actually it begins with self-love, because at birth the infant is a completely self-loving creature. Through being loved by others, he then gradually develops the capacity to extend his love to others. From self-love the love the baby has next extends to his mother or whoever substitutes for her. Next, the child extends his love to others in the immediate environment. Then comes the period in his life when love is reserved largely for members of his own sex and age. This period is followed by adolescence and the gradual development of love for members of the opposite sex. Later we will look at these periods in greater detail.

One measure of emotional maturity is the degree of healthy unselfishness in loving. The term healthy is included here because a superficial kind of unselfish love may actually be quite unhealthy. An example of this is the mother who "martyrs" herself for her children in the belief that she is loving unselfishly. In reality, her love may be quite selfish because she may be doing this to obtain the praise of others.

When considering emotional development as it is presented here, step by step, there is danger of interpreting it as a series of well defined steps in which one period is left before another period is entered. This is not true. Rather the movement from one stage to another is gradual; all of the characteristics of one stage are not lost before the next stage is entered. Various emotional and environmental factors produce regression also. This means that a mature individual as a result of various circumstances may go back in his behavior and attitudes to those of an earlier stage of development. Or in his progress toward maturity he may move ahead, slide back a little, then move on again. Furthermore, emotional development is a cumulative process. As one moves ahead from one stage to the next, characteristics of all of the previous stages will be retained. For instance, given a normal situation of mother-child love, the child will retain some of his own love for his mother throughout his lifetime. A certain amount of self-love is retained; without it love for others would not be possible. It is equally true that human beings retain love for members of their own sex. Life for average men and women would be strange indeed if they no longer had friends of their own sex with whom to share interests. It is an important part of normal development that human beings cling to a little of all of these love experiences they have had in their developmental stages. The deviation from normal comes when these early loves remain strong enough to prevent the maturing of adult heterosexual relationships which exist between men and women.

What this knowledge offers nursing

Although the process of emotional development is interesting in and of itself, our primary concern with the subject is to utilize a knowledge of it effectively in nursing. In order to do this, three aspects of emotional and social development should be clearly understood and especially remembered. First, it is important that an individual achieve satisfaction at each level of development. If he does not, much of his energy, both conscious and unconscious, will have to be devoted to seeking in some form the satisfaction he missed. This accounts for a large proportion of undesirable, immature behavior. Second, it is possible for an individual, because of emotional and environmental reasons, to remain fixated at any one of these levels; instead of moving on in his development to the next more mature level he remains at an earlier level. Usually a person who shows this kind of immaturity is fixated in a specific way. For example, a young woman may have so much love for her mother that she is unable to leave her in order to develop friendships with young people her own age. At the same time she is mature enough in other areas, to go out to work and earn her living. Third, under certain circumstances people regress to earlier stages of development. *People always regress in illness.* The most mature, the most well adjusted people, will regress in varying degress 'when they are ill and are thereby faced with the necessity of once more becoming dependent on others. When nurses are able to recognize and understand these facts they will be able to accept their patients better and will be better prepared to give them the comfort, care and support they need. To show the significance the above three factors in emotional development may have for nurses, let us consider three patients cared for by one student nurse.

THREE SIGNS OF REGRESSION

Miss Brown is on duty on a women's medical ward. Before going to class she used a few spare moments to check on each of her patients. She stopped first to speak to Mrs. Kane. When Miss Brown went to leave, the patient said, "Here, take this; go buy yourself something with it." She spoke abruptly as she attempted to place a folded bill in the student nurse's hand. Refusing the money as graciously as she could, Miss Brown left Mrs. Kane's bedside and moved on to her next patient. The patient here, Mrs. Smythe, was sitting by her bed. As the nurse approached, Mrs. Smythe gave her a sheepish grin. "Caught in the act," she said, as she put a half-eaten cookie back into the box. After a brief conversation Miss Brown went to the next bed. Miss Bell was straightening up the top of her bedside table, which was already far more neat and tidy then most of the others in the ward. As she lay back in bed when the nurse approached her, she carefully smoothed out her neat covers.

Later on, as Miss Brown prepared for her weekly conference with the ward instructor, she pondered over the strange ways of the three women for whose care she was currently responsible. Why should Mrs. Kane offer her money? She certainly was not usually very courteous or kind. No matter how much Miss Brown attempted to do for her it was never quite enough; she rarely expressed any thanks. Any time or attention given to Miss Brown's other patients Mrs. Kane openly resented. And now she was offering Miss Brown money! It was difficult to understand.

Mrs. Smythe was so different. She was usually pleasant, although she had a very worrisome home situation. She talked a good bit about this to Miss Brown; it sounded like a desperately unhappy home. In spite of this, Mrs. Smythe was a "good" patient, easy to get along with, cooperative. Cooperative? Well . . . she was, except where her diet was concerned. Mrs. Smythe was a very heavy woman and was on a strict diet. She realized the importance of adhering to it, but somehow she could not resist the temptation of food. It seemed strange to Miss Brown that a patient as cooperative and eager-to-please as Mrs. Smythe could not be trusted where her diet was concerned.

Miss Bell was not like either of the other two patients. She was fussy, particular, worried about the smallest details. Everything had to be "just so." Any change in her routine was extremely upsetting to her. Her fussiness was a source of annoyance to everyone around her. When her meal was brought in, she meticulously wiped all of her silverware with tissues before she began to eat. Her washcloth had to be kept wet at all times so that she could wash her hands. If the nurses and attendants had time, Miss Bell would have liked to use her basin and soap for a more thorough handwashing job a dozen times a day.

What made them regress?

Each of the three patients, while not critically ill, was ill enough to require hospitalization. Each of them was reacting in her own unique way to the dependence on others made necessary by illness. The reaction, regardless of its kind, grew out of an attempt of the patient to meet the emotional needs which had been present since birth and would persist as long as there was life. These patients provide examples of the influ-

ence of family background on personality development, and of
the role unmet needs play in adult behavior.

TO LOVE AND BE LOVED

People like Mrs. Kane in all probability have spent their
childhood with adults who had never learned how to love. By
loving, remember, we mean the ability to give of oneself in a
warm, affectionate relationship in which there is a deep and
abiding interest in and concern for others. Equally important
is the ability to receive such warm, self-giving love. Not having
received this kind of love, Mrs. Kane could not develop the
capacity to give it. Like everyone else, however, she still needed
to give and receive love. Since she could not demand love, she
substituted a demand for constant attention, with the result
that she was less lovable. As a substitute for the love she was
equally unable to give, she gave material things.

Often children who are deprived of parental love will attempt to buy the companionship of other children with gifts,
treats, even money, if they have it. This pattern, too, may have
been learned from their parents, who used material gifts as a
substitute for the comforting, unselfish love they themselves
were unable to give. Thus the "Mrs. Kanes" in human society
(unfortunately there are many of them) struggle through life
seeking something they have never known but that they need
desperately, and destroying their chances of finding it by using
the only methods they have learned from childhood experience
to use. A vicious circle, indeed!

ORAL PLEASURE INSTEAD OF LOVE

The beginning of the story of the "Mrs. Smythes" in the
world is not too different from the situation described above.
The newborn infant is a completely self-loving organism who
finds his pleasure and satisfaction entirely through his mouth.
As the early months go by and he receives the oral pleasure of
sucking in conjunction of hunger, he begins unconsciously to
equate the receiving of food with the receiving of love. As he

grows older, he may turn to some other form of oral gratification. In early childhood this is usually thumbsucking or the sucking of a blanket or favorite toy. The pattern of seeking pleasure by oral means and of attempting to use oral satisfaction as a substitute for love and security persists in adult life. Even the relatively secure adult has some "oral" habits. The adult who has not developed a feeling of security through receiving the love and attention he needed in early childhood will carry these patterns of behavior to extremes. Thus we see the young man who is unsure of himself (that is, unsure whether or not he will be liked and wanted) chewing gum or chain smoking or biting his nails as he awaits a job interview. We see a woman, like Mrs. Smythe, made insecure by a currently unhappy home situation, reverting to the pattern of finding security in eating, just as she did in childhood.

PLEASURE VERSUS REALITY

To find the probable source of Miss Bell's pattern of behavior we need to move beyond the oral stage of life to the next period of development which is sometimes called the anal stage. When the baby is about fifteen months old his interest centers on the anus and excretory functions. By now the nerves which make it possible for him to learn bowel and bladder control have developed to the point where toilet training is possible. Until this time, the infant has been a relatively uncontrolled human being. When he was hungry he had been fed; when he was cold he had been given warmth; when he was lonely, frightened or in pain he had been comforted; when he felt the urge to defecate or void he did so when and where he wished. In our civilized society, however, it is not possible to have our physical wants satisfied at our own pleasure. It is an infantile pattern of behavior that follows the "pleasure principle," having what one wants right now, regardless of consequences. The mature person is able to postpone the satisfaction of his needs until the proper time. He can relinquish immediate pleasure in favor of future goals; this is living by the "reality principle."

Introduction to this more mature way of life comes with the early efforts on the part of the mother to toilet-train her child. The loving, generous mother now becomes a symbol of the society which demands that a child conform to its dictates. This period of life is characterized by conflict between a child's natural desire to retain pleasure as he has experienced it in the past, and a fear that if he does not conform he will lose his most important possession, his mother's love. Life becomes a struggle between his own wishes and the desires of his parents. While the focus of the struggle is on toilet training, the struggle includes all of the other areas in which the child is having to face reality. He is forced to recognize the meaning of authority. He is learning to distinguish between bad and good, which results in his introduction to feelings of guilt.

In civilized societies emphasis on cleanliness is strong, and many American mothers are outstanding in this emphasis. As a general rule, a child wants to conform, but he does need time. As is true in all areas of child development, it is important that he set his own pace. Sometimes the child is forced to move more quickly than he comfortably can, his failures are met with disapproval, and he feels threatened with the loss of his mother's love. In an effort to prevent this happening he gradually begins to place as much emphasis on this part of his life as he believes his mother does. Love and approval soon become equated with cleanliness and neatness, a belief related not only to excreta, but usually generalized to all aspects of living. Here, also, many "normal" adults retain some of the habits acquired during this period of their development. When this pattern of behavior is carried to an extreme, the result is the meticulously neat, compulsively clean person like Miss Bell.

Taken at face value, the abrupt, demanding behavior of a woman like Mrs. Kane, or the untrustworthy sneaking of forbidden food by someone like Mrs. Smythe, or the annoying perfectionism of patients like Miss Bell can all be most irritating and frustrating to a nurse. But it is part of a nurse's responsibility not to take patients at "face value." To give her utmost in care and comfort to her patients, the nurse must see beyond the obvious to the factors that cause irritating behavior. She will in this way not only be giving more to her patients, but also find immeasurably greater satisfaction in her work.

Emotional development continues

In presenting these illustrations we have by no means completed the picture of how human beings develop emotionally. Another stage of development with which the nurse should be familiar, because of her work with children, is called the genital stage. This period follows the anal stage. Once again the emotional need for pleasure and satisfaction is apparent. The child has discovered, partly as a result of toilet training, that handling his own genitals gives a sense of pleasure. Masturbation at this stage is a perfectly normal part of one's development. The sense of touch is an important one in adult sexual adjustment, and the foundation for good adjustment is laid early in life, in the genital stage of development. If the child is punished, scolded or threatened for "doing what comes naturally," he learns to repress his normal sexual desires and interests, with potentially serious results later in life. It is important that nurses be aware of the needs of this period for two reasons. First, the sick child may seek pleasure in this way because his security has been threatened by illness. The child who is ill is usually anxious and frightened, and must not be frightened even more by the scolding and punishment of a nurse who doesn't understand his needs and fears. Second, parents who are alarmed by masturbation may turn to a nurse for help or advice, and the nurse should be able to explain the child's behavior in a way that will help the parents understand and accept it.

About the time the child is ready to start to school, when

he is between five and seven years old, he usually loses his open interest in his own body. He has begun to identify with the parent of the same sex. This is the period in which the little girl has an interest in doing the things her mother does and she draws closer to her. The little boy wants to be with his father and to participate in the activities he associates with masculinity. There is nothing biologically responsible for this division of interest. It is a purely cultural phenomenon. By the time a youngster has lived six or seven years he has learned from watching others that his sex role in life involves certain kinds of activities, responsibilities and interests that are characterized as being masculine or feminine. Assuming that he has a sound identification with the parent or some other adult of the same sex, he usually moves without question into his role in our society as either male or female.

There are variations

Under certain unusual circumstances the direction of a child's development may be altered by environmental pressures. For instance, if a father has a little girl instead of the little boy he wanted, he may deliberately channel her interests into masculine areas of activity. Or in a home where the little boy has no adult male figure with which to identify he may pursue feminine interests. As an illustration of some of the difficulties which may grow out of the reversed developmental trend, the writer recalls the following:

Fred, now a young man, grew up in a family of several boys. By the time Fred had arrived, after several older brothers, his mother was almost desperate in her desire for a girl. With grim determination she made as much of a girl of Fred as possible. He wore dresses and long hair until almost school age. In the assignment of household tasks in their farm home, Fred was given all of the chores which are normally considered a girl's. The effeminacy his mother so carefully nurtured carried over (with her help) into his school life; she used her influence in having him given female parts in plays and entertainments, and rejoiced in the opportunity to dress him appropriately for the parts. By the time Fred reached adolescence, with its normal awakening of an interest in members of the opposite sex, Fred was floundering in a state of confusion about his own sex role. Never having identified with males, he had not learned to make himself acceptable to them. Never having related to females except as one of them, he could not easily learn how to accept his male role with girls. Fortunately, Fred's education created a desire to find out what was wrong; he did not accept his life as it developed, but sought help to "find" himself.

There are many others, unfortunately, who never become aware of what happened to them and who are struggling through life with a conflict for which they can see no solution.

Moving toward adolescence

The stage of development that begins with a child's identifying with the parent of the same sex is sometimes referred to as the homosexual stage. It is a period of natural interest in members of one's own sex. There are exceptions, of course, but in general this is the age of gangs and clubs, when the most important people in the child's life are members of his own age and sex group. It is a normal part of our development. Like the earlier periods, this one also provides part of the foundation of a stable adulthood. The period usually lasts until puberty, the physiological beginning of adolescence.

When the child is between the ages of ten and twelve years, the onset of activity of the sex glands results in physiological changes which have both social and emotional significance. This is the age of puberty, a period lasting usually two or three years. The physical changes which include developing breasts in the female, growth of pubic hair and voice changes in both male and female, may result in a certain amount of physical awkwardness. This is most apt to be true where the young people are teased about these changes. The major physical changes are menstruation in girls and nocturnal emissions in boys. If young people are not prepared for these maturing processes, they may prove to be very upsetting.

Conflict and anxiety produced by the physical changes tend to stir up the forces that have been repressed in early childhood. Emotional problems, which were not completely solved then, emerge once more, accompanied by some of the fantasies and pleasurable wishes in which the young child indulged. Old hostilities reappear also. The adolescent unconsciously attempts to handle some of these feelings in the ways he found satisfying earlier, with the result that some of his behavior is like that of his early years. For instance, he may handle his hostility the way he handled it in the preschool days —behavior akin to temper tantrums being frequently in evidence.

The adolescent must not only work out the changing relationship with his parents and develop satisfactory relations with members of the opposite sex but must also contend with new social pressures. As a rule, at this stage the youngster is faced with making vocational plans for the future. There is pressure toward preparing him to accept mature responsibility. Success and ambition require a certain amount of aggression which, in the past, the child has been taught to inhibit. These factors contribute to making adolescence the difficult period of life that it is generally considered to be. The teen-ager struggles toward independence, being constantly reminded by well-meaning adults that he is "too old" to behave in this way or "too young" to do that. Being lost in a chronological no-man's-land, where he is neither child nor adult, adds to his confusion and frustration. The result of these emotional and environmental pressures is usually a very mixed-up, irritable, unreasoning young person in tremendous need of support from his elders. It is unfortunate that at a time in our lives when we are especially in need of being loved we are often least lovable.

In resolving the problems of adolescence there are two choices. One is regression to infantile patterns of behavior, i.e., running away from facing the reality adulthood requires; the other is giving in to society's pressures and maturing as quickly as possible. There are some adults, perennial adolescents, who never face reality. It has been said that human beings are children for so long that they never get over it. Compared to other members of the animal kingdom, human beings are, indeed, protected and cared for for a very long period of time. However, the average person moves toward the pleasures of maturity while accepting the reality of adversity that the responsibility of adulthood brings.

The patient's adolescent phase

Even though a person reaches a relative degree of adult maturity, he still may not have seen the last of his own adolescent behavior. Most people regress to adolescent behavior during hospitalization. Rarely do we find a patient who does not. Illness brings with it, particularly in the hospital situation, circumstances of reality that force the patient to assume the role of an adolescent. Therefore, we should not be surprised or annoyed by patients playing the part to the hilt. The newly convalescent patient is more likely to do so than the acutely ill patient.

Adolescence is characterized by rapid spurts of growth followed by quiescence. It is also distinguished by other marks, one of which is the need of the adolescent to emancipate himself from his parents; another is to accept himself as the person he is; and yet another is to establish his independence. An adolescent is particularly sensitive in his relations with adults, resistive to force and manifestations of dependence.

In the hospital situation, the adolescent's role is re-enacted. Most patients go through a period of sickness when they are totally or partially dependent on medical and nursing care for their very existence. In the normal life experience, this situation is characteristic of the infant and young child. As the patient recovers from the acute phase of his illness, we expect changes in his behavior appropriate to his stage of recovery.

Seldom will we tolerate it otherwise. If we find the convalescent patient clinging to the behavior of the actually ill, we hasten to change this behavior to fit his new status, and rightly so. It is the method we use that is important.

What behavior is acceptable for the convalescent patient in the hospital? We know that convalescence is usually sporadic, not even and not always well-tempered. We see our patients feeling fine one day and feeling absolutely miserable the next day. This is similar to the growth spurts and remissions of adolescent days. The hospital parents are the doctor and nurse. They want the convalescent patient to emancipate himself from his dependency state, so useful and easy to maintain. Whether or not the physician and nurse are the "good" parents will be judged by the "good" or "bad" patients. The doctor-nurse team encourages self-help physically, and the truly "good" team encourages self-help emotionally.

In addition, the convalescent patient must learn to accept himself as the person he is, and to love that person. Be the patient an amputee, a cardiac invalid, a diabetic or a young hysterectomized wife, we encourage and teach constantly that the patient must learn to live successfully with his disability and accept it and accept himself. We want the cardiac patient always to remember that he has the angina pectoris; the angina pectoris does not have him.

AN ADULT CLINGS TO CHILDLIKE BEHAVIOR

Mrs. W., aged 42, had been treated medically for many years for ulcerative colitis. At last the drugs and diet to which she was adhering were no longer effective and her doctor admitted her to the hospital for extensive studies of her intestinal tract. Mrs. W. was small of frame and slender. She had been married for 15 years to a dynamic vigorous man who was a salesman for a leading plastics manufacturer. The couple had no children. They lived in a village which had earned the reputation of being an "artists colony." Mrs. W. was well educated, sophisticated and charming. She had studied art and her oils often appeared at various sales in the village but mostly she painted for her own satisfaction. Mrs. W's doctor was meticulous in his care of her and spent at least an hour with her every day. He ordered numerous X-ray and laboratory studies, telephoning to the nurse's station every night to have the reports read to him. The nurses were cautioned to be constantly on the look-out for the dreaded signs of perforation.

Mrs. W. was an easy patient to handle although she remained tense despite her medications. Every morning she would ask the nurses when her doctor would be in, and if he was detained and was late in visiting her she became visibly upset. Every afternoon she asked if her husband would be in that night. Her days, despite reassurance by the nurses, were spent in anxious waiting.

Medical treatment did not seem adequate to control Mrs. W's symptoms and she gained and lost strength uncontrollably. Her doctor called in a surgeon on consultation and he recommended performing an ileostomy to relieve the condition. Her doctor was very hesitant to suggest surgery to Mrs. W. because of her constant apprehension. However when an operation was recommended to her, her reaction was one of complete agreement, resignation and acceptance. Hearing the details of the ileostomy had no apparent effect on her. She seemed to understand and expressed the desire to do anything or to put up with anything if it would enable her to go home.

Mrs. W. was an excellent pre- and post-operative patient. Her operation was uneventful; she quickly learned to take care of her ileostomy. Ten days post-operatively, however, when the doctor was preparing her for discharge she began to run a fever each afternoon ranging from 101°F to 103°F. She was immediately placed back on chemotherapy. After three days of such therapy Mrs. W. continued to run a temperature elevation, but only at four o'clock in the afternoon. Because of this, Mrs. W's doctor deferred discharge, a decision Mrs. W. took in stride.

Numerous blood studies and X-rays showed no pathology, but the fever persisted.

One day the student nurse who was taking Mrs. W's four o'clock temperature pulled aside the curtain in front of the door to Mrs. W's private room and saw, to her consternation, Mrs. W. take the thermometer out of her mouth and touch it furtively to her burning cigarette. Carefully Mrs. W. examined the reading, shook it down a bit, looked again, touched the tip of the thermometer again to the tip of the cigarette, re-examined the mercury and, satisfied, popped it back again into her mouth. The student nurse, barely able to believe her eyes at this behavior also felt guilty for having spied on Mrs. W. The student would have to confess, too, her own lack of responsibility to the head nurse. The student well knew that she had been at fault by leaving Mrs. W. alone with the thermometer. "But Mrs. W.! who would have thought that she . . ." Mrs. W. was purposely prolonging her stay in the hospital and was, for reasons of her own, behaving in a manner that was unacceptable.

In the same way that sickness can bring out extreme dependency patterns in adults accompanied by a regression to an immature way of dealing with the hospital situation, sickness can bring out abnormal maturity, especially in the behavior of a hospitalized child. Such behavior astounds the inexperienced nurse, and she needs guidance in handling her own reaction to it.

A CHILD RELINQUISHES HIS CHILDLIKE BEHAVIOR

Danny was a five-year-old boy who was in the first grade in school. One week in spring, Danny came down with what appeared to be mumps. He was treated by his family doctor for mumps, and, after ten days in bed began to lose some of the swelling on both sides of his neck. Upon resuming normal activity for a boy his age, the swelling again appeared on both sides of his neck, accompanied by a sudden loss in weight. The family doctor referred him to the hospital for diagnosis. Histologic examination of a lymph gland removed from the side of Danny's neck, revealed the diagnosis—lymphosarcoma. Treatment for Danny was largely palliative. It began with X-ray irradiation to the neck. Can you imagine, being five years old and exposed to X-ray machines, which by their very size and strangeness are frightening even to an adult? Can you imagine being five years old and suffering from irradiation burns on your already bursting neck? Can you imagine being five years old and suffering from irradiation sickness? Even when you are only five years old you can guess why Mommy cries so often, and Daddy looks so stern? They are sorry you are sick. But Mommy doesn't need to turn her head when she cries, nor does Daddy need to try to make you laugh too much—you understand.

Danny did understand; he had a sense of understanding that was mature far beyond his five years, which was disquieting to the nurses. There was only one thing Danny wanted—to go home and no nonsense about it. He would clench his teeth and submit to anything if it would help him to go home.

The irradiation brought little or no remission of symptoms. When the series was over, the lymph glands in Danny's neck didn't seem to get any larger and yet his dyspnea and pallor increased. Insidiously the glands were growing bigger, but their growth was inward, encroaching upon Danny's trachea and esophagus. Soon breathing became so difficult that a croupette, a child's oxygen tent, was ordered by the physician. Cold moist oxygen is circulated through the tent. The child is placed inside the tent, a frightening and confining experience. Danny fought the croupette with all his remaining strength. He hated it. This was one treatment he refused to understand or accept. No amount of coaxing, or joking or patience on the part of the nurses would change Danny's mind. Danny would become so disturbed when his dyspnea increased to the point that the croupette was needed, that the beneficial effects of the oxygen were counteracted; the dyspnea increased when he was placed in the croupette. The physician, understanding Danny's fear, ordered the croupette discontinued.

Then began treatment with cystotoxic agents. Danny benefited greatly from this intravenous medication, and nearly miraculously the swelling receded, the dyspnea vanished and the dysphagia was less pronounced. Most obviously, his heavy noisy breathing, so characteristic of Danny since his admission, was gone. Danny began to prosper and day by day gained back strength and five-year-oldness. Finally he was so improved he was allowed to go home and to return to the out-patient department for close follow-up. The day Danny left the hospital, walking erect, holding his parents' hands, one on each side, he looked neither to the left nor right; nor would he have said goodbye to his nurses without his mother's reminder. There was no doubt about it—Danny was going home!

One evening about two weeks later, the student nurse working the evening shift was finishing up her notes. It was about ten-thirty. The children were nestled all snug in their beds when the phone rang. An anxious intern in Accident Ward warned hurriedly over the phone, "Flood the croupette, you've got a sick kid coming up." Miss S. flew to the private emergency room across from the nurses' station. Quickly and deftly she prepared the croupette and the room for occupancy. She was just finishing when the elevator door opened. At that moment she heard and recognized the sound of the child's breathing—loud, brassy, labored. Blue in his father's arms lay Danny. Danny couldn't breathe. His neck was swollen badly, his abdomen was distended with fluid, his feet edematous.

Miss S. took Danny from his father and began to unwrap the blankets from around him. She realized time was at a premium. And Danny, hater of the croupette, struggling desperately for air, wiggled adroitly out of his blankets, and, with a little sigh of complaint, crawled into the croupette and drew it close around him. He went on all fours into the corner, assumed the fetal position and smiled. He smiled not at his parents, nor at the frightened nurse—he smiled all for himself.

Such evidence of knowledge, of abnormal maturity, of acceptance of the inevitable in a five-year-old child can be quite shattering. Within two hours, Danny was dead of lymphosarcoma. Cancer had triumphed despite the heroic battle of its little victim. The picture of Danny, bravely huddled in the despised croupette, his nurse will never forget.

These two cases illustrate the influence of illness on emotional development, on emotional maturity. There is the woman who has found so much satisfaction in her childlike dependence on doctors and nurses that she does not want to relinquish this comfort to return to the world of adult responsibility. Illness has made her regress and she does not wish to move again toward maturity. And there is the exact opposite: A small child in illness has become mature beyond his years, with the capacity to fight for independence while he is able, and the capacity to accept the inevitability of dependence at the end. The message these illustrations carry is surely clear. A nurse to do the best nursing of which she is capable must understand how people develop emotionally, so that she will be able to help patients when, because of illness, they deviate in some way from average behavior. There is much more that might be said about the way in which human beings develop emotionally and socially. The purpose here has been to stress the interaction between behavior and attitudes and emotional development. An understanding of such interaction will help nurses in contributing to improved interpersonal relations, particularly in their work with patients.

3

Growing Up in the Family

The nurse contributes to mental health

So far we have considered the formation of personality and the course of emotional development, a knowledge of both of which can be valuable to the nurse in understanding herself and in enhancing her work with others. One of the goals of improving interpersonal relations is to help more people reach an effective adult maturity and emotional stability. The mental health picture of our population is an alarming one as evidenced by the tremendous number of people with various emotional and adjustment problems. If every nurse can lead herself and even one other person to greater emotional maturity and a better adaptation to life, think what a contribution this would be to a better society! And we may hope that every nurse, through her human relations skills, will be guiding many people to improved mental health.

The nurse's contribution, of course, can be only part of the effort which will be required to make a substantial change in our society's mental health status. The importance of the early years of life has already been demonstrated. If an emotionally healthy, mature, stable personality is to develop from the impulse-driven organism produced at birth, the burden of responsibility rests upon the family, particularly upon the parents. It is the parents, primarily, who provide, or fail to provide, the wholesome family life which is a healthful environment, emotionally and socially as well as physically. This chapter will be devoted to some of the family life factors which help children progress toward emotional maturity, toward what is accepted as desirable adult behavior.

The family life factors have significance for nurses for

several reasons. When a child is hospitalized, the nurses and doctors become parent substitutes. Because of this, the nurses have a direct influence on the child's development during his hospitalization. Obviously, unless the child is in the hospital over an extended period of time, the relationship between nurse and child will not have nearly the intensity of that between parent and child. Except for this fact, the principles which will be presented here as applying to parents apply equally to nurses, or to anyone else, concerned with the care of children. An understanding of these principles may also be helpful to nurses in dealing with adult patients who have regressed in illness and who behave like children.

Finally, nurses are frequently looked upon by parents as fonts of knowledge and information about child development. This means that nurses have the responsibility of helping parents understand the needs of their children, and of interpreting for parents what is involved in a wholesome family environment. Such help and interpretation should be given as uncritically as possible. Parents as a group have been the target of so much criticism, some of it just and some of it unjust, that many of them are terrified of making mistakes with their children. Their fear of doing irreparable damage to the "little psyches" of their youngsters often prevents their being the natural, spontaneous, comfortable people they need to be in order to instill confidence in their children. Some parental mistakes are pretty bad, but children are wonderfully resilient, and there is no point in a professional person (a nurse, for instance) making a parent feel more inadequate than the mistake warrants, or than the mistake has already made him feel.

The contributions of wholesome family life

With this word of caution, let us look at some of the conditions ideally considered to be part of wholesome family life. A human being must have certain specific opportunities during his developmental years so that he may develop into an adult whose behavior contributes to the general good of humanity, whose attitudes are accepting and relatively free of destructive influences, whose value systems are based on both individual and social integrity.

THE NEED FOR A VARIETY OF EXPERIENCES

He needs the opportunity, first, to have a variety of experiences that allow him to test the reality of the society in which he will grow and develop, the society to which he must relate, if he is to reach a desirable state of maturity. Many parents, in an effort to protect a child, will deliberately prevent him from having experiences that are part of a normal child's reality.

In one family, well known to the writer, there were four active, normally aggressive boys. The parents were most anxious to have a little girl. Their prayers were answered with the arrival of Jean, the fifth child. The parents, particularly the mother, had a very definite belief that little girls must be little ladies. After several years with lively, masculine boys, this was a natural reaction for parents who hoped their little girl would be the embodiment of femininity. The interest the boys showed in their new sister was short-lived due to constant parental admonitions to treat her gently, not to include her in their boisterous activities because she might be hurt, since little girls were different from boys. The boys played ball, rode bikes, roller-skated, went off on picnics and hikes. Jean was kept close to her mother and father, finally reaching the point where she preferred to be there. She was afraid to try anything new. During her preschool period, this situation was not abnormally far removed from the reality of our culture. School age girls, however, participate today in most of the activities open to boys. They *do* ride bikes, roller skate, go for hikes. Realistically, in our culture there is little difference between activities open to boys and those open to girls. When Jean entered school she was totally unprepared, both physically and psychologically, to take part in sports activities. So she withdrew, first ·in fear of being hurt, but later in fear of failure. Physically there was

no reason why Jean could not have excelled in at least some
of the school sports. Emotionally, she was not prepared to
participate, let alone excel.

Lack of opportunity to have needed experiences can be
of many kinds. Youngsters who are never separated, even temporarily, from their parents are not prepared for the possible
reality of loss of their parents through illness, separation or
death. When the illness is the child's own, and *he* is the
one taken to the hospital, the child's inability to accept the
necessary separation from his parents may make his nursing
care very difficult. A kind and loving nurse, who is just as
aware of the child's emotional suffering as she is of his physical
condition, can do much to help the little patient accept the
reality he has never before had to face. Children whose parents
do not share with them a difficult family economic situation
will have trouble facing the reality of financial management.
Young people who do not have the experience of knowing
that their parents have differences of opinion (sometimes honest-
to-goodness fights!) will be shocked when faced with the reality
of this inevitable truth. The child who is protected from the
experience of any kind of pain will accept with difficulty the
fact that pain is another of the inevitable realities of life.

What *is* reality for children will vary with different cultures, and, within a given society, with the demands or expectations of various sub-cultures. In spite of continued movement
toward democracy in our country, the experiences the subur-
ban-raised child of a prosperous business man must have to
prepare him for reality will differ in many ways from the
experiences needed by the city-born child of an unskilled
laborer.

The nurse must realize that the reality of her own cultural
background and her own standards may be quite different from
those of a patient. In working with a child not her own, the
nurse needs to remember the child's background and the home
to which he will return. This point may be illustrated by a
case which one student nurse will never forget.

A NURSE'S STANDARDS MAY NOT BE ACCEPTABLE

Believing in the importance of the good nutrition the young student knew in her own home and about which she learned more in her classes, she put conscious effort into improving the nutritional habits of her pediatric patients. One little boy was discharged from the pediatric ward to return regularly to the out-patient department. When the youngster was not brought back to the clinic for his first scheduled check-up, a social worker was delegated to investigate what had happened to him. The story she learned was amusing, but might have been alarming. The child while hospitalized had a total aversion to meat of any kind. This constituted a real challenge to the nutrition-conscious student, who persisted in her efforts to get him to eat meat. One of his orders during convalescence was House Diet, and House Diet included meat. With frightening stories of what might happen to people who ate no meat, and insistence that when he went home he must urge his mother to have meat for him every day, the student nurse was successful in her efforts. The child began to eat meat. At first it was without much enjoyment, but gradually he seemed to like it. What the student had not learned was that the boy came from a completely vegetarian family. His parents had strong feelings against eating meat and were horrified at the insistence of the youngster that at the hospital he was told he *must* eat meat in order to be well. They were also angry at the hospital. They refused to bring back the child to the clinic until they were finally assured that the hospital would not attempt further to destroy this one part of their way of life.

What reality is will vary also with one's physical condition. A child who has a physical defect, either congenital or the result of illness, will need experiences that will help him to accept the reality of his own physical limitations. Well-meaning adults, in their efforts to protect him, sometimes deprive the physically defective child of experiences he should have. In so doing they accentuate the differences between him and the average child. A more healthy approach to this is to emphasize the ways in which he is like "normal" children. This will lead to a much more desirable attitude of self-acceptance on the part of the child. An astute, understanding nurse can help the defective child in two ways: Without placing undue emphasis on his defect, she can *directly* help him accept his limitations. *Indirectly* she can help him by capitalizing on all aspects of his body and mind that are normal, and by her own acceptance of the child. This provides support for the child and an example for the parents.

To summarize: In order to know what constitutes reality within his own physical and mental limits and in his own particular segment of society, the child must have the opportunity for varied experiences of a realistic nature. The nurse who is caring for a sick child must know some of the realities of his particular social life and background, especially if she is going to help provide realistic experiences for him while he is in her care.

THE NEED FOR FREEDOM

As a child learns more about the realities of his cultural and physical milieu, his next need is for a gradually increasing freedom to determine and manage his own behavior. This should include the acceptance of responsibility for his own decisions, for the results of his own actions. Early in life a youngster is rightfully allowed the freedom to climb. When he is endangered by his faulty judgment he is rescued from harm. But if he goes on being rescued from the consequences of his decisions and actions, he will never have the opportunity to develop reliable judgment. Most adults who have become accustomed to this kind of "protection from themselves" reach a point in life where fate deprives them of their protectors, and they flounder on the brink of uncertainty and indecision. Although, admittedly, there are some adults who do go entirely through life with the assurance of protection from others. To some people, when they are beset by the need to make decisions or to take a risk, it might seem wonderful to have someone protecting them from their own errors of judgment. On the contrary, the adult who has never learned to think for himself and to be responsible for his own behavior and to accept the consequences of it, is only half alive. For part of the satisfaction of living comes from confidence in one's ability to achieve.

THE NEED FOR RESPONSIBILITY

This brings us to the third opportunity needed by human beings. Every child needs to feel a gradually increasing responsibility, not only for himself but one which has social significance also. By this is meant a responsibility for socially constructive enterprises. He needs to feel that at least some of his activity is making a contribution to society. The "society" of the small child is his family, and here is where his ability to make a contribution begins. If one compares the old autocratic family with the modern progressive family, one might wonder why the children who grew up in authoritarian homes and did not have the advantages of our knowledge of child psychology, were not more maladjusted. One reason is that the children often had to make a contribution to the well-being of the family group. Children were given chores to perform, not because the experts said it was good for them, but because the family was dependent upon their help.

In a hospital situation an alert nurse may help a child to develop a sense of responsibility.

SAM IS HELPED TO GROW UP

Sam was a twelve-year-old boy who was almost too overgrown to fit into a pediatric ward. Large, awkward and ungainly, he had great difficulty in his relationships with others in the hospital, both patients and staff. Not being an attractive boy in either personality or appearance, Sam used all sorts of disturbing behavior in seeking the attention he needed. He bullied the younger children, and behaved in a spiteful, nasty way with the doctors, nurses and other personnel. Most of the ward staff felt they were far too busy to have to put up with his unpleasant behavior. They scolded, threatened and sometimes when he was intolerable, would punish Sam. Among the nurses, however, Sam had one friend. As annoying as he was, Miss Wells felt sorry for him, and she accepted understanding him and helping him as her particular challenge. Using every opportunity to talk with him, accepting without condemnation his wild stories, but placing definite limits on destructive behavior, Miss Wells gradually gained Sam's confidence. She learned, through carefully listening to him and to his mother, that Sam had always been a problem at home. An only child, his mother was overprotective, and she never gave him the opportunity to make decisions or to accept responsibility. His father expected too much of Sam, and vacillated between cruel punishment and ignoring the boy in disgust. Miss Wells realized it was little wonder that Sam behaved as he did. Slowly tearing down Sam's distrust of himself and others, Miss Wells helped him gain confidence in himself. She began to ask his help in various little chores, not scolding when things went wrong, but praising any job well done. The first chores she selected were those which Sam could accept as being helpful to her. Gradually she asked his help in doing things for the younger children. As he became more helpful and cooperative, both staff and patients responded to him in a more positive way. This in turn was an added stimulus to further helpfulness from Sam. The interaction circle was established to the benefit of all. Although his parents recognized and appreciated the obvious improvement in Sam's behavior, it is doubtful that they were emotionally able to give him the same kind of healthy support Miss Wells had offered him. But at least during his four-week hospital stay he had the opportunity to experience the satisfaction of being given responsibility and feeling worthy of it. He was helped to grow even in this short period. All of this happened because one nurse recognized the needs of a frustrated child and decided to do something about satisfying these needs.

THE NEED FOR SUCCESS

Experiences in which a child is rewarded with a feeling of success promote the development of a sense of personal worth. Success helps develop attitudes of self-confidence which are part of good mental health. Failure in a child's every under-taking leads to lack of self-confidence and to a defeatist attitude which discourages the child from further effort. Sometimes parents are so anxious for a child to be outstanding that they actually cause him to fail consistently. This is frequently true when parents use a child to satisfy their own emotional needs. The standards they establish for the child are designed to bring them a reflected glory. When a child consistently fails because the standards are beyond his reach, he loses all motivation. This is the child about whom it is often unjustly said, "He isn't trying."

Fulfilling the child's needs

Providing the child with the foregoing experiences and opportunities is primarily the responsibility of the adults in the child's family. Other adults and community institutions also have a responsibility for providing the child with a variety of experiences. Whether the most efficacious experiences are provided depends upon the individuals involved. For example, the policy of a school may be to provide enough individual attention so that every child has an opportunity to experience success in some form. Unfortunately, many teachers tend to overlook this need of a child. Through failure or threat of failure, rather than through success or promise of success, they attempt to force a child into the conformity which makes teach-ing "easier." The result is that many potentially capable chil-dren leave, or are graduated from, school with a mediocre record. After that, they slip into a rut of adult mediocrity, lack-ing both motivation and belief in their own abilities. One might wonder how many student nurses are discouraged be-

cause they are frustrated by ambitious instructors who use failure instead of success as a motivating force.

Nurses working with children have a dual opportunity for
providing the young patients with desirable experiences. Admittedly, the nurse's task may be complicated because the child
is ill, already struggling against greater odds than the well
child. Most nurses have learned that they can achieve better
cooperation from children if some of the responsibility for their
own welfare is placed upon the children themselves. As we
have seen, in a ward situation a child may beneficially be given
limited responsibility for the welfare of others. Or a child may
"help" the nurse by sponging his own arm or leg when being
given shots. It is undoubtedly easier and quicker for a nurse
to do things herself than to be helped by a child, but in so
doing she is depriving the child of desirable, satisfying experiences. Thus, part of the contribution a nurse makes in providing experiences for the child is made directly in her work with
him. The other part of her opportunity (and responsibility) is
in her work with parents.

Some of the errors made by parents are a result of ignorance of a better way. Others are the result of the parents' own
insecurity, or of their efforts to satisfy their own unmet emotional needs through their children. Nurses are among the
professional people to whom parents turn, either directly or
indirectly, for help. Sometimes the help they seek is information to dispel their ignorance; sometimes it is the comfort of
leaning on someone else in whom they have confidence. In both
of these needs, nurses who are themselves adequately prepared
are able to give the needed help and support. In a later chapter,
we will look in detail at some of the specific methods we may
use for helping parents and others who turn to us for help.

Foundations of wholesome family life

All of the functions and purposes of family life have their
roots in the two major objectives of providing the experiences
described above and in meeting the specific emotional needs

discussed earlier. The degree of wholesomeness in family life is determined by the extent to which the family is successful in meeting these objectives for its members. It has been said that the best way to reach a high degree of emotional maturity is to have emotionally mature parents. Certainly it is true that the parents hold the key to the happy, satisfying family life which results in security for their children. The most desirable family situation is one in which the parents are themselves really grown up and secure. Their marriage, based on a mature, unselfish love, has the goal of giving happiness to each other. The arrival of children is a visible expression of that love. The parents sincerely want their children. This would be the ideal situation. Most people do not grow up in a family situation that is ideal from all standpoints. Their own experiences as they grow up—and older—and their own developing insight help them move toward maturity in spite of the lacks in their childhood backgrounds.

EMOTIONAL ADJUSTMENT OF PARENTS

One accepts others only to the extent that he accepts himself. A "good" parent needs to maintain a high level of self-acceptance, of self-esteem. He needs to feel that he meets society's expectations of a "good" husband or wife, of a "good" father or mother. A man, to give his best to his children, must feel confident that he is an adequate, worthy representative of the male sex. Similarly, a woman must feel sure of herself as a respected, competent representative of the female sex. Not only are their reactions to their children a function of these attitudes, but the development in their children of feelings of self-acceptance is dependent upon them. The most significant contribution parents may make to their children is the feeling of belonging. Once again, these same points may be applied to nurses. A "good" nurse is self-confident, self-assured, self-accepting. Just as "good" parents are able to develop these feelings in their children, a nurse is able to contribute to their development in her patients, whether children or adults.

All the activities of a lifetime demand adjustment. Parents —who really want children—look upon the requirements of parenthood as another adjustment to be made. Obviously, there will be changes resulting from the arrival of children which will call for adjustments. If the changes are "taken in stride" by the parents with a matter-of-fact acceptance of the limitations imposed by the arrival of children, the children themselves will feel accepted. At the opposite end are the parents who outwardly want children because this is part of their own and society's expectations of them. They look forward consciously to the joys and satisfactions of parenthood. But, perhaps because of their own feelings of inadequacy and their own immaturity, they unrealistically fail to anticipate the responsibilities that accompany parenthood. When children arrive, instead of seeing the requirements of parenthood as one of the many adjustments necessary in life's fulfillment, such parents see them as limiting factors to their own current enjoyment. Thus, a husband begins to resent the time given by his wife to the children; he misses the satisfaction of fatherhood because he looks upon his children as rivals for his wife's time and attention. To him, fatherhood means a disorganized household and a deprivation of the leisure-time activities he used to share with his wife. The immature, insecure wife, instead of finding satisfaction in the child care motherhood brings, looks upon it as perhaps meaning the end of outside activities, the end of her youth and attractiveness. Whether these feelings are part of the conscious awareness of the parents, or whether they are operating unconsciously in the parents, the children may have difficulty in developing feelings of being wanted, of belonging, of being accepted. Nurses will feel the results of these different parental attitudes when they care for a patient, whether he is a child or adult.

ACCEPTANCE

Acceptance, like many other feelings, is a matter of degree. We ideally strive for total acceptance of others, but, realistically, there are parts of others which, consciously or unconsciously, we reject. There are several factors which influence the ease with which a parent accepts a child. Physical resemblance of the child to a family member who is particularly loved and accepted aids in acceptance. Resemblance to an undesirable family member may impede acceptance because of the fear it arouses. Resemblance may even influence the way in which a child develops as a result of adult reaction to the resemblance. A child sometimes tends to become what adults say he is. "That *poor* child, she has always looked like her Aunt Molly, and now she is beginning to act like her too. It's too bad." If a child hears that sort of comment consistently enough through her developmental years, she begins to take on the characteristics she thinks she is expected to show. On the positive side, it is equally true that the child who is referred to as "sweet and kind and gentle, just like her grandmother" will tend to become that because of the expectations of the significant adults in her early life.

Sex and position in relation to others in the family is another factor in the acceptance of a child by the parents. In most civilized societies for centuries, high value has been placed upon the first-born being a son. While the reasons behind this desire for the first child to be a male no longer exist in our modern society (which boasts equality of the sexes), parents even today seem to prefer to have a boy first. (The effects of this centuries-old emphasis are still exhibited among women who have difficulty accepting their womanhood, who unconsciously resent it as they struggle to compete with men.) Whether the parents want a boy or a girl in any specific pregnancy, their having or not having a child of the sex they want is of real importance in their acceptance of the baby. An understanding nurse may be able to help the parents in their acceptance of the new baby. The nurse may help by accepting the right of the parents to feel as they do. Parents who feel rejection for a child already feel somewhat guilty. The nurse can help relieve these feelings of guilt by accepting as normal and understandable the parents' disappointment that the baby is not of the sex they preferred. If the parents are made to feel more guilty by a thoughtless, condemning remark of a nurse, they are likely to become even more rejecting. On the whole, people tend to reject the thing or person that is responsible for creating feelings of guilt in them. Fortunately, the average parent, becoming involved emotionally in the care of a totally dependent infant, soon accepts the baby regardless of sex or position in the family.

The readiness of the parents for a child also influences their acceptance of him. Children who are wanted because the parents are ready emotionally and economically to have a child, whether the first or a later one, will accept him more easily. The arrival of a child to parents who are burdened with debts, who are struggling with emotional or environmental problems for which they can find no solution, or who are in poor physical health, is a mixed blessing, if a blessing at all. At the very least, these adverse circumstances make acceptance of the child difficult.

Not only the health of the parents but the health and general ability of the child enters into the ease with which he will be accepted by his parents. Although occasionally parents may fear the possibility of producing a child who is not mentally and physically perfect, most parents anticipate that the child will be a strong, healthy baby. It is a shattering experience when this expectation is not met, an experience which may lead to the rejection of the child. The rejection may be permanent or temporary. Frequently it is compensated for by an over-protective attitude. Whether the baby's incapacity is present at birth or whether it develops later, it is likely to give rise to feelings of guilt on the part of one or both of the parents. They blame themselves for producing a defective child, or for allowing a child to develop a defect, especially so when they did not want the baby in the first place. The self-sacrificing overprotectiveness which may follow is a form of self-punishment to assuage the guilt feelings. Where a child is defective, either at birth or as a result of accident or illness later, nurses are likely to be in a position to give help and support to the parents, the child, or both. Sometimes to a nurse the demands of parents seem unreasonable. But if she can understand the motivating factors—the oppressive guilt feelings of the parents, their over-whelming concern for the child, perhaps even some feelings of shame or embarrassment—the demands will seem less unreasonable and easier to accept. Understanding the motivations of the parents opens the way to helping the parents and the child directly, and to showing the parents how they can help the child.

THE PERIOD OF "MATERNAL CARE"

From the material covered so far, it can be assumed that the kinds of people a child's parents are will be the main determinant in the degree of maturity a child will attain, because they will determine the extent of wholesomeness in the child's family life. There are exceptions. Many youngsters, for example, do not grow up in a family setting. But on the whole, the contributions the parents make to the child's progress toward maturity will be felt in every experience the child has. A few of the many areas in the child's life in which parental influence is of particular significance will be considered. Some of these areas are closely related to the emotional phases of development. The first among them is the area of maternal care. Actually, this care may be parental rather than maternal care alone, for often it is care given by both parents or even by parent substitutes. It includes the child's feeding, weaning, toilet training. It involves the learning process he undergoes in developing the ability to communicate, to walk, to feed himself, to begin to care for his own personal needs. Most important, it involves learning how to receive and express affection. During these early periods the child needs attention, but he should not be swamped with attention and supervision. He needs to be guided to do things when he indicates that he is ready for them, but he should not be hurried. Many parents are concerned about the ages at which a child accomplishes various tasks, the controversy between breast and bottle feeding, whether he is fed on demand or on a rigid schedule, and other specific phases of his development. But these things are not as significant in the life of the child as are the feelings and attitudes the child senses in his parents' approach to him.

A NURSE RELIEVES A WORRIED MOTHER

One mother, Mrs. Q., remembers well a public health nurse who gave her a great deal of help when she was worried about the development of her second child. Mrs. Q. was an energetic, active young woman with a tendency to be high-strung and quick in her reactions. Her first child, a boy, was much like her. He was bright and quick to learn. He sat up, walked and talked at a remarkably early age for each of these accomplishments. Now, at four years of age, he was a little "dynamo of energy," a replica of his mother. The second child, a girl, was not like this at all. She was late in getting teeth, slow in sitting up; at thirteen months, her present age, she was standing with support but not making any effort to walk. Miss Allen, the public health nurse at the child health center where Mrs. Q. brought her children, began to be aware of a great deal of tension in Mrs. Q. The tension was beginning to react on the baby girl who previously had had no special problems. Now she was beginning to be difficult to feed, and was crying a great deal. As Mrs. Q. talked to the doctor and nurse at the clinic she seemed terribly agitated by the baby's relative inactivity. In spite of the doctor's assurance that the baby was well, Mrs. Q. did not seem satisfied. Not having time in the busy clinic for a long conference with Mrs. Q., Miss Allen decided to make a home visit. After a short time in the home, with Mrs. Q. pointing out all of the accomplishments of her son by the time he was the baby's age, Miss Allen realized that the mother was genuinely troubled because she believed the second child must be subnormal because she was different from the boy. With the help of some literature, Miss Allen was able to relieve Mrs.

Q's mind. The nurse reminded the distraught mother of individual differences between adults as well as children. She questioned Mrs. Q. about her husband, and upon learning that he was a slow-moving, easy-going person, Miss Allen used this as a talking point. Of course, Mrs. Q's anxiety was not relieved immediately, but by the end of the second conference with Miss Allen she was more understanding and accepting of the reality of different rates of development among children. An auxiliary gain was her ability to see how her own agitation and anxiety were upsetting the baby, possibly causing an even greater retardation in her speed of development.

We see that one contribution nurses can make toward wholesome family life is in relieving anxiety growing out of these developmental phases. By helping parents relax, the nurse makes possible more constructive feelings and attitudes in the parent-child relationship.

Most behavior problems in children stem from emotions aroused within the child during the period when he is dependent on maternal care. Sometimes problems grow out of painful experiences during feeding. An adult who is in a hurry, who is lacking affection for the child, or who is frustrated, sometimes angry, because the child does not eat as well as the adult thinks he should, can be quite ruthless in his feeding methods. The child associates the pain of having a nipple forced into his mouth, or having his lips jabbed with a spoon with the lack of affection he senses. There *are* times when a parent must hurt a child for the child's own welfare, during illness, perhaps, or following a minor accident. When this is true, love is present, the hurting is done with an affection which the child understands.

"MATERNAL CARE" IN THE HOSPITAL

In the hospital, a child's behavior problems may grow out of his dependence during the early period of maternal care and later. Recognizing how busy a pediatric department may be, it is easy to see why hospitalization may increase a child's or baby's problems. When nurses and aides are attempting to feed a whole ward full of sick children at one time, it is difficult for them to remember that hurried, ruthless feeding methods with no demonstrable affection may have damaging effects on the children. While the damage may be only emotional at first, it may be followed by physical effects if the child turns against food as a result of the rough feeding regime. A nurse may indeed be busy and hurried, but the child can accept this, as he can accept pain, if underneath the pressure of work the nurse shows a genuine concern for the child. A child fully senses the difference between the hurt administered in impatience, anger, or outright rejection and the hurt that is necessary but administered with love.

One of the feelings a child receives through loving maternal care is a feeling of certainty that he can depend upon his mother without fail. The destruction of this certainty, regardless of the reasons for it, is another source of behavior problems. Even though the infant is not consciously aware of the extent of his dependence upon his mother, removal of her support constitutes a threat to his life. Without her he cannot exist. The mother as a dependable protector, provider, love giver and love object may lose her dependability through environmental circumstances over which she has no control. Or she may, for some reason, not be able to continue giving the child love. Whatever the cause, the child's life actually is threatened, insofar as his own experience is concerned. He is forced to struggle for existence, and out of his defensive struggle the behavior problems develop. This possibility exists in a hospital too, because the patient, whether child or adult, is dependent upon the care of his nurses and doctors. The removal of the care constitutes an emotional threat to the patient similar to the anxiety of the child who is threatened by the loss of his mother's care. When a patient is nervous and apprehensive, failure to take his dependency and anxiety into account may result in a very disturbed and upset patient. He may attempt

to build up a defense against his own fear by retaliative, uncooperative behavior.

EMOTIONAL CLIMATE

The emotional climate of the home, even in the early
months of life, often plays a part in the causation or prevention
of behavior problems. The smallest infant is sensitive to dissension in the home because of the interaction of feeling within
the mother-child relationship. Anxiety and the tension it arouses
in the mother are conveyed to the child in all of the care given
—an emotional interaction that is apt to result in an unfortunate seemingly endless cycle. The child attempts to relieve his
tension in the only way he knows, by crying, which adds to the
anxiety of the mother. Although his life may not actually be
threatened, the child's emotional comfort is destroyed. He
seeks his way out by clinging to infantile patterns of behavior
which eventually become problems. The anxiety a parent may
feel about a child who is hospitalized also may be transferred
to the child. Nurses should attempt to alleviate the anxiety of
the parents so that it will not retard the child's recovery or
upset his routine.

EMOTIONS—THEIR CONTROL AND EXPRESSION

There is another area related to the maternal care part of
the child's life in which parental attitudes are especially significant. This is the child's introduction to both the control and
the expression of his own emotions. The child needs to express
his emotions for the relief of tension, but he needs also to
control them to participate as a constructive member of a
social unit, which is his family. Or, if he is hospitalized, his
social unit becomes the people with whom he is associated in
the hospital—the other children and the hospital personnel.
His handling of his instinctive drives and needs must conform
to society, to group living. In teaching control and expression
of emotions, parents accomplish far more by example than by
any other means. So, of course, do nurses. If parents demon-

strate, without embarrassment, their positive emotions, the
child will be comfortable in doing this also. If the parents
give way to violent expression of negative emotions, the child
responds in kind. His response, however, will be even more
intense than the emotion exhibited by the parent because it
is complicated by the fear and anxiety the child feels. Many
adults can look back, almost with horror, to occasions when
they were threatened as children by the experience of seeing
their parents carried away or overcome by emotion, usually
anger or grief. Faced with a real situation of insecurity, the
child usually reacts not to the situation itself but to the
emotions shown by the parents. When the grandparent of a
young child dies, even though he may have been greatly beloved by the child, the child responds first to the emotional
reaction of others in the family, not to the loss of his grandparent.

One night a baby-sitter for several children in a family
was called into the bedroom by the youngest child, a six-year-
old girl. Two months prior to this a twenty-two-year-old half-
brother had died. Through her tears, the child managed to
blurt out that she wanted her brother. Actually, because this
boy had been at home very little, the child did not know him
well enough to feel very close to him. What seemed like grief
on her part was her reaction to (an identification with) the grief
of her mother, who, at times, seemed almost inconsolable.
Similarly, when one parent dies or deserts, the child's immediate reaction is usually to the emotional response of the remaining parent; later on, however, the effects of the death on the
child himself may be quite pronounced.

THE IMPORTANCE OF DISCIPLINE

The early discipline of a child is another area in which
parental influence is of major importance. To some people
the term discipline brings to mind the concept of punishment.
Correctly, the term should apply to training, which may or
may not include punishment. The goal of discipline should

be to develop within the child high standards of self-discipline. While parents are the early "conscience" of the child, they are not able to accompany the child forever. Discipline of the parents can merely form the foundation of the standards that the child will later adopt on his own.

A competent child psychiatrist has said that the one single factor which is of most importance in promoting feelings of security in a child is consistent discipline. It must be consistent in two ways: from day to day and from parent to parent. How many children—once they are a few years older —have not gone from one parent to the other, in an effort to play one against the other, to achieve what the child wants! Mother says, "You had better ask your father." The child goes to daddy and tells him, "Mommy says it's all right, if you say I may." If the father believes in agreeing with his wife in matters of training, the child gleefully runs to the mother and says, "Goody! Daddy says I can go!"

Where there is basic conflict between the parents which pervades the atmosphere of the home, disciplinary problems may become acute. The child is apt to be used as a pawn or perhaps even a weapon in the problems of the parents. A child may be permitted to do something by one parent because it is known to be something that will aggravate the other parent. One example of this occurred following the divorce of a wealthy young couple. When their two little girls were sent off for their periodic visits with their father, they were always beautifully dressed in clothes chosen and paid for by their mother. When they returned to her, they were equally beautifully dressed in clothes chosen and paid for by their father. An amusing example of childish behavior in adults, but a tragic experience for the two little girls. Of all the aspects of married life in which togetherness is important the training of the children should come first.

Just as necessary as consistent discipline from parent to parent is consistent discipline by either parent from day to day, from hour to hour. As an example, let us consider the toddler whose recent introduction into a whole new world of exciting objects and experiences keeps his curiosity in a constant state of stimulation. Just barely within his reach, on the edge of a table is a colorful, shiny ashtray. He reaches for it and it falls on the rug. There is no harm done. Mother picks it up making a comment about "that child" getting into everything. Later when the child reaches again for the ashtray, both child and rug are showered with ashes and cigarette butts, and the mother is very angry. A small incident, but when it is repeated over and over in many forms, a child will be confused by discipline.

Ever since "experts" in child training first appeared on the professional horizon, there has been controversy about the kind of punishment that is most desirable when punishment is necessary. There are advocates of solitary confinement, of the deprive-of-a-pleasure school, of the old-fashioned spanking, and of various other methods. Possibly each of them has a proper place in child training. The method, however, is relatively unimportant. It is important that punishment be directed toward helping the child develop self-discipline which will enable him to live comfortably and happily with other people. The primary purpose of punishment should not be release of the parent's own emotional tension, although, quite justifiably, this may be a reasonable and valuable by-product. Even more important is the basic relationship between the child and parent. Where this is good and sound, where the child feels secure about the feelings of his parents for him, it does not make much difference whether he is spanked, or deprived or put in his room alone; and it can do a child no harm if a parent shows anger when anger is justified. In fact it is part of his learning to face reality.

Whatever discipline may be necessary for the hospitalized child, it has the temporary goal of control of the child and the ward as a whole, rather than the more permanent goal of establishing standards of self-discipline. Obviously, any training the child may receive during his hospital stay which will help him become a self-disciplining human being is all to the good. But the average hospital stay is not long enough for this to be a major goal of discipline in the pediatric ward. Because of the unusual tension which the hospitalized child is already experiencing, punitive discipline should be kept at a minimum. There must necessarily be restraints on the behavior of a child if it is likely to harm himself or others. Beyond that, the hospital atmosphere should be permissive and accepting enough to allow for the frightened hospitalized child to express his feelings pretty freely. When punishment is necessary in a hospital setting (and this should be so rare as to be almost non-existent), it should *never* be physical punishment, but might perhaps be deprivation of some privilege or temporary isolation from the other children. With good ward management and conscientious personnel who are fond of and really interested in children, punitive discipline will rarely be necessary. A little acceptance, understanding and T. L. C. go a long way with a child—or with any of us, for that matter.

INTRODUCTION TO SEX

Discipline or training undoubtedly is a major factor in determining the kind of adult a child will become. There is one kind of discipline which possibly has a more pervasive influence on the child's whole life than any other single phase of training. This is sexual discipline, usually referred to as sex education. Here again, what parents teach by the attitudes they exhibit is far more penetrating than any verbal instruction they may give. In order to do a wholesome job of sex education, the parents themselves need to have wholesome attitudes about sex—an accepting, shameless feeling that sex is a clean, desirable, natural and necessary part of human life. Having these attitudes, parents are able to answer questions at the time they are first asked, which is when they should be answered. The earliest questions are simple ones, usually related to where babies come from. The answers should be straightforward, honest and unemotional. The first questions usually come around the beginning of the genital stage of development. To the three-year-old, these questions are no more emotion-producing than any of the other questions he asks about life and the endless stream of new things he is meeting in it. Only when adults shy away from these questions in obvious embarrassment do small children begin to feel emotional about them.

Certainly the place of sex in human life should not be belittled. But neither should it be given undue importance, which is probably happening if parents attempt to shield their children from knowledge of sex. Apparently it is human nature to be more curious about and interested in those things that are hidden from us than those that are out in the open. Parents who do not feel comfortable in speaking about sexual matters with their children may be helped by being themselves encouraged to talk about these feelings. They may also be directed to the many excellent books on the subject, some of them designed to be read by the children themselves, and others intended to help parents in presenting the subject to their children. Children may ask nurses about sex because during illness a child's attention quite naturally turns to his body and various body functions. A nurse should be prepared to answer the child's questions as well as questions parents may have about how to explain sex to their children.

INTERPERSONAL RELATIONS WITHIN THE FAMILY

Another area in the child's family life in which the parents exert tremendous influence for good or ill is that involving siblings (a term denoting brothers and/or sisters). Their interpersonal relations within the family group have not been discussed so far. The relations between siblings are determined by several factors: the relationship between the parents; the relationship of each child to each parent; physical, mental, personality and age differences between the children; and, most significant, the preparation of the child, or children, for the arrival of a new brother or sister.

No matter how much effort is made to prepare children

for a new arrival, the new baby will be a threat to the positions of the other children, especially to the child who is currently holding the position of baby in the family. A child should know in advance that a new baby is coming, and emphasis should be on the fact that it is "our" baby, not just mother's and daddy's. The more the experience is shared with the child, the less likely he is to look upon the newcomer as a usurper of his place in the home. Many parents feel that their good handling of this situation is proven if the child does not direct open signs of hostility toward the new baby. This assurance fails to take into account the use of displacement. Many youngsters will pretend love for the new baby, but will show intense hostility toward other children. Some children will displace their hostility onto their mothers, refusing to show them any affection. Others will displace their hostile reaction onto other women, identifying them with their own mothers. One precocious little boy who had been the very center of his parents' lives for five years before his brother's arrival had been prepared for the new baby. When his father telephoned the news from the hospital he talked to his son. The child asked several questions about the baby, including his weight. Finally when there was nothing left to say about the baby, he said with grown-up dignity, "And how is the mother?" This was his way of expressing the anxiety and the hostility he felt toward his mother at that moment. First he rejected her by not asking about her, and then verbally he disowned her in his use of the impersonal "the."

Another mechanism children use who feel threatened by the new baby, is regression. It is not at all unusual for a child who has been toilet-trained to begin having accidents after the arrival of the baby. Others will begin sucking their thumbs or demanding a bottle. In handling the frightening hostility they feel, they regress to the infantile patterns of behavior which at one time brought them satisfaction and attention. What these children need is not punishment or further threats, but reassurance that they are very much wanted, loved and needed. At least temporarily they need to be showered with attention. Instead of the child becoming "spoiled" by this extra attention, it is the initial investing in togetherness which will some day pay dividends in happy, well-adjusted people who have a feeling of loyalty toward each other.

One of the unfortunate habits among some parents is comparing brothers and sisters with each other. A parent is going to react differently to the different personalities among his children. And the same is true of a nurse in relating to the children in her care. Parents and nurses may try to treat each child exactly alike; it simply is not possible. On the other hand, differences between children should not be emphasized in a way which will make one child conscious of his short-comings in comparison with other children. Consistently prais-ing the "good" child to the others, in an effort to make them do better, may have the opposite effect. The other children may make up their minds to be as different as possible from the good child. If children feel defeated when they compete with another child for recognition of good behavior, they will strive to get attention by other means.

Because nurses are parent substitutes in the hospital situa-tion, children who are sharing the attention of the nurses take on the relationship of sibling to each other.

SIBLING RIVALRY IN THE HOSPITAL

Little Betty had been hospitalized for several weeks to undergo treatment for correction of a congenital deformity of the leg. A lovable, sweet, dark-haired child not quite five years old, Betty was small for her age. Because of her need for care and her pleasant, affectionate ways, Betty soon became the darling of the pediatric ward, and she thrived on it. All of the nurses and aides enjoyed doing things for her, but Betty was especially fond of one young nurse who had been responsi-ble for Betty's care when she was first admitted. The distribution of care and attention on the ward was, of course, largely determined by need. But nurses are human, as parents are, and Betty did have her share of Miss Britt's attention. One evening, a boy a year or so older than Betty was admitted. He had been in an accident and had received a serious laceration on the head in addition to concussion, the seriousness of which had not yet been determined. In the morning, the boy also was assigned to Miss Britt. He required a great deal of time and physical attention. After Miss Britt had completed his care, she took care of Betty and noticed that she was unusually quiet. The only conversation Betty started was about her mother coming on visiting day, what her mother would bring her, and what they would do together. Miss Britt was still too preoccupied with her thoughts of the little boy to realize the significance of what Betty was trying to communicate to her. Later, when Miss Britt spoke to Betty again, she received the response, "Go away, I don't want you." With that, the child began to cry. Gently and slowly, the nurse managed to coax Betty into expressing her feelings. Miss Britt had on her hands a very real case of sibling rivalry, with herself in the role of the mother.

A nurse working with children must be acutely aware of the possibility of sibling rivalry and must understand the factors underlying it. The role of a parent, added to all the other duties, makes nursing complex and challenging. What the nurse does with this challenge may make the difference between a poor prognosis and a good one.

INTRODUCTION TO WORK

The average human being can look forward to spending a large part of his life in some kind of productive work. This does not necessarily mean remunerative employment. House-wives, for instance, are certainly engaged in productive work. The man who uses his leisure time for adding improvements to his home and grounds is engaged in productive work. This brings us to the last of the major areas in the child's life in which parental influence is of particular significance and which provides still more of the foundation of good mental health —the child's induction into work. A major determining factor in a child's looking forward to work with pleasure is seeing his parents work with apparent enjoyment. If a father returns home each evening with a long list of complaints about his job, his boss, how hard life is when it has to be spent in drudgery in order to care for a family, the picture of work the children get is not a pleasant one. The same distasteful picture of work can be produced by the mother who looks upon every household chore as another link in the chain that is binding her to a dull, fatiguing life of toil. Other parents may work equally hard, but do so with a satisfaction which is apparent to their children. This does not mean that they do not get tired, that there are not times when they would prefer doing other things. Nor does it mean that they cannot admit fatigue, or even temporary boredom with a specific task. Once again, it is the overall atmosphere, created by their feelings about work, which influences the way the children see and accept work. On the whole, if parents find satisfaction in their work because it is creative or because the results of it are productive and because it makes a contribution to others, children will accept work in this same light. Ideally, children should be given small jobs as soon as they are ready for them. The jobs should be worked out cooperatively, they should be varied, and they should be shifted occasionally. Whatever jobs are assigned should be an integral part of the whole family living organization, and doing them should bring the appreciation of the parents.

There are many aspects of family life which might be presented in greater detail. What has been included here is a basic foundation of family life. To summarize: Wholesome family life ideally begins with *mature parents;* it is the responsibility primarily of the parents to provide the child with *desirable experiences* which will help him in his progress toward maturity; it is the responsibility primarily of the parents, during specific key stages in the child's development, to provide *training* which will determine the kind of adult the child will be. While the parents exert the major influence on the child's life, there are others who influence the way in which a child develops. *Nurses* particularly, using the factors that are known to promote wholesome family life, can have a constructive influence on child development in their own work with children, as well as indirectly through their contacts with parents.

4

Adapting to Life

Undoubtedly the impression has been given that growing up involves constant strain and struggle. It does. But like most things that are worthy of effort, the satisfactions of maturity bring their own reward for the efforts made. The struggle we experience in moving toward maturity grows out of the constant interacting relationship between the mind, the emotions, the body, and the outside world (our environment, the people in it and the social pressures it contains). Our emotions, our bodies and society are continually making demands on us, and these demands frequently are in opposition to each other. A frightened, apprehensive patient's emotions may be urging him to change his mind about surgery, telling him that the operation is not worth having to suffer this devastating fear; yet his body is urging him to find relief for the physical ailment he is suffering. An exhausted night nurse may be urged by her weary body to sit down in a comfortable chair and put her head back just for a little while; yet her conscience, representing the demands of her professional responsibility, rebels at the thought. Usually the patient does suppress his fear enough to undergo surgery. And the night nurse usually lets her conscience (society's pressure) overcome her tired body.

A human being's eternal conflict

This condition of conflict between what we want and what we have, what we would like to do and what we are permitted to do, how we feel and how we are supposed to feel, does not end at maturity. But with maturity comes increased ability to adjust to the demands of life. Even though the conflict frequently includes the pressure of society or the demands made on an individual by his environment, the conflict is usually an internal one, that is, it takes place within the personality. In order to survive the conflicts happily and in a mentally healthy way, the opposing forces must somehow be reconciled, or the personality may literally be pulled apart. The individual must learn how to resolve some of the internal conflicts he feels, and he must find ways of adapting comfortably to those conflicts for which he can find no solution. There probably cannot be complete emotional comfort while conflict remains, but a person can use adaptive methods which help to keep away shame, guilt, remorse. For instance, if the night nurse, in the example, could not possibly keep herself awake and gave in to her desire for a short nap, she might have told herself that since the floor was quiet she could do a better job of caring for her patients when they would need her by having a short nap now. She could do this without even being aware that in reasoning this way she was using an adaptive technic to protect the person she would like to be.

Every individual must adapt to constantly changing conditions. The greater the conflict, the more strain he feels and the greater his need for finding his own way of adapting. Knowing the various ways in which individuals may adapt to stress situations and conflict is highly significant for nurses. In the first place, nurses themselves experience conflict and stress in their own personal lives as well as professionally. Knowing, understanding and accepting themselves necessarily includes trying to recognize their conflicts and their unconscious methods of handling stress. Both their conflicts and their efforts to resolve them have direct bearing on their interpersonal relations. Secondly, all that has been said about conflict and stress applies to the healthy as well as to the sick. However, any kind of adaptive behavior a patient uses is complicated by the fact that he is ill and dependent; added to his other adaptive methods is the regression which accompanies illness and which in itself is adaptation to stress.

Obviously, there is much conflict in the early years of life. As we talked about the child's development within his family, it was apparent that the strong emotional instinctual drives of infancy would inevitably clash with what society expected of him as he grew up. When the negative emotions aroused by this conflict become too great for the child to face, he automatically represses them; they are waiting in the un-conscious mind for an opportunity, perhaps not until adult life, to burst out and make themselves felt. Stress begins at birth, when the infant is forced to leave the warm, comfortable uterine home he has known for nine months. This stress is followed by that of early training—first learning to live har-moniously with family members and later learning to adjust to the world of playmates. As the child's social contacts expand, he encounters more and more of society's demands. Fortu-nately, it is a gradual process, and his early adjustment ex-periences usually take place among those few people, his family, who know and love him most. By the time the child has made these adjustments, he is ready to face the new experience of going to school which requires his adaptation to a much more rigid, controlled existence. Progressing on toward maturity, an individual continues to face new stress situations as he adjusts to earning a living, accepting various adult responsibilities to himself, his partner in marriage, his family, his community, his nation and to humanity on a world-wide basis. These are external stresses. The internal ones grow out of his own feel-ings, and frequently they present more difficulty in adaptation than do the external situations. The internal stresses lie largely in the emotions which we think of as being primarily negative: hostility, frustration, guilt feelings, shame, anger, anxiety.

No one is in full and complete harmony within himself or with his surroundings. There is always some discrepancy between one's desires and needs and the fulfillment of them. The discrepancy is expressed in the degree of unhappiness one feels or exhibits, in the emotional tension under which one lives and works, in the number and intensity of psychoneurotic symptoms one has. Because the adult unconsciously repeats in his relations with others the childhood feelings he had toward his parents, his way of reacting will be guided in part by the sort of discipline he had. Where there has been too little discipline or training, or where it has been lax, perhaps lacking altogether, the child may develop into the infantile, impulse-ridden adult who is making himself and his associates unhappy by trying to continue to live by the pleasure principle. Where there has been too much discipline, possibly combined with cruel punishment, the child is apt to move into adult life in one of two well-defined patterns. Either he will be anxious, timid, frightened, lacking initiative, inhibited and burdened with an overactive conscience, or, going to the opposite extreme, he will be extremely hostile, belligerent, always wanting to get even, facing life with a "chip on his shoulder." Inconsistent training—rigid discipline one day and none at all the next—is likely to produce an indecisive, confused, insecure adult who is afraid of making and accepting his own decisions.

The struggle toward independence

The drive toward independence from childhood into adult life is, in part, in the direction of economic and social independence, but the greater problem is produced by the drive toward emotional independence. Ideally there is a balance in maturity between dependence and independence. It is just as indicative of psychoneurotic behavior to be overly independent of others as it is to be too dependent upon others. Many people are unaware of this truth, and in their unconscious attempt to deny their need of dependence, will show behavior in aggressive, hostile ways, resenting any help offered by others.

SOMETIMES THERE IS OPEN REBELLION

Peter was the youngest patient on a male surgical ward. Only fifteen years old, he had become involved with a terrorist teenage gang, and was shot in the leg by police during an attempted holdup by the gang. In the hospital he was surly, abusive toward the nurses, particularly, but also toward the other patients, the doctors and the orderlies. He boasted and bragged about his past activities, and arrogantly talked about what he would do in the future when he "beat the rap" which he confidently expected to do.

What about Peter's family? He didn't have much family. His father had disappeared when Peter was a pre-school child. His sister, two years younger, was ashamed of Peter and did not have any more to do with him than was necessary. Like her mother, she was attempting to create a better life for herself that could not include Peter and his anti-social activities. Peter's mother was unlike his sister in one respect, however. His mother did not reject him. Following her husband's desertion she had directed her energies toward two goals. One was pulling the little family up toward a more desirable social level. It meant working hard all the time, which she gladly did. She wanted her children to have some of the "finer things in life" which she had missed. Her other goal was making a fine, upstanding boy and man of Peter. To this end she guided him, made decisions for him, attempted to choose his friends, babied him, keeping him dependent upon her. On some social levels, or in certain neighborhoods, this prolonged dependence in a boy might have been less unacceptable. But in their low income neighborhood, where many of the boys were left to fend for themselves, where independence was highly prized, the intense care given Peter by his mother resulted in his being teased and rejected by the other boys. Peter consciously hated this. His growing dependence on his mother was frightening to him even though it was not part of his conscious awareness. Unconsciously, his dependence did exist and was shameful to him. Peter had two choices. He could allow his dependence upon his mother to take over his life, or he could rebel. Without knowing why, he chose the latter course. Unconsciously, what was going on inside Peter was the development of the feeling that dependence on the mother was a weakness. Weaknesses and limitations in oneself are painful to accept, and Peter angrily attempted to show strength instead of weakness, turning eventually to gangsterism which in his peer group was an indication, albeit distorted, of strength.

Having already had his life pattern determined, in part, by his dependence on his mother, his hospitalization forced Peter to become more dependent. More shame was aroused, and Peter's reaction to this was more rebellion. Because he identified the nurses with his mother, they became the unwitting targets of his hostility. When a patient's emotional problem is as deep-seated as Peter's, there may be little that nurses themselves can do during his hospital stay to help him modify the patterns of behavior he has established. But by understanding his behavior nurses will find it easier to accept; they will also be better able to accept the patient as a person. To be able to "get through" to such a patient requires a complete, unqualified acceptance of him.

What is a stressful situation for one person may not be for another. Each individual has his own areas of vulnerability. In some ways, entering nursing school or any other vocational field, for the first time, contains elements of stress. Examples of student nurses may be used to illustrate what is meant by specific emotional vulnerability. Among the many adjustments which have to be made on entering "training" are an adjustment to a regimented, routinized way of life, and an adjustment to the fact that a nurse has to accept tremendous responsibilities, frequently for human life. One young nurse will battle the rules and regulations throughout her training days (sometimes having to drop out because she is not emotionally prepared to adapt to this particular kind of stress). Yet, offered the responsibilities of being alone on a ward at night, of thinking for herself, of work in the accident ward or operating room, she may stand out as an efficient, capable, self-assured person. Another student may slip into the regimented life of rules and restrictions, finding a certain comfort and security in them. She finds the regulations just, and has no conflict about accepting and living by them. But placed in positions of responsibility for life and death, she may find the stress of responsibility too great for her to take.

Reacting to stress

For the reasons behind these individual variations of re-action to stress we look in the family life of the individual. It is probable that extreme independence at an early age was in some way fostered in the first student. She had grown up placing such a premium on her own independence, perhaps even feeling that she could not rely on any one else, that she had never learned to live comfortably with others or under restrictions established by others. Gradually she developed pride in her independence and in her refusal to conform. Yet it is balance between dependence and independence that is so important. Under some circumstances extreme independence can be valuable, but in other circumstances it may be danger-ous not to recognize one's own limitations and need for some dependence on others. In contrast, it may be assumed that the second nurse was the product of a domineering mother who discouraged in her daughter any tendency toward aggression, any desire to take responsibility, or even to think for herself. These examples illustrate two extremes in the reaction to the stress produced in entering into a new experience.

All people are emotionally vulnerable in some way. When the pressures exerted on the vulnerable areas become too great, even the average person shows psychoneurotic reactions. He reacts with fight or flight. Everyone is familiar with the physi-ological reactions to stress, evident in cold sweat, blushing, palpitations, or shortness of breath. During this mobilization of the body forces, the individual feels either anger or fear with resultant feelings of anxiety. The fight reaction may be exactly what the words imply—hostile, resentful, belligerent behavior which may or may not involve physical activity. In adult life, fight is more apt to be expressed non-physically, through irritability and verbal battles. Flight, as the term suggests, is expressed by withdrawal from the conflict or stress situation. Under circumstances in which withdrawal is not possible, flight may take an emotional form, such as regression to infantile reactions, eating disorders, illness or a loss of capacity for responsibility. No matter how well concealed or controlled they may be, dependent, regressive tendencies are common to everyone. Even the well-adjusted, mature person faced with a crisis or a change to which he finds it difficult or impossible to adjust will regress. As we have seen, illness is an example of such a crisis.

An amusing example of this is recalled in a student nurse's account of the post-operative behavior of one of her surgical patients. She was thoroughly disgusted with his childishness. He demanded attention, he whined, he complained of pain in excess, the nurse felt, of what should have been true for someone with his condition. In discussing this case and how she might help the patient, the student expressed finally what really bothered her most. In genuine amazement she blurted out, "But he's a Ph.D., not only that, but he's a Ph.D. in psychology." Her implication was definitely that anyone as educationally advanced as a Ph.D. in psychology knew better than to behave like a child. Furthermore, she felt that he did not have to do this, that his superior intelligence should make childish behavior unnecessary. What she failed to take into account was the fact that, regardless of what he was outside of the hospital, in the hospital he was simply a patient with all of a patient's conflicts, needs, anxieties and dependence.

Handling hostility by repression

Another of the hurdles, which must be cleared on our way to maturity, is our own hostility which is closely related to stress, conflict and regression. Hostility is the basis of criminality, war and social unrest; a limited amount of hostility, however, is essential for survival. The terms hostility and aggression are sometimes used as having the same meaning. They should be differentiated. Aggression is wholesome and desirable; without it progress would not be possible. Aggression may be hostile, but is not necessarily so. Aggression without hostility denotes a self-assurance which enables an individual to move ahead to his goal on his own merit, to stand up for his own rights, to face opposition. The goal of aggression with hostility is to hurt others. Hostility includes the raging violence which results in cruelty and destruction; it includes also anger, resentment, bitterness, malicious gossip, and exploitation of others. Few people recognize how hostile they are. Hostility is involved in conflict because overt signs of hostility in childhood are one of the kinds of behavior that society, through the parents, attempts to control. Where control of hostile behavior is too rigid, the child soon begins automatically to repress his hostile feelings. But we know that repressed emotions do not disappear. They are removed from the conscious mind, but continue to operate in devious ways. *Repression* is an *unconscious* process which takes place automatically when a person entertains thoughts, or desires which are contrary to society's dictates. Repression is valuable to us as a protection from some of the less desirable demands of our emotions; its danger lies in being used to extremes.

For example, a little girl during the genital phase of development quite naturally explores her body, discovers pleasure in her handling of the genital area, and begins to masturbate. She shows an interest in the bodies of other people. She enjoys being nude, and is curious to see her parents nude. All of these interests are a normal part of a child's development. When her parents punish, scold, or threaten her for masturbating, when they react with horror to the idea of nudity, she will take her first steps toward repressing a natural and desirable interest in sexuality. It is easier for her to bury this interest in her unconscious mind than to be threatened with the loss of her parents' love and approval. As she progresses through the stages of her development, she may be told, in tones which suggest that she lacks native decency, that, of course, she cannot marry Daddy! Still later she may be made to feel that menstruation is a painful, unpleasant "curse" which females have to undergo. When her interest in boys develops (if it is allowed to develop at all), she may be warned about the dangers of becoming too closely involved with them emotionally. Assuming that, in spite of all this preparation, there are other influences in her life to counteract it, the girl moves toward marriage and the sexual activity she has a right to expect in marriage. Consciously she looks forward to a good and satisfying sex experience, but often, in such cases, something goes wrong. Sexual activity does not hold the pleasure and satisfaction for her which she had anticipated. Frustrated and unhappy, she is unaware of the role her repression during early childhood is playing in her marriage. Consciously she wants a normal sex life, but unconsciously she rejects it. A marriage ceremony cannot, in itself, wipe out the inhibitions her repressed childhood desires have built up.

An example of repressed hostility and aggression is the little boy who is never allowed to take what he wants, who is punished for expressing hostile feelings. Later in life when he exploits others to gain what he wants, he will not understand the drive that motivates him or the unpopularity it produces. On the surface he may appear to himself to be a man of integrity, not recognizing his sneaky, ruthless methods which have grown out of the lack of opportunity to express any hostility as a child.

Repression is very close to a stimulus-response mechanism, excluding from conscious thought feelings, ideas and desires which are shameful, painful, or in some other way unacceptable to society. Things that are repressed are banished from consciousness and cannot be recalled like ordinary memories. The emotion, however, which accompanied the repressed material persists even though it is not recognized. *Suppression* is *consciously* controlling and putting out of mind feelings which *are* recognized. A nurse may be consciously aware of finding a certain chore distasteful to her, but she deliberately suppresses her feelings of dislike, and continues with her work. A student may prefer to anticipate with pleasure the weekend date she is expecting, but she consciously suppresses these thoughts so that she can concentrate on studying for an examination.

Everyone uses suppression and repression. The former is used to enable us to concentrate on what is important, to clear, deliberately, our minds of distracting, or unpleasant thoughts. Repression is an unconscious device used automatically to protect us from seeing ourselves as we really are, human beings who are driven by socially unworthy desires and motives.

The foregoing by no means advocates giving vent to our true feelings all the time. This would certainly not be feasible. Only by recognizing and accepting the existence of true feelings (no matter how undesirable they may be) can they be handled constructively. It makes no sense to fight something about whose existence one is ignorant. Hostility, especially, finds an outlet of some kind. Repressed hostility frequently is directed inward to establish the self-punishing behavior known as masochism. The masochistic person, without his awareness, constantly places himself in a position where he will be hurt. A common example is the martyred mother who sacrifices herself for her family; as a rule, she talks freely of her martyrdom, thus punishing herself still further by incurring the displeasure, and sometimes rejection, of others.

There are nurses who consistently use this pattern also. They give and give of their time and energies, but in a way that makes other people feel obligated and uncomfortable. Furthermore, the nurses working with this self-punishing nurse have to listen constantly to her complaints.

Using emotions constructively

Everyone has emotions, negative as well as positive. Emotions are an important part of us, forming the basis of opinions, of perception, of action. They add a desirable zest to life, but they can also cause difficulty—particularly if they are ignored. Emotions are responsible for internal conflict. We do not always feel the things, or the way, we believe we are expected to feel. Sometimes we like things we are not supposed to like, or we may not like things society says we should like. For instance, we are brought up to believe that we should love and respect our parents. Parents, too, err in judgment, occasionally doing things that are not worthy. When this happens our feelings of love are in conflict with the distaste we feel. The distaste can be handled by repression, promoting a "my-parents-can-do-no-wrong" attitude; the repressed material is relegated to the unconscious where it smolders, awaiting the opportunity to burst into full flame. More wisely, this conflict can be handled by openly facing the fact that the parents did do something unworthy, which did, justifiably, bring forth our negative feelings. Looking at the situation realistically, one can, however, admit that parents are human and entitled to mistakes, and that the mistakes need not destroy whatever good feeling exists between parents and child. The child who learns this from his parents is well on the way to a mentally healthy attitude about his negative feelings.

In a profession which covers as wide an area of human life as nursing does, it is inevitable that a nurse will meet many kinds of behavior she does not like. It is especially important that a nurse be able to separate her negative feelings about what a patient does from her feelings about the patient himself. She must be mature enough to accept the patient as he is, but this does not mean that she must *like* whatever he does, or that she must even *pretend* that she likes it. If you do something which someone you love does not like, he may simply let you know that he does not like it and that he hopes you will not do it again. This you can accept. But if he rejects or turns away from you as a person, not separating you, in his mind, from your act, you are deeply hurt, and rightly so.

The results of guilt feeling

One of the most important factors involved in conflict is guilt feeling. Like hostility it is one of the motivating forces in our lives. Because of society's attitude of disapproval of hostility, the normal person feels guilty when he feels hostile. Guilt feelings, in turn, are always followed by a need for punishment. Being punished provides absolution, carrying with it the assurance that, although rejected for the "bad" act which brought on the guilt feeling, one may be restored to favor by paying for the act. There are many ways in which adults "ask for" punishment. If they are not punished by the environment in some way, by circumstances, or by other people, they will punish themselves. For years, studies in industry have been underway to determine whether accidents really are accidents, or whether the emotions are responsible in some way for making some people more accident-prone than others are. In all probability we shall learn some day that guilt feelings and a need for punishment play an important part in crises that are currently believed to be accidents. Illness is another way in which people punish themselves to alleviate guilt feeling. Chronic failure in one's undertakings is another way.

GUILT AND THE NEED TO FAIL

Charles and John were the children of an unhappy marriage which was held together in the belief that it would be better for the children if the parents did not attempt to solve their problems by separation. Discipline of both the boys was of a chaotic, inconsistent nature. But on the whole, Charles who was two years older than John was given what he wanted. Aggressive, determined and hot-tempered like his father, Charles was the pride of his father who encouraged these traits in his son. Because of the dissension between the parents, Charles' mother resented having her husband duplicated in their child, and she unconsciously rejected Charles. Instead, she turned to John, giving him the love and attention she was unable to give to Charles. Charles' resentment of his younger brother was expressed in a fairly open, uninhibited way. The outgrowth of this was a deep hatred of John for Charles. But because of his mother's influence, John's feelings of hostility had no avenue of escape. His mother instilled the idea into him that it was wrong for a "good" boy like John to feel hostile. But the feeling was there, directed against both his father and brother whom he identified with each other. Accompanying the hostility was the inevitable feeling of guilt and need for punishment. In adult life, Charles' aggressive manner of self-assurance, backed by his father's support, brought him outstanding success in the business world. John, though the more intelligent of the two, met failure in every undertaking. His self-punishment was carried to the point of finding employment with persons whose characteristics were similar to those of his father and brother so that, in a way, his failure was preordained. Had he been aware of his own hostility, and had he been given the opportunity to face it openly, he would not have had to punish himself with repeated failure.

Motivating forces such as those responsible for John's behavior tend to lead to cycles from which there seems to be no escape: Failure is succeeded by frustration, frustration by increased hostility; following this there is guilt, leading to the self-punishment by failure—and the cycle begins again.

Working compulsively is another means of self-punishment. Like the martyr, these people complain about the amount of work they have to do, criticize their superiors for making unreasonable demands upon them. They develop feelings of hostility, and feel guilt about it. Their guilt results in the feeling that they are not really worthy of any respite from work, and they punish themselves by driving harder than ever. Another example involves envy. When an individual is extremely envious of another, he resents that person, feels hostile towards him. The punishment he uses to alleviate the guilt feeling is apt to be self-depreciation with a concomitant building-up of the person he envies. Out of this build-up grows further envy, and the cycle continues.

It was said that there *seems* to be no escape from these emotional conflict cycles. An escape does exist, of course. It lies in understanding one's emotions, in facing them and accepting them. Only in this way is control of emotions possible. Complete freedom from inhibition is not desirable in civilized society. Everyone needs the security that comes from emotional control, and emotions are more easily controlled if they are recognized. But it is as undesirable to deny the existence of emotions as it is to give vent to them in a way which will hurt oneself or others.

Protecting ourselves from ourselves

In handling emotional conflicts we use mechanisms of adjustment, or methods of adaptation, which are usually referred to as "defense mechanisms." These mechanisms will be considered briefly so that we may have some understanding of how they operate in interpersonal relations. The objective of defense mechanisms is to defend ourselves by concealing our real motives from the conscious self, thus sparing us social or personal humiliation. Because defense mechanisms are used for self-protection, they are by no means maladjustments unless they are used in excess. Basic to the use of defense mechanisms is repression. Painful or shameful impulses, or impulses that are too difficult for us to control need to be repressed before the mechanisms of adjustment can operate. It should be reemphasized that all normal people use repression, but not to the extent that their capacities for action, their ability to face reality, are blocked. Repression, a necessary part of all the others, is in itself the major defense mechanism.

Displacing our emotions

Another defense mechanism, which is common to some, but not to all of the others, is displacement. It is probably the most common method of handling emotions. It is socially and personally dangerous to express some emotions toward some people; to protect himself, a person involuntarily chooses some safe object as a target for his negative emotions. Displacement is the shift of an emotion, wish or idea from the object or person who aroused the emotion (and toward whom it would normally be directed) to some other object or person. Many examples of this can be found in the life of everyone. How many of us have not slammed a door, or kicked some inanimate object out of our way, or have angrily torn something up when our anger was aroused, not by these objects but by another person? Usually this other person is one whom it is not safe or feasible to fight back. Suppose a student nurse has a date which involves going somewhere with a group of people who are expecting to meet her at a specified time. Just before she is due to go off duty a new patient comes in, and the head nurse, in the absence of ample help on the ward, asks the student to go ahead with the admission of the patient. It is natural for the student to feel both anger and frustration, but neither the head nurse nor the patient, who would both be the natural targets of her anger, would be safe targets. In all probability the student complains little or not at all, but represses the anger she feels. The anger is still there, even though it may not be recognized. When the student finishes and goes off duty, she will subject her roommate, perhaps the bus driver, possibly even her date, to an irritability which neither the student herself nor the targets of her anger can understand. After having repressed it, she has displaced onto them the anger or frustration aroused by someone else.

When the opposite is true

There are several mechanisms of defense that utilize displacement. One of them is called a reaction formation. The "I hate you" becomes "I love you" because it is safer. This occurs in the relationship between an unwanted child and his parent. Society demands that a mother love her child. Sometimes she simply does not. But she has to repress her feelings of rejection of the child in order to protect herself in the eyes of society, and she reacts by avowing her love for the child, going to extremes to demonstrate it. The child who has been punished has the same reaction. If he feels that the punishment is unjust, he will be filled with anger, perhaps even hatred temporarily. If he expresses these true feelings, he faces the possibility of his mother's withdrawal. So, instead of saying "I hate you, Mommy," he tells her how much he loves her, seeking forgiveness in that way. The child who is allowed to express without fear of reprisal the occasional hatred he feels for his mother is a fortunate child indeed.

Protestations of strong feeling are frequently a reaction formation. A nurse, talking about her director of nursing, or the hospital at which she works, may be heard to repeat again and again how wonderful her director is, what excellent working conditions she has, how good the pay is, what marvelous opportunities the job holds. When all of this is overemphasized, one begins to wonder whether she is trying to sell the job to herself because she is not so sure that it is what she wants, or because conditions are actually undesirable. Another illustration is the person who needs to reiterate that something he is telling is the truth. As a rule one assumes that people are telling the truth. When an individual keeps saying, "This is true. . . . You know I wouldn't lie . . . You know I always tell the truth . . .", one is inclined to question whom the person is trying to convince—and why it is necessary. Shakespeare expressed this in Hamlet when he said, "The lady doth protest too much, methinks."

Pre-adolescence provides another illustration of the reaction formation. Not being secure in the newly developed feelings toward members of the opposite sex, young teenagers may be afraid to express their positive feelings. The fourteen-year-old girl is likely to say of the boy she secretly would like to date, "That square! Why, I wouldn't be seen walking down the street with him." The boy of the same age who wishes he had the courage to date may be heard too say, "Dates? You won't catch me spending my money on any dizzy dame." By simply not believing that he wants anything in the first place, he makes it easier for the ego to be spared the possibility of rejection or of being denied something.

Attributing our own faults to someone else

Another common defense mechanism that uses displacement is projection. An individual transfers from himself to someone else an element in his personality which he does not admire and cannot accept in himself. It is a weakness, existing but usually not recognized in oneself, that is seen clearly in other people. We meet the inveterate gossip who is the first to criticize others for this trait; the person who has a tendency to stray from the truth, if it suits his interests, who is consistently suspicious of the integrity of others; the person who struggles to avoid work who is the first to condemn others for laziness. A perfect example of this kind of projection was observed in a hospital ward recently.

"I KNOW HIS KIND . . ."

The patient, J. H., came into the receiving ward at two in the morning on a bitter cold day in December. His complaint was that his feet had been hurting for the past two weeks. Hardly clothed, unshaven, uncombed, his eyes half-open, he apparently had had an alcoholic bout. The odor on his breath confirmed this to the intern on duty.

When J. H. had sufficiently recovered to give a brief history to the intern, he said that he had been on an alcoholic bout for the past month. He had eaten nothing that he could remember for the past two weeks. During that time he had lived in the back seat of an abandoned automobile on a junk lot. The weather had been bitterly cold and had "bothered his feet somewhat,"he said. The police found him in the car that night and brought him to the hospital. A diagnosis was made of "third degree frostbite of both feet" and J. H. was given a bed on one of the male surgical wards. He was trembling violently all the time and pleaded for "something to quiet his nerves." For psychologic reasons he was given one ounce of whisky and an order was written for paraldehyde, 4 cc., to be given whenever necessary. After a good night's sleep, a morning bath, an adequate breakfast, and a shave. J. H. began to resemble a normal human being. He was quiet and cooperative but complained of severe pain. It was necessary to perform a bilateral sympathectomy on J. H. to relieve the pain in his feet. He made a successful and uneventful recovery.

One day he called the nurse to his bedside and told her he had something very personal and unpleasant to report to her. The nurse gave him her attention and he said, "You know that man across the room, Mr. K?" The nurse said she knew him, although not very well, since he had only been admitted last night. "Well," continued J. H., "you'd better stop leaving alcohol in his bedside cabinet. He drank a whole bottle last night." "He did?" said the nurse, who was familiar with J. H's history, "perhaps I had better talk to him about it." "Oh, no, don't do that," hurried J. H., "he'd know it was me who told you. Why don't you just take it away? If you questioned him about it, you don't know what he'd do to me. He doesn't like me because I don't drink my rubbing alcy." The nurse agreed that she would not want to make any trouble for J. H. and that perhaps the best thing for her to do was to report this to the head nurse. J. H. agreed that it might be a good idea to tell the head nurse and the doctor, too. "But don't tell them where you got your information, nurse—that patient really has it in for me. I know his kind—drink anything they can get their hands on."

The nurse gave the head nurse the information J. H. had given her, and the head nurse in turn asked the nurse's aide, when she checked bedside cabinets for supplies that afternoon, to pay particular attention to Mr. K's bottle of alcohol. The aide reported back that the bottle was full. However, J. H. had an empty bottle, "And I know," said the aide, "it was full this morning when I rubbed his back during morning care!"

Not only weaknesses but also wishes are projected onto other people. The man who falsely prides himself on not having had a vacation for years and not wanting one, will tell that his wife is very anxious to get away on a trip. Thus he projects his own desires onto her and his ego is spared the necessity of relinquishing a position of which he is proud. The man, whose youthful ambition to be a physician was frustrated, will project his own unfulfilled wishes onto a son. He will attempt to guide his son into this profession, himself convinced that it is his son's wish, not his own.

Taking unto oneself

The opposite of projection is introjection, in which one accepts into himself the opinions, values, ideals and ideas of others. Some psychiatrists do not approve the term, since nothing can actually be "introjected" into one's self; rather, they think of it as internalization through the process of identification. At any rate, the mechanism begins with the imitation of others based on a desire to be like the person imitated. Gradually the imitator internalizes (incorporates as part of his own thinking and feeling) the thoughts and feelings of others. Identification (or introjection) should be a constructive part of personality development; certainly it is necessary if one is to be educated. The test of identification is the kind of result it produces. If it helps one to be better, to live more effectively, it is good. If it leads to inaction and escape from reality, it is not desirable. An example of the latter is the person who is so closely identified with a loved one who dies, that he himself withdraws from desirable human contact.

Making up for our lacks

Three defense mechanisms are quite commonly used and, therefore, more familiar than others. One is compensation, which is repressing feelings of inadequacy in one area by concentrating conscious efforts on areas in which there is a feeling of adequacy. Examples of this in the physical body are easily understood. If there is an injury to, or loss of, one eye, the other eye compensates for this loss by added effort. When the use of one muscle is impaired, another muscle will work harder to make up for the impairment. The same principle operates psychologically. The individual who suffers from feelings of inferiority will drive himself to appear superior. Many of the people who are referred to as snobs are really suffering from what has been called an inferiority complex. A mother's rejection of her child will be disguised by an over-solicitous, over-protective attitude. The child who is unable to compete in physical activities will devote his efforts to becoming an outstanding scholar. The student nurse who recognizes that she is awkward in nursing skills will concentrate on doing exceptionally good academic work.

Fooling oneself

The second of the common mechanisms of defense is rationalization. This is giving a socially accepted reason for things we emotionally want to do anyway. In our culture things are done because they are right, noble, desirable, not simply because emotionally we *want* to do them. In rationalization we follow our unconscious wishes and desires, and then give a reasonable explanation for it. Rationalizing is not the same as deliberately being untruthful. For example, there may be a movie a student is most anxious to see, while there is also an examination for which to study. The student attempts to study, but because she is not accomplishing much, she suddenly decides she needs the relaxation of a movie. She rationalizes that she will be better able to study if she has had some recreation. Thus she does what she wants to do, sparing her ego the real reason. A person who is fond of sweets will have a candy bar, not because she cannot resist the oral urge, but because she "needs the quick energy the carbohydrate provides." A girl who is reluctant to accept an invitation because she would prefer to stay home, will convince herself that she *needs* to be home for some reason, although consciously she thinks she would like to go out. When we rationalize, we really believe the reasons we give for a certain action are the true ones. But one should try to become aware of his rationalizations, because it is an important part of knowing oneself.

Substituting something else

The third common defense mechanism, sublimation, which is always associated with socially-acceptable goals, involves displacement. It is the displacement of an unconscious deprivation or need into socially accepted channels. The woman deprived of the opportunity to have children of her own will go into kindergarden or nursery school work. Aggressive, competitive sports are frequently sublimations of hostile, destructive impulses. This method of adapting to conflict comes closer to a real resolution of the conflict because it tends to satisfy both sides: it gives in partially to emotional desires, but it also satisfies the demands of society.

Illness provides its own excuse

All of the mechanisms of defense which have been considered so far are of general interest to anyone who wants to know himself better and who wants to increase his understanding of others so that he will be able to work more effectively with them. There is one defense mechanism, however, which depends upon displacement which is of particular significance for nurses. It is the use of the conversion symptom. Occurring with almost complete repression, it forms the basis of psychosomatic illness. A conversion symptom is a displacement of emotional conflict, its fear and anxiety, into physical symptoms: pain, loss of function, illness. Any area of the body may be affected. Which area it well be depends upon the kind of conflict it is, the personality of the individual, and the individual's physical vulnerability. Some people are predisposed to digestive or gastro-intestinal disorders. Others may tend to have respiratory problems, while still others may have an especially vulnerable cardio-vascular system. While some of these predispositions are related to the personality, undoubtedly some of them are based on physiological weaknesses as well. Many of these patients carry their symptoms from one doctor to another vainly seeking a cure. If the symptoms are relieved as a result of treatment there will be either recurrences or other illnesses, until the emotional conflict causing the symptoms is resolved. Where there are enough physical symptoms to relieve the pressure of the conflict, these patients frequently show no other neurotic symptoms. There is no need for other defenses. Illness in itself does an adequate job of protecting the ego. When one is ill he cannot be expected to be independent, to accept responsibility, to give of himself in any way. Thus, illness provides its own excuse.

Nurses are by no means exempt from having psychosomatic symptoms as the result of emotional conflict.

A clear-cut example of this involves a graduate nurse who was working toward her degree. For a period of time during summer school she was concerned because of daily headaches. The strange thing about them was that they always occurred at the same time every day, immediately after lunch. She eliminated in her mind all the usual physiological causes for headaches. Her eyes were all right, she was eating well (her meals were included as part of her compensation for her part-time job), she had no gastro-intestinal difficulties. With all the physiological leads ending in dead-ends, she had to turn to the possibility of an emotional cause for the severe daily headache. She found it in the class which immediately followed her lunch. She didn't like the class, nor the professor. Although she was a bright student, in this one class she did not do as well as in her other work. On the other hand if she wanted her degree this class was required. Herein lay her conflict, a conflict between what she wanted and what she had to have. The conflict had no resolution, but it had to find some means of expression, and it did—in her headaches. It would have been difficult for a good student and a mature person to have to say that she was doing poorly because she did not like the class or was not capable of doing this work well. The daily headaches spared her ego from having to face this "shame." They provided a reasonable excuse for not doing well. In this example we see repression and displacement clearly. Before her headaches could function to protect her ego, the real reasons for her poor work had to be repressed. But repressed feelings have to come out somewhere, and these did, displaced into headaches.

There is a tendency among some nurses to consider emotionally-based illness imaginary. Nothing could be further from the truth. A gastric ulcer *is* a gastric ulcer, complete with the pain-producing physiological changes, whether it is emotionally or physiologically caused. A severe headache caused by anxiety, frustration, or guilt is just as distracting and unpleasant as a headache caused by concussion. People with emotionally-based illness need the same symptomatic relief from pain and discomfort that any other patient needs. They need more than this. Obviously, nurses are not prepared to do psychotherapy with these patients but they can offer support, comfort, and empathy.

All of the methods of adapting to life which have been considered in this chapter apply to the patients for whom nurses will care, to the co-workers, and to the nurses themselves. In life's struggle, various methods of adaptation are necessarily used by all human beings, by those who are healthy as well as by those who are sick, but sickness adds complications to the already existing struggle. To help in the removal of some of the complications in their patients, nurses need to understand not only the way in which people develop but also the methods used for adapting to life.

5

Family Adversity
and the Nurse

Every family is struck by adversity at one time or another. No matter how mature the parents are, regardless of the care and advantages they give their children, despite a desirable interacting love between family members, adversity will attack any family. It does so in many ways: It may strike in the form of illness, death, economic reversals, marital friction, or it may grow insidiously out of the normal process of aging. Nurses cannot always wage a successful battle against adverse conditions in their own families and lives, let alone in the lives of their patients and their families. Nevertheless, nurses frequently will be looked upon as sources of help in time of family trouble. This is so because many of the crises are related to illness, and because nurses, generally, are considered to have good judgment, growing out of their close touch with the drama of life.

Obviously nurses cannot take the place of doctors, clergymen, lawyers, or social workers trained to help families and individuals with specific problems. In some situations it would be highly unethical for nurses even to try to substitute for other professional people. But because nurses have such close personal contact with patients and families, they have two responsibilities and opportunities to help troubled families. One is through supplementing the efforts of other professional people by lending support, reassurance, and a willing ear. The other is in referring those who need help to the specific professional resource the situation requires.

SURGERY AFFECTS THE FAMILY

Miss West was a general duty nurse on a semi-private surgical floor in a large suburban hospital. Mrs. R., one of the patients on the floor, had been admitted to the hospital for the removal of a lump in the breast. She was an attractive young woman, married less than a year to an attractive young man. Their beginning life together was filled with promise for the future. Mr. R. was off to a good start in his own business, they were in love, and they were enthusiastic in their plans for the years ahead. This was the state of their life when Mrs. R. discovered the lump in her breast. Of course she was upset. So was her young husband. Intelligent people, they recognized what the lump might mean. Taking the advice of Mrs. R's family doctor, she was examined by a surgeon who recommended removal of the lump and a biopsy. The small lump was successfully removed. Until the operation, Mr. and Mrs. R. had taken the whole event in their stride, secure in their confidence in the doctors, and filled with the hope that the condition would be benign. Unfortunately, it was not. The biopsy indicated malignancy, and the surgeon recommended an immediate radical mastectomy. When Miss West went in to see Mrs. R. late that afternoon, instead of being greeted with the usual pleasant smile, she found Mrs. R. pensive and unhappy. Miss West already knew of Mrs. R's diagnosis and recognized that this in itself would be frightening. She sensed that there was more involved in Mrs. R's unhappy frame of mind (some people would refer to it as intuition) but she also was experienced in observing the reactions of people under stress. Miss West realized that Mrs. R. had accepted without too much difficulty the need of surgery before; she had even accepted the possibility that her diagnosis might be cancer. As Miss West talked to the patient and gently attempted to draw her out, this opinion was substantiated. Mrs. R. actually had no fear of surgery, nor even an unusually strong fear of cancer. Her depression, however, continued. It was Miss West's well-placed, but casual, comment about Mr. R. coming in to visit that evening which finally brought out the real cause of Mrs. R's dejection. How could Mr. R. continue to accept her if she was deformed? Was it fair to him to go through life with a woman whose body was not complete? How would her attractive clothes look on a woman with only one breast? These may seem superficial things to worry about for those of us who have never faced them. But to the individual involved they are a genuine emotional threat. Miss West was able to understand these feelings so readily because she was aware of the family life factors involved in Mrs. R's feelings. Here was an attractive, vivacious young woman whose appearance and the sexual appeal she held for her husband were especially important to her because of her relatively recent marriage. With great difficulty, Mrs. R. finally blurted out her feelings, a genuine concern about Mr. R's reaction to her deformity. When Mrs. R. had been given ample time to express herself, Miss West talked to her about the use of prosthetic appliances, explaining how and of what material an imitation breast is made, describing accurately and honestly the appearance of it. This in itself did not result in a sudden change of feeling about the operation and its results. Miss West did not expect it to, but her talk with the patient was the beginning of the removal of Mrs. R's fear. Mrs. R. was in a much better position to face her husband and even to help him in accepting this new event.

During evening visiting hours, after Miss West ascertained that Mr. R. had already been told by the surgeon of the need for further surgery, she spoke to Mr. R., giving him opportunity to express his feelings. Naturally, his concern was for his wife, rather than himself, and he did not have as much need to release feeling. Miss West also told Mr. R. about the use of prostheses, pointing out that sometimes women need help and understanding in accepting the necessity for these. With the help and reassurances that each of these young people had received from the nurse, they were able to face Mrs. R's surgery with much less tension and apprehension.

In this particular situation there was no one to whom Miss West could have referred the R's for the kind of help Miss West herself was able to give. Mrs. R's *emotional* problem was not one which could be handled directly by medicine or surgery. Her physician or surgeon might have been able to help her with it if either had known of it. But frequently a worry of this nature will be revealed in the intimacy of nursing care, whereas it will not appear in the relative formality of a doctor's visit. Mrs. R's problem was neither spiritual, nor legal, nor social. To tell Mrs. R. that she should talk about her fears to someone else would have been turning away from the patient, and could justifiably have been interpreted by the patient as rejection. Referring Mrs. R. to someone else could also have been interpreted by her as meaning that the problem was bigger and more serious than was true, or, just the opposite, that it was too insignificant to be upset about. Nurses need to remember that no problem is insignificant to the person who is upset by it, regardless of how the nurse *thinks* she would react were she to face the same problem.

Mrs. R's problem was one with which no one professional person was specifically trained to deal. And yet, the removal of even a small amount of Mrs. R's tension made for a more satisfactory recovery from surgery. In helping Mrs. R. to bring out her fears, to "verbalize" them as the psychiatrists say, and then to offer her concrete information which would help to alleviate some of her fear was supplementing the work of the surgeon, even more effectively than if Miss West had been assisting him in the operating room. In acquiring knowledge and developing skills of the kind used by Miss West, a nurse has to accept a good bit of responsibility herself. These phases of nursing are not easily taught.

Many times the emotional problems patients will reveal to nurses are not problems with which a nurse can help, beyond offering the comfort of a willing listener and referral to someone more highly trained. Nurses in every branch of the profession are faced with this situation many times.

EMOTIONAL PROBLEMS AFFECT THE FAMILY

Miss Daly was a senior student nurse on affiliation with the visiting nurse society of a large city. One of the patients in her district was a middle-aged widow, Mrs. W., whom Miss Daly visited twice weekly to administer intramuscular injections. Mr. W. had been killed in an accident at work four years ago, and Mrs. W. received a small pension from the company which had employed him. Supplementing this amount with her salary as a part-time cashier in a super-market, Mrs. W. managed to support her four children. The oldest boy had completed high school and was in the army. The next oldest, a senior in high school, had a Saturday job with which he helped support himself. The third child, a girl, was a freshman in high school. The youngest was a boy in fourth grade. While Miss Daly visited Mrs. W. over a period of several weeks, she gradually learned a great deal about this family. Mrs. W. looked upon her visiting nurse as a friend and confidante, talking freely of the progress of the children and the problems entailed in raising four fatherless children. The three older children had always done well in school, and since the death of their father had taken on additional responsibility willingly and were generally quite well adjusted. They created no problems, and Mrs. W. was warm in her praise of them. Jack, the youngest boy, was, according to his mother, a real problem child. Mrs. W. felt that a good bit of her nervous tension was the result of his misbehavior. She placed a great deal of emphasis on the fact that she had always been a good mother to him in spite of the difficulty she had had with him ever since his birth. Having been married rather late in life, she was forty years old when Jack was born.

During one of Miss Daly's visits, Mrs. W. described the difficulties of the birth itself and pointed out how much harder this one had been for her to bear because she really had considered her family complete with the other three. It seemed to her that Jack as a small child had had more illness than all the others combined. Because of this he was spoiled, having received far more than his share of attention. Having been particularly close to his daddy, his father's death when he was six years old was a terrific blow to him. Even before Mr. W. died, Jack used to get into mischief, but since then he was worse than ever. The scrapes he was getting in now were much more serious. In fact, his mother said, he could no longer be considered just mischievous, he was now really a bad boy. Unlike her other children who had excellent school records, Jack was doing progressively poorer work. In the past year he had been reported twice for truancy. Mrs. W. had threatened and punished Jack in a variety of ways, but his behavior did not improve; in addition to this, the gap in understanding between him and his mother grew wider and wider.

The episode which resulted in Mrs. W's desperate out-pouring to the nurse of all the details of her difficulties with her son, was stealing from various other children at school. The things he took were not important at first, but eventually he stole money. Much to Mrs. W's indignation, the school author-ities instead of disciplining the boy themselves, had turned the situation over to Mrs. W. to handle. Miss Daly was pro-fessionally mature enough to recognize the influence Mrs. W's disturbed emotional state might be having on her physical con-dition. She further recognized that Jack's behavior was that of a disturbed, unhappy child. Mrs. W's state of health was part of Miss Daly's responsibility, but she was not sure how much responsibility she should accept for what was obviously a family life—not a health—problem. She listened thoughtfully to what Mrs. W. had to say. Although she was not in a position to offer advice, or even reassurance, her very interest reached through to the patient, who felt relieved by the opportunity to share her burden with her nurse.

When Miss Daly left the home, she made a mental note to discuss this case with her supervisor. She felt genuinely sorry for Mrs. W. who had tried so hard to do her best for her chil-dren. On the other hand, she realized that the many sacrifices

Mrs. W. had made for this youngest son might have been in compensation for not having wanted him in the first place. Miss Daly wanted very much to be able to do something constructive, not only for Mrs. W. but for the boy as well. As she and the supervisor discussed this situation, Miss Daly was helped to recognize that in public health, as in other nursing fields, a nurse has limitations. The causative factors in family life were brought into sharper focus. Here was an unwanted child who had felt deserted by his father at a time in his life when he normally would be identifying closely with him. Young children do not differentiate emotionally between malicious desertion and the separations caused by death, illness, or other environmental factors. The child also felt the rejection of the mother. In spite of her unawareness of this rejection, the rejection was realistic enough to make her compensate for it by giving Jack an abundance of material things and over-protective care during his early years. But he needed also to feel wanted, to feel that he really belonged. His stealing was symptomatic of his efforts to share some part of other people, in an effort to make up for the emotional ties he was lacking at home. Because of the complexity of interaction between mother and child, this was not a situation in which a nurse could help directly.What she could do, and did, was to refer the child to a child guidance clinic. There the trained personnel worked with both the mother and the child in helping them to an understanding of each other and of themselves, with the hope that a serious delinquency problem might be avoided.

If the nurse had not taken the time to look behind the patient's words to what lay behind the behavior of the boy and his mother, she might easily have been misled into giving potentially harmful advice, sympathy, or reassurance. She might have agreed with the mother that this was indeed a bad boy who ought to be punished for bringing his mother so much suffering. Or she might have made the mother feel guilty by prematurely pointing out or interpreting the mother's uncon-

scious rejection of her child. Or she might have lulled the
mother into a temporary false security by reassuring her that
this was just a phase of the youngster's development which he
would later outgrow.

In this situation the nurse referred the patient to another
source of professional help, but she also lent support and
understanding to the mother in her steps toward seeking help.
It is not always easy for people to acknowledge the need for
this kind of help. One of a competent nurse's responsibilities
is to interpret counseling or psychiatric help in such a way as
to make it acceptable. Sometimes people who are referred for
such help feel that the need for help is a sign of their own inadequacies and incompetence.

When Miss Daly suggested to Mrs. W. the possibility of
her taking Jack to the child guidance clinic, Mrs. W. took this
to mean that she had failed as a mother. The talk with her
supervisor had prepared Miss Daly for this reaction from Mrs.
W. Knowing that Mrs. W. had always given her children good
physical care, the nurse asked Mrs. W. whether Jack made
regular trips to the dentist. Mrs. W. looked surprised, but
answered in the affirmative. Miss Daly went on asking whether
Jack had ever had any cavities in spite of the care Mrs. W.
had attempted to give his teeth. Jack had had cavities. Miss
Daly asked whether Mrs. W. felt this was her fault. When
Mrs. W. said she did not see how it could be her fault, the
nurse pointed out that sometimes something goes wrong no
matter how much care is given; that it happens not only to our
teeth and other parts of the body, but also to our emotions as
well. Miss Daly asked why Mrs. W. took Jack to the dentist
regularly even when he did not have any cavities. Mrs. W.,
though she thought this was a strange question under the circumstances, explained that she took him to prevent anything
serious developing. This was the answer Miss Daly had waited
for, and she was quick to use it in explaining that taking Jack
to the clinic now could be a precautionary move. Mrs. W's
acceptance of Miss Daly's interpretation was followed by a

consultation with the familiy doctor, who gave his approval of the plan, and a referral was made.

To help, first understand

This was a family life problem, but like many family life problems it was also a mental health problem of great signifiicance, not only to the child and his mother, but to society. Had this nurse not been aware of the way in which family problems develop into emotional problems, she might have stuck strictly to nursing procedure. In so doing she would have failed in one area of her professional responsibility. Because she understood the problem, she was able to interpret to the patient the need for skilled help of a kind the nurse herself was unable to give.

In contacts with patients and their families nurses have often been able to help them arrive at wise decisions about specific care, even where other professional people have failed. For instance, a tuberculosis patient may decide to accept sanatorium care, helped by the nurse's understanding of what this means to him and his family. Or parents may be motivated by a nurse, whose opinion they respect, to place a retarded child in an institution, for his own sake as well as to protect the natural development of other children in the home. In situations including care or treatment, the initial opinion, obviously, is not the prerogative of the nurse. But frequently even after a doctor has made his recommendation, a patient or family will still be reluctant to take steps that are potentially traumatizing because they disrupt normal family living. Since a nurse's contact with people is apt to be much more intimate and informal than that of a doctor or social worker, it is easier for the people under her care to reveal their feelings, worries, anxieties. Also, secure in the knowledge of her genuine interest in them as individuals, people will respect her opinion and her efforts.

A knowledge of the intricacies of interpersonal relations within a family is of particular importance in two referral situations. One of these has already been discussed in the example used, namely, motivating people to seek and to accept any kind of psychiatric care. Because of the stigma which still is, in the minds of many lay people, attached to any kind of emotional or mental illness, a nurse needs a tremendous amount of understanding and empathy in this situation.

Similarly, a stigma is frequently associated with the acceptance of financial or other material help from a social or welfare agency. While it is the opinion of some ill-informed individuals that the clientele of welfare agencies have no pride about asking for and accepting help, actually, for many people, pride is a barrier to obtaining needed available economic aid. In order to motivate anyone to ask for such aid, a nurse must attempt to understand what the feelings of the individual are, and what influence the steps the nurse is advocating will have on the family constellation. In addition, of course, the success of the nurse's efforts will be dependent upon her own attitudes, because her attitude will determine the approach she will use.

The young and the old

Of all the adversities which may strike at family life undoubtedly one of the most devastating is chronic illness. Long-term illness presents seemingly unsurmountable obstacles to wholesome family life. Although the event may be most serious when the family breadwinner is struck, it can be equally upsetting when any of the other family members is the patient. When the patient is a child there may be strong guilt feelings on the part of the parents, which the parents will then attempt to alleviate with various defense mechanisms. Their overcompensations or rationalizations may do even more harm in an already undesirable situation.

Often, the long-term patient is of the older generation, a patient living with a married son or daughter. Think of the complex mesh of interacting feeling in this situation. The patient himself will feel hostile and resentful because no "normal" individual wants to be dependent on anyone. His hostility has to be directed somewhere, so it is displaced onto the people on whom he is dependent. On the other hand, he knows he should be grateful for the care he is receiving, but his resentment is too strong to allow gratitude to enter in—and he feels guilty. The young people with whom he is making his home are laboring under a similar configuration of feelings. If nothing more, a sense of duty tells them they should be grateful for all the care given them at one time by the parent. But they feel so hostile at the interruption of their own family life by the arrival of a parent, and a sick one at that, that they, too, end up feeling guilty because they inwardly want to reject the person on whom at one time they leaned.

THE NURSE IS CAUGHT IN THE MIDDLE

This was the situation in which the B's found themselves when Mr. B's mother who lived with them had a stroke and had to be hospitalized. The B's were a couple of young middle-age. They were economically stable, middle-class, and "comfortably fixed." They owned their own home, and their children, ranging in age from ten to eighteen years, were expected to receive a college education for which money was being saved regularly since the early years of the first child. By the end of the older Mrs. B's third week in the hospital she was out of danger, and the doctor said that she would be able to leave the hospital in two or three days. It was at this point that the morning nurse, who had been largely responsible for this patient's care, found herself in the middle of a subtle, but disturbing, family feud.

The patient had made occasional comments about how hard it was to be dependent on someone else, the difficulties inherent in giving up one's own home, and her extreme dislike of being a burden to anyone. Her initial reaction to hearing that she would be able to go home was one of great pleasure. She talked excitedly to the nurse about the plans that would be made for her care. With her limited income she would be able to have a practical nurse until she was able to care for herself, which she firmly believed she would be able to do again some day. She spoke warmly of her grandchildren and her son, who obviously meant a great deal to her. As Miss Ronson, the nurse, assisted her with her morning care she shared the joy her patient was feeling. This was on a Friday, and as far as Mrs. B. was concerned the ideal time for her to leave the hospital would be on Sunday. Then her son would be free to come for her and to help her get settled at home. This would also give the family time to arrange for a practical nurse to begin work on Monday. To Miss Ronson this seemed like good planning and a very real possibility. Although the thought did occur to her that it was strange that Mrs. B's daughter-in-law had not been mentioned in Mrs. B's happy presentation of her home-going plans.

As the morning nurse, Miss Ronson had had very little contact with Mrs. B's family, and thus she was totally un-prepared for the events that were to happen. Even if she had seen her patient's visitors more often, she still might not have recognized the undercurrents of feeling, particularly between Mrs. B. and her daughter-in-law. They were always carefully polite to each other. Young Mrs. B. brought her mother-in-law small gifts, spoke to her about family activities, and always gave Mrs. B. a kiss on the cheek upon arriving and leaving. Miss Ronson had finished helping Mrs. B. with her bed bath and was getting her up in a chair, preparatory to making the bed, when young Mrs. B. arrived. There was the usual exchange of pleasantries and then Mrs. B. asked her daughter-in-law what time her son would come for her on Sunday. Young Mrs. B. looked hesitantly at her mother-in-law, glanced hastily at the nurse and replied: "Well, mother, we've talked it over and we feel that it would be better for you not to come home right now. We are all so busy, and we don't feel that we can give you the care you really ought to have. In fact, John is out right now looking for nursing homes where you can be well cared for. We'll find one not too far away, and we'll be able to come and see you, just as we do here. It will really be better for everyone, especially for you." She was a bit flushed and was talking very rapidly, as though she were afraid to stop.

All of this happened too quickly for the nurse to make a graceful exit, and she was distinctly uncomfortable, even though the other two women did not seem to be aware of her presence. At this point she began to leave the room, but the younger Mrs. B. said, "Please don't go; mother thinks so much of you, I know she'll want you to know of her plans." As the nurse turned back to her bed making, the visitor went on with her remarks to her mother-in-law, "There's a really beautiful place out near . . ." The patient, with a stunned expression, interrupted her: "This wasn't John's idea. This was *your* idea! This is your way of getting me out of your home. You never did want me there." She started to cry and would not listen to the other Mrs. B's attempts at explanation or reassurance. Miss Ronson did not know what to do now. She wanted to put her arms around the old lady and comfort her. Feeling embarrassed to be a witness to this family scene and yet reluctant to run away from it, she finally left the room with the soiled linen, saying she would be back in a few minutes. She hoped these two people would work out their problem themselves, because she already knew that she was leaning in the direction of her patient, and she did not want to interfere.

Soon after Miss Ronson left the room, young Mrs. B. came to her at the nurses' station and said: "I might as well leave. I'm not getting anywhere. This is our one opportunity to move her somewhere else and have a chance to live our own lives again. But she's just too stubborn to want to make a change. Well, if my husband wants her at our house, he can take care of her himself. I'm not going to do it. He'll be in later." Miss Ronson listened, but made no comment. When Mrs. B. turned to leave, she apparently felt badly about what she had said, and spoke to the nurse again: "I hope you'll be going in there soon. She really is upset. Maybe you can help her. I can't do anything with her. I never could. I wish now I hadn't come in." Miss Ronson also wished Mrs. B. hadn't come in, but she merely said kindly that she would return to the room right away, and that she understood how difficult this situation must be for both of them.

When the visitor had left Miss Ronson returned to Mrs. B. She found the patient emotionally exhausted and just beginning to recover from her crying spell. The nurse asked if she could do anything for her, but Mrs. B. shook her head. The nurse patted her hand and said to call her if she needed her. A while later Miss Ronson returned to the room to help Mrs. B. back into bed. Mrs. B. talked a good bit about her feelings of not being wanted and the nurse let her know she understood, by saying that it must be awfully hard to think you are not wanted. Two or three comments of this kind helped Mrs. B. to continue to express her feelings until she quieted down, seeming very tired.

Early in the afternoon John B. came to see his mother. After he had been with her for a while, he came out in search of Miss Ronson. He asked her what had happened between his wife and mother. Instead of directly answering his question, Miss Ronson asked him if they had both told him about it. He told her briefly what each of them had told him, and Miss Ronson agreed that this was essentially what had happened. This saved her the possible embarrassment of having anything she might say misinterpreted, and is a very useful technique, indeed. As Miss Ronson recognized with Mr. B. that this must be very upsetting to him, he continued to talk about the conflict between the women and the resultant tension at home.

This case is another example of a situation in which a nurse becomes involved simply because she is there and people have confidence in her. The case is typical of some family problems in that there is no solution which will be satisfying to everyone. Furthermore, it deals with a situation that is steadily on the increase. Partly, this is so because people are living longer; partly because changes in family life have overlooked the needs of old people. While in the large houses of the past there was room and work for the older generation, we are more and more becoming a society of small-home and apartment dwellers. Activities have tended to become more individual-centered than family-centered. Each family member has his own activities and his own social interests. Unfortunately, most of these activities do not include older people. Thus, in addition to having little or no room to house older people and no constructive work to make them feel worthwhile, today's families do not even have interests they can share with their aged. Because illness is likely to complicate the problems involving the aged, nurses are often forced to be more than interested bystanders.

Once again, the finding of solutions for such problems is not the responsibility of the nurse, but the well-being of the patient is definitely her responsibility. Too often the two conditions cannot be separated. It was part of Miss Ronson's obligation to help Mrs. B. back to health. To attempt this without an awareness of Mrs. B's feelings of frustration and rejection would have been futile. In this instance a compromise was reached whereby Mrs. B. stayed in the hospital a few days longer, left to enter a desirable nursing home on a temporary basis, and was to return to her son's home when she was well and able to take care of herself. Usually in such cases there is more behind the story than the nurse is told; if she is wise she keeps her mind open to all sides of the story. In the B. case, the daughter-in-law was jealous of the patient because she felt her husband was overattentive to his mother. To some extent she was realistic. Mr. B. had brothers and sisters who could have taken his mother, but she preferred to live with him, and he had been willing to take this responsibility. The nurse's responsibility here was largely listening with understanding. Admittedly, this did not contribute directly to solving the problem, but talking about it helped each of them to clarify their wants and needs and to reach a decision.

In other situations involving the interaction between family members a nurse may step in quite actively in an effort to help the family find a solution for a problem.

THE NURSE AS FAMILY PEACEMAKER

Following Mrs. Yost's hospitalization Miss Day, a public health nurse, went to the home for supervisory visits. As she knew in advance from visits to the family of Mrs. Yost's daughter, Miss Day found an elderly woman living with two bachelor sons. The house was owned by the elder son, who was at home during this visit. During their three-way conversation Miss Day received her first hint of family contention: John Yost seemed almost to be competing with his mother for the nurse's attention. Whenever Mrs. Yost referred with obvious fondness to Thomas, the younger son, John brought the conversation back to himself.

At subsequent visits when both men were working, Miss Day learned that Thomas was, indeed, his mother's favorite in spite of the fact that she was supported almost entirely by the elder son. Mrs. Yost was aware of the difference in her feelings for her sons and attributed her favoritism to the suicide of her husband when Thomas was a baby. Her motivations were probably quite complex. Consciously, she felt the situation had developed because she tried to be both mother and father to her baby to compensate for his loss.

After several months Mrs. Yost was hospitalized again for a brief period. Shortly before she was to be discharged from the hospital Mrs. Yost's daughter called Miss Day. The daughter was terribly upset because John had told Thomas to take his things and get out of his house. Furthermore, since Mrs. Yost thought Thomas was so wonderful, she could make her home with him from now on. As for John himself, he was going to sell his house and furniture and find himself a room somewhere. The Yost family was in the low income group. The sons made a living but no more than that. The married daughter had a large family of her own with no extra room in her modest home. She was very distressed about the possible effect of John's ultimatum on her mother and, of course, concerned about where her mother could live. Miss Day listened sympa-

thetically, then, saying that she knew how difficult it would
be for the daughter and her family, she asked if the daughter
could possibly make a place for her mother and Thomas for
just a few days. In the meantime, Miss Day would see John to
learn more about his plans.

Having been a willing listener in the past, as he talked
about his physical ailments and problems, Miss Day was a welcome visitor in John's home. Part of Miss Day's talk with
John follows.

"I wondered if there was something I could do for your
mother? The hospital notified me that she has been discharged."

"She isn't here."

"Oh? I must have misunderstood the message. I was sure
they had said she was discharged!"

"She was—but she is at my sister's. So is Thomas."

"Well, do let me know when she returns home. I would
like to see her."

"She won't be coming home, not here, anyway. I chased
Thomas out. He's always been mother's pet. Let him take care
of her for awhile. No matter what I've done for her, it's never
been enough. She never gave me any credit. It's always Thomas,
Thomas, Thomas!"

"This is hard to take, isn't it? Especially when you feel you
have done so much for your mother. These are trying situations
when parents get older and aren't well. I suppose she will be
looking for some other living arrangements now, won't she?"

"She doesn't know about it yet, I guess. My sister just
suggested that she come there for a few days after she got out
of the hospital. Oh, she can come home, if she wants, but I
don't want Thomas."

"I'm sure she would be more comfortable here than anywhere else. Your mother is so grateful to you for all your kindness to her and thoughtfulness. She has often told me how
much she depends upon you. In fact, sometimes she felt she
was asking too much of you, but you were always the one who

seemed to know what to do about things. She never put this into words but I got the feeling you took your father's place as someone she could lean upon. She did say once that with Thomas too young to remember his father she was glad you were able to be a good example for him. She's going to miss you. But I am sure you know what is best for you. After all, you have your own health to think about."

"Well, I'm not *that* sick! I can take care of her. You know that! I didn't know she felt this way about me. I wouldn't do anything to upset her. Maybe she needs me as much as she needs Thomas. But . . . well . . . I'm going to think some more about my plans."

"All right. And you'll let me know where your mother goes, won't you?"

The ultimate outcome of this interview was the return of both Mrs. Yost and Thomas to John's home. John's new-found belief that his mother really appreciated him enabled him to relinquish some of his martyrish traits, with the result that his mother found it easier to give him attention. Mrs. Yost's physical condition, in spite of her age, improved immeasurably until she was able to care for her son's home, which she enjoyed doing. At the time of Miss Day's last contact with the family, harmony continued to prevail to the benefit of each of the Yosts.

This kind of direct action, involving, as it did, some subversive planning on the part of the nurse cannot be used in every family situation. It worked with this family because they were accustomed to using the public health nurse as a pillar of strength upon which to lean. Outside of medical help they availed themselves of few of the limited resources offered by their small community. Trusting the nurse, and not knowing where else to turn for help, they were suggestible. They accepted without question her role, whereas others might have interpreted what she did as interference.

There are many ways in which family life influences the illness (or health) of a family member, and, conversely, in which illness influences various phases of family life. And there are many situations in which a nurse's knowledge of family interaction can be of help to her in assisting a troubled patient or family. The principles brought out in our examples can be applied by nurses in many family-based problems. There are, however, two major areas of difficulty; they contain emotionally-charged elements which make their handling more complex.

Some illnesses complicate family problems

One of these areas includes all conditions that may be thought of as guilt-producing, and the other, closely allied to the first, is the area related to sex or sexual activity. Through the years, doctors and nurses have had to combat the barrier of morality in order to fight certain diseases.

This statement is by no means intended to reduce the importance of morality. The concept of good, wholesome morals is a valuable one for all of us who are concerned with the welfare of society as a whole. Yet, morality sometimes interferes with the promotion of health and the prevention and treatment of disease. Two clear-cut examples of this side effect of morals are to be found in venereal disease and alcoholism.

Venereal disease is simultaneously a health problem, a family problem and, possibly, a moral problem. For centuries the venereal diseases have been associated with sexual activity outside of marriage and, therefore, with immorality. It was finally recognized that venereal disease could not be controlled until it was brought out in the open, and emphasis placed on treatment of the patient rather than on the stigma of immorality. Gradually the stigma has decreased, although vestiges of it remain in the minds of many. For those of us who assist the medical profession in treating venereal diseases, in interviewing patients and in locating their "contacts" there can be no moralistic or judgmental attitudes about the people involved. If the moral aspects were emphasized by doctors and nurses, in all probability a patient would be hesitant about presenting himself for treatment. He would also feel much too guilty and ashamed to name his contacts, so that they could be treated, or, if he were married, to face his wife with the fact that she too needed to be examined, and possibly treated.

Sometimes it is a nurse's responsibility to interview venereal disease patients for the purpose of interpreting the diagnosis, explaining the treatment, and, most important, obtaining the names of contacts. For every venereal disease patient there is someone from whom he contracted the disease and possibly someone to whom he has given it. The nurse, therefore, must be aware of the significance the patient's diagnosis has for his family life situation. When the patient is a married man or woman, and the disease is the result of extramarital sexual activity, the patient frequently is already guilt-laden. Any censuring on the part of the interviewer, either by word or expression, will add to the patient's guilt, and will make him feel less cooperative about giving the names of contacts. A successful approach presupposes a thoughtful consideration of the patient's reaction to his diagnosis; it conveys a deep-seated interest in the patient and his welfare. There is no substitute for a genuine interest in arousing confidence. A constructive approach includes starting the interview where the patient's thoughts and feelings are at that particular moment, rather than attempting to bring his thoughts to a starting point that may be convenient for the interviewer. In dealing with a patient's emotional reaction to a diagnosis as significant as that of venereal disease, there is no room for small, petty thoughts and prejudices. The nurse, as an interviewer, must retain humility and a certain objectivity, for becoming emotionally involved may becloud her judgment. Yet, the nurse must be able to feel with her patient if she is really to reach through to him.

Frequently when a patient has his first interview, the diagnosis of venereal disease is not as upsetting to him as the consequences the disease may have in his family life. The nurse who is conscientious and perceptive can tactfully uncover these worries so that their disclosure may be an important factor in the patient's ability to accept his diagnosis and treatment. In the event that the patient is married and his home has been a comparatively placid and happy one, the shock and mental anguish caused by the thought of a possible breakup, intensified by his feeling of guilt, is particularly devastating. Only the nurse who can visualize the whole situation, who can understand what the diagnosis means to a patient morally, socially, physically, and especially in his family relationships can effectively deal with the venereal disease problem.

Many of the points which have been discussed here apply equally in the treatment of alcoholism. The attitude of the public and the feelings of the patient about the diseases are similar. Even more than is true of the venereal disease patient, the alcoholic when sober, is characterized by self-derogatory, self-condemning attitudes. The etiology, even a definition, of alcoholism is still open to question. Among the people engaged in research on alcoholicm are those who are convinced that there is a biochemical basis for alcohol addiction. There are others who feel that alcoholism is the result of an inadequate personality structure in which the victim attempts to satisfy emotional needs through the use of alcohol. Still others feel that alcoholism must be a result of both of these conditions. Emotional needs may drive some people to seek satisfaction and release from tension through drinking. Some of these, because of basic biochemical factors, will become alcoholics, others will not. Regardless of what is known or not known about alcoholism as a disease, it is recognized as a devastating condition emotionally and socially, having a particularly disruptive influence on family life. The alcoholic, like anyone else who is acutely suffering from guilt feelings, needs most of all to be accepted as an individual. His family, either sharing his suffering with him or suffering as a direct result of his alcoholic behavior, needs to be supported and to be helped to understand alcoholism as a disease rather than a moral weakness. Alcoholism today is considered to be the third largest public health problem. For this reason, a large part of a later chapter will be devoted to it.

There are other conditions that involve guilt feelings and

are related to family interaction. Miscarriage and stillbirth frequently are guilt-producing, especially when the mother has unconsciously rejected her developing baby. Illegitimate pregnancy is another. The unwed mother who has been made to feel accepted and worthwhile is far less likely to make the same mistake again. If she feels misunderstood and rejected, the motivation to seek any kind of relationship in which temporarily she feels loved and desirable will continue to be present. When the unwed mother has been blamed, criticized, perhaps even ostracized by members of her own family, her need for kindness, empathy and understanding from an insightful nurse is even more necessary.

SUPPOSE SHE WERE MY DAUGHTER?

Silence hung over the bed like an ominous cloud as Mrs. Eaton busied herself with the admission routine for the new maternity patient. The atmosphere was heavy with hurt; hostility, sadness. Mrs. Eaton, sensing the tension and conflict between the young patient and her mother, did not trust herself to say any more than was necessary as she helped the girl into bed. Keeping her distance, both emotionally and physically, Mrs. Lynch watched the proceedings with a cold, impenetrable expression. Mrs. Eaton sized her up as a tough customer who might lash out in brutal anger if she let go of her feelings. Mrs. Lynch was heavy, stolid, with a no-nonsense air about her that was emphasized by the current situation. Having left in a hurry to bring her daughter to the hospital when the pains started, Mrs. Lynch's unpleasant appearance was worsened by her hurried dressing. Her graying hair was uncombed and her housedress was mussed. When her daughter was settled in bed, Mrs. Lynch said abruptly, "I'll be going, nurse, you won't need me." For the first time the girl spoke, plaintively, "Mom, don't leave me here alone!" Sharply her mother answered, "Now, look here, Lucy, you didn't need me around when you got into this mess, so you can do without me now. I've got to go to work in the morning." When she went out the door, Lucy stretched

out her arm with a pleading, "Mom, please!" As the door
closed and the sound of the plodding steps receded down the
hall, Mrs. Eaton grasped the outstretched hand firmly in her
own, thinking, "Suppose she were my daughter?"

What a small soft hand! It had the smooth, fair, un-
blemished look typical of a teenage girl's hand. The hand
matched the little-girl face. Tears were running down the
rounded cheeks—and now the face was distorted with pain.
"Poor kid," thought Mrs. Eaton, "not sixteen years old yet
and she has to face this alone."

Twenty-four hours later the delivery was over. Adoption
arrangements had already been made, and according to plan
Lucy did not see her baby girl. When Mrs. Eaton came on duty
at 3 o'clock, she wondered if Lucy would be less tense and
anxious now that it was over. She was not. She was lonely,
frightened and depressed, appearing more childlike than ever
and strangely out of place in the ward filled with grown women.
The activities of the busy maternity ward and the babble of
voices—nurses', patients', visitors'—drifted around Lucy without
seeming to touch her at all. Mrs. Eaton wondered if Lucy's
hurt was so great that no one could reach her. The nurse
wondered also what the patient's life would hold for her when
she returned home to the rejecting mother.

Six days in the hospital is not much time for a busy nurse
to help with such a tremendous emotional problem as Lucy
was experiencing. It took three days of patient understanding
on Mrs. Eaton's part to give Lucy the courage to tell a little of
her experience and her feelings about it. When the girl realized
that she could talk freely to Mrs. Eaton without being censured
or condemned, she was able to talk of the much more distressing problem of her relationship with her mother. The eldest of
four children whose parents had separated several years before,
Lucy had been forced to carry a heavy burden of responsibility
in the family. Her mother, with an air of martyrdom, drove
herself and her children desperately hard in an effort to maintain the family in a semblance of decency. Decency was a by-

word with Mrs. Lynch, and she pounded into her children the necessity for constant hard work to keep up decent standards. Good children, in her estimation, were necessarily busy children. Lucy, in particular, was expected to keep her nose to the grindstone in order to "keep out of trouble." There was no time in Mrs. Lynch's Spartan regime for expressions of affection or understanding.

During Lucy's gradual sharing of her feelings with Mrs. Eaton, she was repeatedly emphasizing how she had let her mother down when her mother had sacrificed so much for her. Lucy was carrying an almost intolerable load of guilt. Just as Mrs. Eaton was accepting of Lucy as a human being, she was accepting, too, of Lucy's right to feel guilty. When a person *has* to feel guilt, whether the cause of the guilt is imaginary or, as in this instance, very real, a counselor has no right to snatch this guilt away or to deny its existence. The guilt needs to be recognized, faced, expressed and accepted. All of this Lucy was able to do before she left the hospital.

Lucy's mother came in only once to see her. Although pressed for time, Mrs. Eaton was concerned enough about Lucy to waylay Mrs. Lynch for a short talk. Still stolid and unyielding, Mrs. Lynch provided a real challenge for the nurse's counseling skills. Instead of talking about Lucy, Mrs. Eaton concentrated on how difficult all of this had been for Mrs. Lynch. The mother's whole approach to life was so defensive that she anticipated blame and condemnation. Unconsciously seeing herself as a failure because of Lucy's difficulty, she expected to be judged by her own self-evaluation. Mrs. Eaton's warmth and empathy, instead of anticipated criticism and instructions, threw the aggressive Mrs. Lynch off balance and she began to thaw slightly under the warmth of the nurse's understanding. When they parted, Mrs. Lynch indicated that no one had ever cared before how *she* felt about this situation. Mrs. Eaton took this opportunity to say, "That's a terrible feeling to have, isn't it? I've wondered if Lucy feels a little bit this way, too? I know this has been pretty hard on both of you."

Although there is no way of estimating the value of Mrs. Eaton's wise counseling, it is reasonable to assume that Lucy and her mother were better able to adjust to a trying situation and to each other because of Mrs. Eaton's efforts. Basic to what the understanding nurse did was her total acceptance of these two people and a complete absence of condemnation. *Depending upon her own attitudes,* any nurse could and should do as much.

In view of the large amount of illness that is emotionally caused, the medical team, including the nurses giving care, needs to be alert to the influence of family life factors on such patients. Frequently there can be found a correlation between increased discomfort of the patient and the visits of certain members of the family in the hospital. The asthmatic patient who inquires anxiously all morning as to the exact time for visiting hours and who requires his PRN aminophylline suppository after his wife goes home; the woman admitted for Menière's Disease who has a severe attack of vertigo and vomiting just before her newly engaged daughter is expected to visit her; the two-year old who toddles deliberately to the opposite end of the crib and stares out the window when his mother comes to visit him on the pediatric unit; the young woman admitted for investigation of her low back pain looking appropriately wan when her husband sits quietly by her bedside, holding her hand. It is for us, as nurses, to interpret this behavior for the patient's benefit, not for the patient's condemnation.

In this chapter various conditions affecting family life or being influenced by family life have been considered. They are examples of the many possible situations. The important things to remember when attempting to help a family in time of adversity are: A patient's physical condition cannot be separated from other aspects of his life; whatever influences a patient's family has or has had on his life will be reflected in his progress or lack of it; nurses frequently will be called upon through social as well as professional contacts to give help in family problems or crises; in order to be able to give the help she is asked for the nurse must know her own limitations; a nurse to make her optimum contribution must understand the family dynamics lying behind the family problems.

Sometimes nurses may *learn* a great deal and be helped themselves through their contacts with a family affected by the illness of one of its members. Bravery, forbearance, patience and fortitude in the face of destitution can be observed daily in the hour-by-hour routines of the hospital situation. Families can be faithful and protective of the members of their family who are ill, for many reasons. We have discussed the negative reasons—guilt, hostility, over-dependence. But there may be a highly positive reason for such reactions, that is, love—love not tinged with guilt or hostility or any negative feeling whatever. The manifestations of love, however, may be difficult for us to handle.

LOVE AND COURAGE IN ACTION

Sue R. was the mother of four young children, ranging in age from seven years to one year. The family lived in the country. The parents had renovated a barn that had been standing on their acre, and of it they had made a charming home. Sue R. was a lovely woman, but, by the time of her husband's hospital admission, she showed physically the wear of her husband's illness. Jim was an engineer in a nearby city—successful, out-going, productive. At the age of 41, Jim entered the hospital, never to be discharged. The diagnosis was acute leukemia.

Death did not have an easy time with Jim. Jim had the one quality that death has the most difficult struggle to conquer, the will to live. Jim had a will to live, and a great deal to live for. It took six weeks for him to die, and for six weeks from morning until night his wife was by his side. Sue bathed him, fed him, turned him, read to him, in short, she tended to his every need both physically and emotionally. The nurses were at first thankful for her help, then amazed at her perseverance, then more and more concerned about her as she daily grew more pale, more tense, more quiet. Her hope never wavered. She would say to the nurses, "Tomorrow, maybe tomorrow they'll find a new drug." One tomorrow came, not bringing with it a new drug, but taking with it her husband. Even at death Sue did not cry. The pathetic acceptance of Jim's death by his wife was as difficult and as disquieting for the nurses to accept as the overt grief so frequently seen. Behavior such as Sue displayed may be beyond our understanding. It certainly is beyond our judgment. It makes us hope that tomorrow, maybe tomorrow there will be a new drug. It makes us believe more firmly that human beings can adjust to nearly any situation that is clearly defined and inevitable.

6

At Home in the Hospital

Perhaps the thought of being a human relations expert might be frightening to a young nurse. If being an expert in human relations to her means assisting people in solving severe emotional or guidance problems for which she has not been professionally trained, any nurse, not only a student, might well be frightened at this prospect. But in our consideration of human relations we mean something much broader, much less specific than this. A nurse is responsible for improving human relations by making a patient feel at home in the hospital or comfortable with his illness wherever he is.

Did the hospital ever frighten you?

Can you remember back to your introduction to the hospital, to its large and varied staff, to the many confusing procedures that constitute the daily hospital routine? In all probability you, like any other student nurse, had some very anxious moments as you faced these new experiences. Each time you went to a new department for duty, each time you were introduced to hospital personnel you had not met before, or the first time you went on an errand to a different area of the hospital, you probably had some apprehension. You wondered if people would like you, you wondered about your ability to face whatever this new experience brought you, you hoped you would not do anything foolish or make any serious mistakes. Ordinarily a student nurse has entered this strange hospital world because she has wanted to. She is already interested in what it has to offer her life, and she hopes and expects to learn through her experience and to enjoy it. Furthermore, she is young, well, strong, healthy and relatively independent. If a well motivated student nurse who voluntarily enters a hospital to receive her education in nursing is anxious about the hospital setting and the procedures being carried out, how much more anxious will a patient and his family be about the mysterious atmosphere and activities within the hospital. It takes a good many weeks before the average student nurse has sorted out in her mind the various personnel involved in work with patients, what all of these people do, where they are located, how and when the strange-looking pieces of equipment are used. Eventually, however, partly through the trial and error method and partly with the help of others, she becomes oriented to hospital life and activity. What is more important, she becomes familiar with what is expected of her in relation to the work of all of the other hospital personnel with patients.

A patient is much more frightened

Looking at the hospital life from the patient's angle is quite different. He may never have been in a hospital before. Even if he has been hospitalized before, he has not had the opportunity to become familiar with all of the activities carried on within a hospital. On the occasion of each admission he will face some new experience. The average patient will be involved quite superficially with a number of members of the hospital staff. Too often he will not know what these people want of him or what they are going to do to him. The unknown is always a little frightening, and in the hospital situation there is not just one unknown experience for the patient to face but usually a whole series of them. When he is not prepared for them, each one increases the anxiety, tension and apprehension the patient had at the beginning. Let us consider some of the things which may happen to the average patient in a hospital.

PUTTING OUT THE WELCOME MAT

Mrs. J., a middle-aged woman who has never been hospitalized before, is admitted to the hospital for various diagnostic studies. She enters the hospital late in the afternoon and is shown to her bed in a four-bed ward. The other three beds are occupied, but the busy nurse who is admitting the patient does not take time to introduce the other occupants of the room. They look curiously at Mrs. J., but do not speak to her. After what may have been only a few minutes but seems a long time to Mrs. J., a young man dressed in white comes into the ward, and introduces himself as Dr. somebody. He mumbles it so badly that Mrs. J. has no idea what his name is. As he proceeds to examine her and to ask her all over again the same questions she has already answered for her own doctor, she knows only that this is not *her* doctor and she feels a little resentment. A short while after the young doctor has left with a pleasant but uninformative "good-bye," a young woman, also dressed in white, approaches Mrs. J's bedside with a basket full of little tubes and bottles, and asks briefly whether this is Mrs. J. Upon having the patient's affirmative answer, the young woman, with actions so quick and deft that Mrs. J. cannot follow them, sponges Mrs. J's finger with alcohol. As she does this, she says matter-of-factly, "I'm going to stick your finger." Before Mrs. J. can react to this, she winces with the unexpected jab of the technician's small blade. She watches with awe the technician who with her lips quickly pulls the drop of blood into a tiny tube, and then squeezes more blood out of the finger. When the young woman finishes, busying herself with more of her strange equipment, she tells Mrs. J. to hold the sponge against her finger. Thankful that this new experience is over, Mrs. J. is startled all over again when the technician suddenly pulls Mrs. J's arm out straight and announces that she is going to take some blood from the arm. Mrs. J. automatically follows directions, opening and closing her fist without having any idea why. As silently as she came, the young woman leaves. Except for giving directions to Mrs. J. she did not say a word. In an hour or so a young woman in a green uniform comes in with supper trays. She speaks pleasantly to Mrs. J. and leaves a tray of food for her which the patient eats, but without much relish. And so the evening goes. Two more nurses come in. One gives Mrs. J. a capsule and tells her to sleep well. The other one, whom Mrs. J. correctly assumes to be the night nurse, comes in to check on the patients around midnight. These were the major experiences—all of them new—of Mrs. J's first afternoon and night in the hospital. There were many strange sounds and unfamiliar activities throughout the night, which did not affect Mrs. J. directly, but the very unfamiliarity of which helped to increase her apprehension.

With the aid of the medication Mrs. J. has some intermittent sleep. In fact, she is sound asleep in the early morning hours when the nurse comes in to take her temperature and to give her an enema. An enema, of course, is not a new experience for Mrs. J. But to have one lying in bed is new, and she is frightened that she may soil the bedclothing. The nurse does not seem to be aware of this as she efficiently and quickly goes about her work. Nor does she explain why Mrs. J. who is not constipated should have an enema. Mrs. J. does not question it, nor does sne express her anxiety about the bedclothing. The nurse seems to be too busy to answer questions or to listen to Mrs. J's foolish anxieties. Mrs. J. merely adds this to the anxiety she was beginning to build up about being in the hospital, and her apprehension increases.

Later in the morning still another woman in a green uniform, an older woman this time, brings in breakfast trays. She gives Mrs. J. hers and moves back to her cart. Then she rushes again to Mrs. J's bedside and snatches her tray away, saying, "Here. You're not supposed to have that!" For some reason the aide's tone of voice makes Mrs. J. feel guilty about having accepted the tray in the first place. She also feels a little resentful that she does not know why she is not to have her breakfast.

Other visitors in the morning include a friendly student nurse, the head nurse on the ward and a different intern from the one who had been in the night before. Soon after Mrs. J. has bathed herself in the lavatory, another green-clad woman comes into the ward with a wheelchair and announces that she is going to take Mrs. J. to X-ray. With no idea of where X-ray is or when she will return, Mrs. J. is wheeled through seemingly endless corridors, and taken down in an elevator. In the X-ray department she finds herself one of several people waiting in a corridor, while technicians and doctors rush around, preoccupied with their own pursuits. After what seems to Mrs. J. an interminable length of time, she is wheeled into the X-ray room. Here she is given abrupt orders as to what she should do. When the X-rays have been completed, Mrs. J. is wheeled out into the corridor again. No one tells her whether she is to have further X-ray studies or to be returned to the ward. She nervously realizes she would not find her way back anyway. After another long wait, by which time Mrs. J. has become hungry and irritable in addition to being apprehensive, the aide who had brought her there returns to wheel her back to the ward.

Just before lunch when Mrs. J's doctor comes in to see her he finds his patient at the point of tears. The head nurse, after being questioned by the doctor about what had upset Mrs. J. reaches the hasty conclusion that this is a frightened, nervous woman who is going to be difficult. This opinion filters down through the ward staff, with the result that even those staff members who have had no contact with Mrs. J. are forming preconceived ideas about her behavior.

When we know in advance that someone is going to give us a hard time we become defensive. All interpersonal relations involve *inter*action. In this instance we have a woman who is justifiably apprehensive about a new experience, in addition to whatever apprehension she may have about the results of her diagnostic studies. Needing desperately to have some support and alleviation of her anxiety, she finds herself instead in the indifferent hospital atmosphere at its worst. Her anxiety grows with each new experience for which she is unprepared, and soon her anxiety takes the form of anger.

This is *her* reaction. The ward staff, sensing her anger, but unfortunately not looking for the cause behind it, react to the patient's reaction with defensive behavior. Unconsciously they are attempting to defend themselves from their own guilt feelings. What shows on the surface, however, is a hostile reaction, the natural reaction to unconscious guilt feelings. Mrs. J. reacts to their hostility-tinged behavior with increased anxiety, manifested by tears and a more intense irritability. Thus, at the very beginning of her hospital stay, hostile interaction is established. All of this developed because the hospital staff looked at Mrs. J's experience *through their own eyes*. Because they had learned to accept the hospital routine without fear, they took for granted that a patient would be equally able to accept it.

Emotional comfort is part of nursing

The illustration used here is an extreme one. It is unlikely that one patient in twenty-four hours or less would undergo this much "objective" treatment at the hands of everyone she is meeting in the hospital. On the other hand, every patient is faced with at least some of these experiences or similar ones. And every patient experiences at least some of the negative feeling which victimized and characterized Mrs. J. Any nurse will readily admit that part of her professional responsibility is to make a patient comfortable. But too often a nurse fails to recognize that emotional comfort, freedom from apprehension and anxiety, is of equal importance with physical comfort. In fact, one might question whether there can be complete physical comfort where emotional comfort is lacking.

Of all the times when a patient needs to be made emotionally comfortable, there is none more important than that of his entrance into the hospital. He has left the relative security of his family, his home and his friends. He is plunged, sometimes quite unexpectedly, into the midst of strangers, on some of whom he will be dependent for an indeterminate period of time. Almost anywhere else a person goes to spend any length of time, he meets and talks with other people. He is made to feel at home. With few exceptions, he makes visits to places, other than the hospital, voluntarily in the line of business or in search of recreation or perhaps for study; and his decision is not complicated by ill health. Ordinarily he has some idea, too, about the length of his prospective stay.

A person entering a hospital is already frightened about his state of health. Added to this are questions for which there may be no answers: How long will I be here? Am I going to be cured by my stay in the hospital or will I get worse? What will happen to my home, to my family, to my job as a result of my being ill? He may be worried about whether he will ever leave the hospital alive. Many patients carry this terrifying thought to the hospital with them. The fear of death, in many instances, is too realistic for the patient to want to think about consciously, but unconsciously it is frequently present and underlying much of the tension and anxiety the patient feels. These are some of the factors with which the hospital personnel, as well as the patient himself, must contend when he is admitted to the hospital.

In the illustration of Mrs. J., there were many people who contributed to her discomfort. Can a nurse be responsible for the failure of other hospital personnel to add to the patient's comfort? Obviously not. However, with certain members of the hospital team the nurse may set an example. By precept she may teach aides and other non-professional workers on the ward; also her actions and attitudes may counteract the actions and attitudes of others. Let us consider some of the ways in which a perceptive nurse may do this. First, a nurse may—and should— introduce herself, adding some brief explanation about her position on the ward, such as that she is the morning nurse, or the afternoon nurse, or a relief nurse. A patient frequently wonders when he will see a nurse again, whether the same nurse will continue to care for him, whether he will have different nurses every day. It's a simple (and courteous) matter to say, "I'm Miss Smith. I'll be here until eleven o'clock and then Miss Jones will be on duty." As the nurse is getting the patient settled she may ask him about previous hospital experience, recognize his apprehension, assure him of her desire to make him feel at home. Learning from the patient why he is in the hospital, or having this knowledge from the admitting physician or the admissions card, the nurse may explain the hospital routine, say probably a laboratory technician will come to take blood samples, and so on. When a patient is admitted to a ward or a semi-private room, common courtesy demands that he be introduced to at least those patients who are in nearby beds. This is assuming, of course, that the newcomer and the patients already there are well enough to acknowledge and care about the presence of someone else.

Nurses who ignore these small courtesies often say they are time-consuming. They are not. Even if they were, they would pay dividends in time saved later on, because of the patient's desire to cooperate with the people who made efforts to help him. But rarely do these gestures require extra time. Most of the small comforts can be offered while admission procedure or nursing care is accomplished. Rather than time, what a patient requires is a genuine interest in his total welfare, a sincere desire to make him comfortable, and a nurse's perceptive ability—the ability to put herself into his bedroom slippers.

Hospital versus home

A hospital is a poor substitute for the comfort and security of a home. At home, a patient (usually) knows that he is being cared for by someone who loves him. He feels a certain measure of security in this, believing that his loved ones will do everything in their power to help him. In the hospital he is in the hands of strangers, trained yes, but strangers nonetheless. At home he is restricted only by the limitations imposed by the illness itself, not by rules necessary in running an institution. If his condition permits he may have visitors at ten o'clock at night or at eight o'clock in the morning. His morning temperature may be taken just as effectively at seven o'clock as at five or six. If he cannot sleep, and wishes to listen to the radio or to read at two A.M., there is no hard and fast rule which will deny him this pleasure.

At best, except for the otherwise homeless, a hospital cannot take the place of a home. Adding to this the fact that, when a patient is admitted in a hospital, his life is usually complicated by serious illness, we might say that, at worst, a hospital can be a house of horror and fright. Because the average patient and his family have more contact with nurses than with any other members of the hospital staff, the nurses have the greatest influence on a patient's concept of hospital life. The way a patient feels about his hospital experience may, in turn, influence the progress the patient is able to make.

Old patients—new experiences

Not only new patients are apprehensive about the hospital experience, but patients who have been in the hospital for some time tend to become anxious over each new experience during their stay. The fact that some of the therapeutic, diagnostic and nursing procedures are definitely painful or uncomfortable serves to add to this ever-present fear of a new experience in the hospital. Under ordinary circumstances patients have not only the need but the right to know where they are going and what is going to happen when they are placed on a litter or wheelchair and taken to some other part of the hospital. Have you ever lain flat on your back and been wheeled on a stretcher for a block or more to an unknown destination, having a distorted view of what is on each side of you, seeing with clarity only the ceiling and whatever equipment is straight above and the upside-down face of the person wheeling you, hearing the voices of people you do not know and cannot see? If you add to this strange method of locomotion the fact that you do not know where you are going or why, your imagination may carry you into the depths of fear, even panic, the patient may be feeling.

Explanation may relieve apprehension

In all probability we will not be able to alleviate all of this apprehension, but we can relieve a great deal of it by simple explanation, "You are going to the X-ray department now. So-and-so will wheel you there, and when you have finished the X-ray department will notify us and someone will come for you." "This is Miss Y. She is a laboratory technician and will stick your finger to get a little blood sample for a test." "Your breakfast will be served later this morning because you have to have an X-ray (or a blood test or whatever it is) while your stomach is still empty." How long did it take you to read each of the above statements? Just that long would it take to make the brief explanations. But the comfort the average patient may receive by having something explained is immeasurable.

In giving an explanation or information of any kind, what we say must be geared to each individual's needs and ability to understand. A patient who has been wheeled to the X-ray department regularly two or three times a week does not need the explanation that a new patient needs. A nurse who is herself a patient may not have to have preoperative preparation explained to her. A diabetic patient need not be emotionally prepared anew for each shot of insulin. Nevertheless, all of these patients have feelings about the experience they are undergoing, and their feelings should be considered. It is far better to err in the direction of giving a kindly explanation to someone who does not need it, than to assume a knowledge and relaxed attitude on the part of the patient that are not there at all. Some professional people think that giving information increases the worry of patients in the hospital. Actually the opposite is true. It is the unknown which is fear-producing.

Any institution easily becomes a breeding ground for rumors. Where there is no information, there is apt to be misinformation based on speculation, eavesdropping, idle gossip and rumors. These are far more damaging usually than is correct information. Sometimes patients hear small portions of a whispered conference between nurses or between doctor and nurse. A few words can be misinterpreted and passed from patient to patient with very upsetting results. An example follows.

A surgical patient was going to be transferred from a very busy ward to a semi-private ward. The man had, attached to his bed, a surgical appliance which had to accompany him to his new room. To facilitate transferring this appliance from the bed to the litter with the patient, he was taken in his bed into the dressing room. While the transfer was taking place the intern noticed that an important tube was slipping out and said sharply, "Be careful!" Then he added, almost sadly, "Well, it's too late now. That one's done for." The tube had slipped out and dropped onto the floor. The patient was then wheeled away to the semi-private ward. When the tube fell down another patient happened to pass the dressing room, the door of which was partly open. He saw an intern, two nurses and an orderly hovering in what he interpreted as an anxious manner around the bed and litter. He also heard the doctor's words. That was enough for him. He passed the word around the ward that "old Jones never did make it to his new ward."

Sometimes a patient who has been in the hospital for a while will have a sudden change of routine which may be frightening.

WHAT DOES CHANGE MEAN TO A PATIENT?

Mr. T., a foreign-born patient who spoke and understood little English, had been ambulatory during his five-day stay in the hospital. One morning as he started toward the bathroom a nurse called to him that he was not allowed bathroom privileges any more. From now on, he was to use a urinal and a bedpan. Mr. T. was one of the "good" patients who never creates any difficulty for the nurses. He quietly went back to bed and used the bottle the orderly brought him. All day long his mind dwelt on this sudden change in routine. You might wonder why he simply did not ask about it instead of worrying. But this fails to take into account the fact that many people are afraid of hospitals, nurses and doctors. Sometimes, people are afraid of what they might learn, or are afraid of asking questions which may make them appear foolish or stupid. In Mr. T's case there was the language difficulty, too; or his foreign background made it embarrassing for him to discuss "bedpans" with nurses. Anyway, he did not ask questions, and when his American-born daughter arrived that evening he was a frightened, worried man. He told his daughter that he must be much worse, and explained why he thought that. It is easy to understand how this idea may have developed. In his brief hospital experience he had learned that the critically ill patients were not able to go to the bathroom, while many of the less critically ill were ambulatory. The young woman, who had heard from her father's doctor that he was improving daily could not understand this. Receiving no enlightenment from the patient, the visitor spoke to a nurse who explained that the doctor would like to have urine specimens measured for a few days. How much less time it would have taken to explain this simple fact to the patient in the beginning, and how much easier it would have been for the patient.

Sometimes a patient is too upset, frightened or worried to be able to accept an explanation. The nurse's handling of this more difficult kind of problem will be considered in the next chapter. Nevertheless, explanations whenever possible and not contraindicated by the patient's doctor or by the patient's mental or physical condition, do help to relieve realistic anxiety.

The nurse as hostess

Most nurses, after a few months, feel at home in the hospital situation. In other words, a nurse is a regular member of the hospital family and as such is responsible for making strangers comfortable in her hospital home. In our own home, two strangers are not left wondering about each other but are introduced; a stranger usually is also introduced to other members of the family. So should patients, the "strangers" of the hospital, be introduced to each other and to members of the hospital staff.

Even as we consider this analogy we know that a hospital is *not* a home. Having to be in a hospital certainly does not constitute normal living for anyone. Patients are separated from their friends and loved ones. They are cut off from their work and other usual activities. They are sick, dependent, regressed. Their families are worried, frightened, feeling isolated and helpless. It is a highly abnormal living situation. But there is no reason for making the situation even worse. Any gesture or word or act which can ease the minds of the patient and his family, which can contribute to making the atmosphere more normal will help to promote the comfort of a patient. It seems so simple, and yet the personnel in most hospitals refuse to act normally in their interpersonal relations within the hospital because it *is* a hospital situation. There are positive factors in hospital life also, factors which tend to counteract the abnormality of it, and they are the ones that should be stressed: Kindness and understanding, a genuine desire to help others, sincere efforts to create emotional and physical comfort for the patients.

Perhaps it would help the total hospital atmosphere if these positive factors were stressed a great deal more in the interactions of hospital personnel with each other. Where staff interrelationships are characterized by warmth and consideration, inevitably some of this good feeling will filter down to that VIP, the patient, for whom presumably the hospital exists. It may be that personnel, as well as patients, need help in their efforts to feel at home in the hospital. This is essentially true of the newcomer to an established hospital situation. A supervisor in a large urban hospital tells of an experience in helping a new member of the nursing staff in her adjustment difficulties in her new position. This illustration points out also that a counseling interview cannot always be anticipated as such.

EVEN THE BOSS HAS FEELINGS

For nine years I had been supervisor of the pediatric unit in the hospital from which I graduated. When I took over the ward, it was in pretty bad shape from the standpoints of physical plan and equipment and the morale of the ward personnel. This was a real challenge to me. With the backing of administration, medical staff and nursing office, I was given a free hand to build the ward into one of the finest pediatric departments in the city. I realize now how childishly I reveled in the praise and appreciation the new department called forth. Almost defensive about "my" unit, I resented any criticims of it.

Into my satisfying professional situation there entered a new director of nursing. Most of the nursing staff had hated to see the former director leave. We all had known of the undercurrent of friction between the director and the hospital administrator, and our sympathies were with the director. Knowing that the new director was the choice of the administrator did nothing to help us accept the director or make her welcome. There was no effort on anyone's part to make her orientation to the position easier; the administration, except in individual cases, did not introduce her to the staff; she herself seemed too busy becoming familiar with office routine to meet the nurses; the nursing staff and school faculty openly avoided her.

It was several weeks before she finally came to my unit. I had instructed my staff to be on their best behavior and I was eager that she receive a good impression. Throughout the tour, in which I proudly pointed out the innovations that had been most recently adopted, she remained cool, aloof and professional. At the end of the tour, she turned to me and said, "And this is the fabulous new pediatric ward? It requires a lot of work, doesn't it?"

I was stunned! I interpreted the first part of her comment

as sarcasm; in the rest of her comment I felt she was saying there was still much to be done in the ward. I could hardly wait for the day to end; I was so anxious to go home and write my resignation. This was a personal insult. My roommate, a head nurse, agreed wholeheartedly with me, since she had the same preconception of the woman that I and most of the others had.

When I made the appointment to see her, I went into the office all ready to take a defensive stand. Promptly submitting my resignation I proceeded to denounce with anger the inference she had made concerning my unit. She looked completely baffled at first, but after my ten-minute speech, prepared in advance, she pushed back her chair and began to laugh, exclaiming, "My dear girl, how very stupid I was!" The director explained that she had meant that rebuilding the ward must have meant a lot of work on my part—which, indeed, it had. She sounded so sincere that my anger gave way to shame and embarrassment. When she came to the unit, I had been so negative and defensive I could interpret what she said only in the light of my own hostile feeling toward her.

Suddenly I was able to see exactly what had happened to me and the others on the staff. We were so thoughtless and unfair we never gave her a chance to prove her ability, nor had we taken her awkward position into consideration. As I tried briefly to explain this to her, she occasionally nodded her head, then said, "I can understand how you all felt. These past weeks have been difficult for you." There was a long pause. I wasn't sure whether I should leave, but she made no move to indicate that the interview was over. Somehow I felt that she wanted me to stay. I glanced at her and saw that her eyes were filled with tears. In a moment she broke the silence by saying, "I'm so glad you came in. I've wanted and needed so much to talk to someone. It's been a long and lonely few weeks." I told her I was in no hurry, and would love to talk with her.

She told me how she had felt when leaving the position she had been in for a long time to come into a strange hospital in a strange city, but that she had made the change because the new position represented a challenge to her. Our school of nursing was losing its accreditation and she, being a nationally recognized coordinator of nursing education and nursing service, had been selected to bring our standards back to what they had been in the past. She told of the very cool welcome she had received from the supervisors in the nursing office, and of being shoved back into a drab office which could hold little more than an ugly desk. On her first day no one offered to accompany her to lunch. When she walked into an office, everyone seemed to scatter. When she returned to her quarters in the nurses' residence that first night, she found flowers and cards and notes from members of her staff at the hospital she had left, but there was not a single gesture to indicate any thought of her on the part of her new staff.

Having relieved herself of the negative feelings that had been crowding in on her, the director then looked at her own part in this unfortunate situation. She said that she, too, had been on the defensive, having known something of the previous dissension in the hospital. She had attempted to initiate changes without first getting to know the nursing staff. Afraid of not being accepted in the place of the former director, she realized that perhaps she was attempting to demand respect at least, even if the staff would not like her. We talked for an hour and a half. When we parted we both knew it had been time well spent, for we were now able to see not only each other in a different light but ourselves as well.

At the time of the interview I did not see its counseling aspects, but I see them now. It might have been traumatic to both of us if I had left abruptly when I sensed that she wanted to talk, or if we hadn't respected each other's feelings and needs.

Things have changed since that interview, a year ago. Once more our hospital is accredited. The director of nursing is not only accepted but genuinely liked by the majority of her staff. Many things have contributed to this change, but I like to think that my giving her the opportunity to talk and my not being frightened of suddenly being a counselor for the director of nursing had something to do with the improvement in relationships between the director and the nursing staff.

The patient's-eye-view of the hospital and nurses

In some of the writer's nursing classes she has asked the students to think back to any hospital experiences they had in their pre-nursing days as patients or as members of the family of a patient. The things that were remembered, whether negative or positive, were acts and gestures which influenced feelings and emotions, not those which related to nursing skills. One student vividly recalled two nurses. The student as a child had an accident which involved the use of much adhesive tape in doing the dressings. What she thinks of when she remembers this experience is not the pain of the accident and the necessary surgery or the boredom of being hospitalized for a long time, but rather the attitudes of the two nurses when the adhesive had to be changed. One nurse in an objective, disinterested way criticized her for crying and told her what a baby she was, adding the overused (and frequently false) words, "Now, that doesn't hurt." The other nurse agreed that it *did* hurt, and that it was all right to cry a little because lots of people need to cry when something hurts. Another student who was in high school when her mother underwent a long hospitalization remembers a nurse who always asked how they were getting along at home. She asked as though she were genuinely interested, an act that was appreciated and remembered by both the patient and her teen-age daughter who was carrying the housekeeping responsibilities. A memory of another student took her back to a tonsillectomy in her pre-school years. All she recalled of this experience is a nurse holding her in her arms by the window and pointing out the school the youngster's "big brother" attended. Another student had the experience of her father's terminal illness. When she went on one occasion to see him she was told brusquely by the nurse, "You can't go in now. He is much worse." No explanation, no kindness, no suggestion as to whether she should wait or should go on home—just a blunt order.

These are the things nurses themselves remember from hospital experiences in their pre-nursing days—the kinds of things your patients some day will remember about you. It gives us a small clue as to what patients perceive when they see a nurse. A gentleman asked me once why it was that so many nurses walked around with their arms folded. He said that he could pick out the nurses from among other women because of this one characteristic. Not having given the remark much thought, I began to notice this habit among nurses. Many nurses, I discovered, do walk this way, and I found myself not liking it. Their posture, with the arms folded tight against the chest and the shoulders pulled forward, epitomized a tight, closed-in, do-not-get-too-close air. What a contrast to the open, receptive attitude one senses in the nurse whose arms swing freely, whose shoulders are back and whose head is up, an attitude that expresses the qualities the nurse needs, an expansive, warm, spontaneous, outgoing interest in people and therefore in her work.

The cause of the stiffly-starched, do-not-touch look may be the emphasis placed for many years in nursing education on a desirable objective relationship with patients. Objectivity has its place. But caution not to become emotionally involved with patients frequently has been carried to an extreme where it seems no longer to be objectivity but unemotional disinterest. There is no place in a good nurse's make-up for this kind of attitude. Nurses should make some effort to see themselves as others see them, although they might run the risk of not liking what they see. Remember, it is not the nurse's speed, efficiency and dexterity that will make a patient feel at home in the hospital nor make a lasting impression on him. Rather, it is the warm human touch and the depth of understanding she is able to communicate to the patient and to his family.

7

The Nurse-Counselor

One aspect of the human relations field is that of counseling. It is not a new concept in this book, for scattered throughout the previous chapters have been frequent examples of the nurse in her role as counselor. Some of the simple measures we have discussed, which nurses may take to relieve their patients, may seem to be no more than a humanitarian approach to interpersonal relations—what any sensitive person might do to relieve the emotional suffering of a fellow human being. If we narrow our definition of counseling to the strict professional sense of the word, perhaps these acts may not be counseling. We will use, however, a broad, inclusive definition of counseling, because we are not talking about counseling as a profession but about the use of valuable counseling tools by the nurse. Interpreted broadly, counseling is helping someone by the use of certain skills and attitudes to recognize, face, accept and resolve emotional problems which are interfering with his ability to live happily and effectively. According to this definition, even helping a patient feel at home in the hospital is counseling. The hospital patient's emotional problem frequently is the uncomplicated one of apprehension and anxiety—fear of the unknown—resulting from the hospital experience itself. As we have seen, this problem may not be openly expressed at all. When a patient himself is unaware of his fear, a perceptive nurse may help him to recognize it. Whenever a nurse does this, or helps make a patient emotionally comfortable with his illness, or relieve his anxiety about being away from home, she is essentially doing counseling of a basic kind.

Alleviation of fear

Someone may ask why it is necessary for a patient to be aware of his fear. Would it not be constructive to let his anxiety "rest in peace" rather than stir it up and bring it into his conscious mind? (The person who raises the question may be feeling some apprehension of her own about her ability to help relieve someone else's anxiety.) A feeling is operating in one way or another, it is active, charged with energy. It might be compared to a bolt of lightning. Protecting the barn with a lightning rod, which will attract the lightning in an open, relatively safe way, is far better than assuming that the lightning may not hit anything and then having it strike and destroy the barn. Or a feeling might be likened to a living dynamo of energy—the pre-adolescent child. His aggressive urges may be repressed to the extent that they burst out without warning in a harmful way, or they may be recognized for what they are, very natural feelings for that stage of life, and accepted and directed into useful channels. The patient who is frightened and is not able to express his fear is draining out vital emotional energy which might be used in helping his whole person to counteract the thing he fears. The person who says he is not afraid of some thing or some experience that is definitely fearful is using up his lifesaving energy to prevent his fear from showing, even to himself. Admitting fear is not the same as admitting defeat, on the contrary, it makes it possible for us to mobilize our forces to fight the thing we fear. Patients who are helped to recognize the fear they have, will release energy which can be constructively utilized to fight disease processes, to hasten recovery, to adjust to disease-caused limitations, to profit from rehabilitation efforts.

Before considering in more detail some of the skills we use to help people with their problems, an explanation of why so much emphasis is placed on fear might be helpful. Look at your own life, at whatever problems you may have experienced. Can you find the one consistent thread which seems to run through these problems? Suppose your plans are all made for a big formal dance this weekend, but the dress your mother has promised to send you has not yet arrived. You do not have another that will do. You do not (if you are like most student nurses) have the money to go out and buy one. Home is too far away for you to go get the dress yourself. You have a problem. You are worried, upset, perhaps even a little angry. You are probably also afraid. You are afraid of what people will think if you attend a formal in street clothes. You may be afraid that you will disappoint your boyfriend. You are afraid of appearing different from your classmates. This is not a problem with which we usually associate fear; it is not like facing physical danger, or illness or the unknown, and yet, fear is present. Think back over some of the problems of patients described in this book. The problems vary considerably, and yet each of them contains elements of fear: a woman afraid of an operation, a young woman with no fear of surgery or cancer but afraid of losing her husband's interest, a woman afraid of being considered a failure as a mother, because of a potentially delinquent child, an elderly woman not afraid of being an invalid but of being rejected by her family.

One of the most familiar fears a nurse meets professionally and socially is the fear of cancer. The nurse's approach to this will be influenced by the circumstances, by her feelings about the patient, and by her own attitude about cancer. Frequently the nurse's own feelings about cancer and her anxiety because she is unable to give valid reassurance will cause her to become overactive in a counseling interview lest she appear inadequate in the eyes of the person seeking her help.

DON'T BE AFRAID

Mrs. Paul, who worked as an office nurse for a local doctor, was unexpectedly visited on her day off by a neighbor who had made no friendly overtures in the seven years she had lived in the neighborhood. A warm, sensitive woman, Mrs. Paul felt that Mrs. Kane was disturbed about something and asked her to come in and sit down. A summary of their interview follows.

Mrs. Kane: Probably I shouldn't be bothering you, but I have just had a terrible shock and I *have* to talk to someone. If you're too busy to talk, just say so. After all, I know I haven't been very neighborly. (Mrs. Kane is feeling out Mrs. Paul to see if she can afford to share her problem with Mrs. Paul without being rejected. It sounds also as though she has some guilt feeling about doing this after having not been friendly with Mrs. Paul.)

Mrs. Paul: I'm never too busy to stop and talk. While you catch your breath, let me go fix something cold to drink. It has been so hot today! (In some situations it might have been wise to react to the lack of neighborliness Mrs. Kane brings out. But here, overlooking it was wise because it obviously was not related to whatever was upsetting Mrs. Kane. If this were someone Mrs. Paul knew well and cared about, it is doubtful that she would have offered to fix a cold drink before hearing the problem. Perhaps Mrs. Paul herself needed the few minutes to sort out her feelings about Mrs. Kane dropping in. The delay may have been helpful also to Mrs. Kane in giving her time to think about what she wanted to say to a comparative stranger.)

Mrs. Paul (returning with iced tea) : Now, tell me what the trouble is. (This sounds very abrupt. It would have been better to invite Mrs. Kane to talk by reflecting her feelings in some way. For instance, "I can see that you're terribly upset about something.")

Mrs. Kane: I've just come from seeing a surgeon to whom my doctor referred me. I have to have an operation for a lump in my breast. Even though I know I have to do it, the very thought of an operation frightens me.

Mrs. Paul: Why are you afraid of an operation? (This question serves no useful purpose. Mrs. Kane is afraid of an operation for the same reasons that Mrs. Paul or any of us would be afraid. She is afraid of pain, of possible incapacitation, possibly even of death. Rather than answering this question by thinking through one's fear, the troubled person will frequently answer "I don't know." A better response for the nurse to make here would have been a comment designed to bring out further expression of Mrs. Kane's fears such as, "I'm sure the thought of an operation is frightening to you. It's not easy to face undergoing one." Then wait for Mrs. Kane to go on. Implicit in asking "why" is the feeling that Mrs. Kane is unusual in her fear. This, of course, is not true! Mrs. Kane, nevertheless, attempted to answer the "why?")

Mrs. Kane: I'm worried about the outcome. My routine way of living will be interrupted. And, oh dear, the awful expense of hospital and doctor bills! (This answer illustrates the futility of asking "why." Rather than reveal her deep-seated fears of pain, cancer and possible death, Mrs. Kane hints at them, then points out sources for her fears which are not really the cause of her emotional distress.)

Mrs. Paul: You do have hospitalization, I suppose? (Here the nurse is hunting for some firm ground on which to take a stand. She is afraid to get involved in the emotional side of Mrs. Kane's fears and hangs on to the practical. This may make *her* feel more comfortable, but it does not get at Mrs. Kane's underlying problem.)

Mrs. Kane: Yes, but it won't cover nearly all of the expense. I'm sure I have cancer and they'll have to remove my whole breast. (Even though Mrs. Kane has not received much encouragement from Mrs. Paul, out of her own need to tell about it she again focuses directly on the major fear.)

Mrs. Paul: What makes you so sure of that? Did your doctor tell you so? (What a frustrating response this is to someone terrified by fear of cancer! It is almost like asking for proof that what is being said is true. The response loses sight of the fact that the worst fears are apt to be based on emotions rather than reality. A better response, again, would be a recognition of Mrs. Kane's feeling. "It's the thought of cancer that is most frightening to you, isn't it? I suppose you've talked this over with your doctor?")

Mrs. Kane: He hasn't told me in so many words, but the very way he evades my questions makes me wonder.

Mrs. Paul: Of course, I don't know what he's told you, but you do have one of the best surgeons in the city. He does loads of operations like yours—you have to trust him and you can really do that. The operation isn't rare at all. Even with your whole breast removed you'll be able to live and take care of your family just as you always have. Of course, you're worried. That's understandable. If I can help you in any way, please let me know. I'd like so much to be able to help you through this. Even if it's just talking it over to set your mind at rest. (In this lengthy response Mrs. Paul has two forces at work within her. One is a desire to help Mrs. Kane, the other an extreme anxiety that she cannot help her. This anxiety produces all the words of reassurance, empty words that only belittle the patient's fears. Although the last things Mrs. Paul said were supportive, comforting and constructive, the very nature of her response brought the interview to a close.)

Assuming that Mrs. Paul had additional time to give to Mrs. Kane's problem, and that she had not been immobilized by her own feeling of inadequacy, she might have continued the interview with this response to Mrs. Kane's comment.

Mrs. Paul: Doctors really *can* be evasive. Sometimes it may be because they're not yet positive of something. Would you like to tell me just what the doctor told you? Perhaps I can help to explain what he meant. (From here, the interview could continue with interpretation of the doctor's explanation and with further recognition of Mrs. Kane's feelings.)

When the interview as it had been conducted was ended, Mrs. Kane said she felt much better, and Mrs. Paul was gratified that she had been able to help. The mutual gesture of friendliness would have made Mrs. Kane feel better regardless of the course of the interview, but the relief of her fears would have been more extensive had the interview been handled a little differently.

Listening is important

It is *possible* that fear is not involved in every single emotional problem, but it is unlikely. There are so many things of which to be afraid; there is fear of being considered inadequate, fear of not being wanted, fear of failure, and—in illness particularly—fear of becoming dependent, fear of pain, fear of death. Part of a counselor's responsibility is to look for these fears and to help the other person face them. One of our most useful ways of accomplishing this is through the art of listening. Listening *is* an art, and not an easy one. Unfortunately, many nurses have difficulty in listening. This is not the fault of nurses themselves, necessarily, but it does reflect a one-sided emphasis in their education. Nurses during their professional education are given a basic fund of knowledge with which to help others. Part of a nurse's job is to pass on information to patients when they need this kind of help. There is no argument with this. The difficulty lies in a nurse's becoming so imbued with the idea of teaching her patients, with the aim also of obtaining their cooperation, that she forgets that sometimes cooperation is more easily obtained by listening than by telling or explaining. When a nurse has explained something to a patient, she often thinks that that is enough, and feels irritated or frustrated because her explanation did not "take," and the patient's attitudes or behaviour did not change. Explanation is *not* enough.

We have seen in earlier chapters that some emotional problems have their roots in concrete situations, perhaps in the family or in other areas of life; they are realistic environmental problems. There may also be emotional problems which have their roots in unrealistic anxiety or apprehension. When this is true, explanations will be of little value because the patient is not emotionally ready to accept them. He may not be ready to give up his worry or fear. Frequently when a patient is given the opportunity to talk out his anxiety (to verbalize or ventilate, as the psychiatrists call it) he is able to clarify his own thinking and feeling to the point where he can give his *own* explanation. In addition, he is in a better position to accept the explanation of someone else. If you are going away on a trip and find your suitcase full of old clothes you no longer need, you would not pile the things you want to take along on top of the old things; you would take them out and then pack. Similarly, when the mind is full of apprehension, misconceptions, unfounded worry, unrealistic anxiety, it must be relieved of the burden before it can take in a logical explanation. The relief is achieved by verbalizing or ventilating—by airing our problems. If something happens on the ward and you feel that you have been unjustly or unfairly dealt with by the head nurse, you are angry and hurt. You are so full of your resentment that the logical explanation she offers you for her action falls on deaf ears. If, on the other hand, you have the opportunity first to verbalize how *you* feel about the situation, preferably to the head nurse herself, but, if not, to one of your classmates, you are in a better position to recognize the logic of her explanation and accept it.

Giving information or an explanation that a patient or anyone else is not able to accept or prepared to use is a waste of time and effort. It is frustrating to the person giving the information and to the person at whom it is directed. Looking back over your own education in nursing, you undoubtedly remember times when your mind was on other things, and a doctor's lecture was wasted on you. Perhaps you had received an upsetting letter from home, or your weekend plans with your boy friend had fallen through. With your mind filled with these worries, there simply was no motivation to try to absorb what you were hearing in class. Not until you were able to ventilate your worries to an understanding listener were you accessible to further teaching. It is the same thing with patients. For instance, in the case of Mr. T., a nurse might have explained the need for Mr. T. to use urinal and bedpan. But if Mr. T. had a preconceived idea that patients who were not permitted bathroom privileges were more sick than those who had such privileges, he might not have been able to accept the explanation. The opportunity first to verbalize his own feelings of fear (that patients who are not allowed to go to the bathroom are critically ill) would have helped him to accept it.

Listening helps people find their own explanations

The writer remembers a very different example of the use of verbalization and the success that resulted from clarifying feelings through talking them out. The incident took place in a course given to student nurses in a hospital. Because of the nature of the course the instructor tried to keep the classroom atmosphere informal, encouraging discussion as much as possible. It was her experience that discussion is more active and productive if class members are seated in a circle rather than in rows. On this particular day, the class met in the late afternoon. When the instructor entered the room the students were seated in the traditional rows. Casually suggesting that they move into a circle, the instructor was totally unprepared for the negative attitudes of the students. While they did not openly demur, there was much grimacing, muttering, hostile glancing in the direction of the instructor, all accompanied by the scraping and banging of chairs. When all was quiet, the lecturer took out her notes, but before beginning to speak she asked, again casually, why they objected so strenuously to sitting in a circle. Someone hesitantly began answering, and the answer was picked up and carried on by others. Gradually the group was carried away into a real (forgive the term) "gripe" session. They did not mind sitting in a circle. It wasn't that. It was just one more thing they had to do because someone told them to. They were tired, they had been in class since early morning, and so on with a barrage of assorted complaints. Putting aside her notes, the instructor asked whether they would like to talk about the problem. And they did! There were complaints about the administration; the students' feelings were not taken into consideration; they were not getting good experience; they were treated like kindergarten children; their instructors did not know how to teach (!); most of their lecturers were boring; they were tired of it and just plain tired.

The instructor was not a member of the regular staff, and the students may have felt a little more free to complain as they did. She encouraged them to say whatever they wished. Actually, the instructor said very little. Sometimes she nodded her head; sometimes she said, "Hm-hm." She probably also said, "It must be hard for you some days." "I understand how you feel." "It hurts when we think people don't have any consideration for us." Ten minutes of the fifty-minute class had already been used up for chair moving. The gripe session went on for twenty or thirty minutes. But in the last part of the hour, amid all the clamor of complaint, a dissenting voice was heard. A student spoke up in defense of the school and faculty, saying something about it not being easy for them either. Another student picked the theme up, adding that the faculty had a big responsibility in trying to work out a program that would give the students all the education and experience they needed. A third student reminded the group that the students themselves were not always so cooperative. Gradually this new approach took over the floor, and while it was not a unanimous swing, it was a swing of the large majority of the students. The class ended on a positive and constructive note. Several of the students commented on how much they had gained from this experience, and on the help the instructor had given them. Yet, the instructor had said practically nothing.

From a standpoint of counseling this incident may profitably be studied for significance from several angles. What happened? The students modified their attitudes and felt much better. And yet, what they achieved they achieved largely on their own. The instructor offered to the students an opportunity to verbalize, to ventilate their feelings, and, thus, to clarify them and to separate the logical from the illogical. The instructor knew that the administration was not trying to impose on the students, that the school had an excellent reputation, and that the faculty was doing its best to provide a topnotch education in nursing for these young women. She knew that some of the students' complaints were unjustified and some of them were not. Suppose the instructor, instead of listening, had used her knowledge of the school to interrupt the students with an explanation of the difficulties the administration and faculty had, and had pointed out to them where their criticism was unjust. The students would have stopped talking or would have argued back. Most of them would have felt less understood and more hostile than before. They probably never again would have felt free with this instructor to discuss their real feelings. Remember, the feelings would still have been there, but they would have been repressed. Eventually they would have come out in insidious ways which conceivably might have harmed the school, a patient, or even a student herself. Undoubtedly, a barrier would also have been set up against assimilating lecture material from the instructor in the future. Instead, the opposite happened; the students were far more attentive during her lectures than they had been before, and the class discussions were excellent, because they knew what they said would be listened to and thoughtfully accepted.

A similar situation is frequently seen in marriage counseling. The early interviews center around the faults and the undesirable behavior of the partner, and the counselor mostly listens, offering to the troubled client the opportunity to express his feelings. It is not unusual for the client, after freely expressing his negative feelings about his partner, to begin to recognize some of his own faults and to see how he has contributed to the marriage problems. Had the counselor attempted to point out the client's own shortcomings, before the client was ready and able to see them, it would have placed the counselor on the side of the partner, and put the client on the defensive, so that he would become less and less able to see where he himself might be wrong.

This same phenomenon can be seen operating in nurse-patient relationships when a nurse is willing to listen instead of being compelled to explain. Let us go back to the nurse-patient situation in the first chapter. Mrs. Callen was a frightened pre-operative patient. When she finally went to sleep she undoubtedly felt that the nurse had helped her. Yet, the nurse had said very little, nor had she taken any real action to relieve the patient. The patient had done it herself. The nurse had not reassured her that "everything will be all right." She encouraged the patient to talk by the use of the skills we will later consider in more detail. She had listened, and she had accepted Mrs. Callen's right to be afraid without criticizing or condemning her for her fear. Just as the instructor had known the reality of the students' situation, Miss Terry knew the reality of her patient's situation. She knew that some of the patient's fear was warranted; she also knew that much of it was not warranted, but she made no effort to explain this. She knew that Mrs. Callen would have to adjust to the undesirable in her coming operation, but she did not attempt to *lecture* her on this point. (Nurses have indeed been known to lecture patients about such things. They may say something like, "After all, you are a grown man, you should know that you can expect some pain in this life." "You ought to be ashamed of yourself for crying over a little thing like this." Remarks like this do nothing to lessen the reputation nurses sometimes justifiably have of being cold and heartless!) Miss Terry did not feel compelled to share her knowledge of the impending surgery and her belief that the patient's chances for recovery were excellent. She recognized that the patient was not ready to accept explanations and assurance, but that she needed the acceptance of an interested, understanding person. Miss Terry offered it, and Mrs. Callen talked her own way out of her fears, at least so that she was able to sleep. There is little doubt that after surgery Mrs. Callen will prove to be a "'co-operative" patient where Miss Terry is concerned.

Several years ago the writer did a limited study which aimed at, among other things, discovering how some nurses attempted to help their patients and others with various problems. The nurses were asked what they would do when presented by their patients with certain problem situations. The phenomenally high percentage of situations in which nurses began their answers by saying, "I would explain. . . ," "I would tell. . . ," "I would say . . ." was appalling. It confirmed what the writer was suspecting. Nurses are trained to do health teaching, to give information when necessary, but they are not generally prepared to listen, even though they will often be called upon to do counseling to which listening is fundamental. There is another angle to listening which is important. If nurses are going to give patients optimum care they must know something about their patients. We are not learning anything about someone else while *we* are talking. Listening in a kind, accepting, encouraging way is a technic which a nurse may apply in her work with patients and their families, with her co-workers and in her daily contacts with almost anyone.

A four-block foundation in the helping process

Before we can listen effectively and helpfully we must accept and sincerely believe in four premises. They are as basic to counseling as is listening. First, we must remember that human beings grow and mature through being loved and wanted. We must cling to this fact. Sometimes we will meet people, they may or may not be patients, who are cold or independent, who do not seem to want or to need the warmth and comfort of anyone else. They are self-sufficient, they live unto themselves without seeking or giving favors. If we are to be effective as nurses and as counselors, we need to be alert to avoid being taken in by this. Probably no people need to be loved and wanted more than those who are fighting against it. *All* people need to be loved, wanted and appreciated, in addition to having the opportunity to achieve recognition of some kind. The brilliant scientist has this need as well as the little orphaned boy in an institution. The outstanding surgeon has it and so has the young unmarried pregnant girl. The warm, loving mother has it the same as the children on whom she lavishes her love. These needs may be summarized in the familiar word "security."

The second premise is related to the first one. We must accept that all human beings are sometimes frightened, lonely, anxious. Here again, we cannot assume that because someone is at the peak of success in a chosen profession, because he has attained economic and social stability, because he seems to be happy, to have friends, to be loved, that he has achieved freedom from anxiety and fear. The degree of loneliness or fear varies from person to person and from time to time, but in everyone it is present at some time to some degree. Frequently when these unhappy feelings are present one human being will turn to another seeking help.

A third premise necessary to counseling is the counselor's own optimism about what he is doing. Even though a counselor knows that conseling will not always be successful, he must believe that it is worthwhile. The nurse who says, even to herself, about a troubled patient, "Well—I'll talk to her, but it won't do any good" or "What's the use of trying to work with her, she won't co-operate anyway," can not be successful in her counseling with that patient.

Fourth and last, anyone attempting to help anyone else must remember that any kind of change or growth or adjustment takes time. The patient who is terrified of surgery at three o'clock will probably not be free of fear an hour later, even though the nurse with him has used the best counseling technics possible. The man who is ashamed of having contracted venereal disease is not going to overcome this on the basis of two or three clinic interviews, no matter how skilled the interviewer. In fact, when behavior and attitudes are modified too rapidly, it may be wise to wonder whether these changes are only superficial and temporary. When the counselor is a nurse, it is particularly important that she be alert to this possibility. Once again, the nurse's rather unique relationship to her patient enters the picture. The nurse, as you remember, frequently is a parent substitute whom the patient unconsciously wants to please in order to retain her "parental" love and care. For this reason patients will sometimes modify their behavior on a superficial level. A patient will say to a nurse, "All right. I'll do it for you because you have been so good to me." When pleasing someone else is the sole motivation for changing attitudes or behavior, the change may come about quickly but is usually not a penetrating one. As soon as the motivating force is removed, the patient's behavior will revert to what it was previously.

EVERYTHING'S FINE NOW

It was three o'clock in the morning and the intensive care unit was relatively quiet when an emergency patient arrived. After the admission procedure had been completed and the orders written, Miss Ford settled down at the unconscious patient's bedside to observe vital signs and to watch for any response from him. As she carefully watched, Miss Ford wondered about the young man and his diagnosis. He had a strong, nice-looking face and apparently a healthy well-built body. From the admission notes she learned that he was a law student just about her age, in the early twenties. Why would such a young man want to commit suicide? Aside from Miss Ford's religious beliefs which taught that suicide was morally wrong and punishable in eternity, Miss Ford was bothered by the fact that anyone so personally appealing to her could want to end his life. During the four hours she spent with Donald her perplexity grew, as did her desire to be instrumental in arousing a response in him. According to the instructions she had received Miss Ford intermittently spoke to him, calling him by name. Just before she went off duty, once more she called softly, "Hi, Donald." This time there was a faint flicker of his eyelashes, and the intern who had just entered the room said there was a good chance for his recovery.

When Miss Ford returned on duty that night she was gratified to learn that Donald had regained consciousness and had been talking. He freely admitted that he had taken an overdose of barbiturates, but had failed to give any reason for it. When Miss Ford went into his room it was Donald who said, "Hi!" Miss Ford silently wondered whether he had been aware of her continuous calling him by name on the previous night. Throughout the night Donald talked to the nurse, clinging tightly to her hand, repeating over and over what a coward he was and what a terrible thing he had done.

By morning Donald was bright and cheerful. His whole attitude seemed to have changed. When Miss Ford was ready to leave the unit she stopped at Donald's door to tell him she would see him that night. He called to her, "Thanks for all you've done for me, Miss Ford. Everything's fine now!" Those were Donald's last words to the young nurse. When she returned that night his bed and room were empty. Having satisfied the doctors and psychiatrists that he was all right, Donald had been given ambulatory privileges. An hour later his smashed body was recovered from an alley-way five floors below. Everything was fine—now.

The nurse must be accepting

A nurse who is able to listen, who recognizes the emotional needs and problems of human beings, who is genuinely concerned about the other person's distress, and who believes in her ability to help others through counseling, creates an atmosphere that fosters counseling. The kindly atmosphere makes the troubled person feel that his burden is finally being shared. It is no longer so heavy to him. His feeling of loneliness and anxiety is lessened as he senses his acceptance by the counselor. He is able to bring his feelings or worries out into the open because the environment the counselor has created makes him feel safe—safe from shame, or guilt or fear, and safe from criticism or ridicule. No one is going to say to him, "That's a silly thing to be afraid of—you ought to be ashamed of having thoughts like that." "You're acting like a baby— this is no way for a grown man to behave." If the patient is allowed to reveal his feelings without the counselor introjecting her *own* ideas, directing or attempting to control the patient, he will be able to clarify his thinking and feeling for himself, and as a result to modify his attitudes and behavior.

The situation in which it is most difficult to refrain from introjecting our own ideas and opinions is the one in which we are involved in helping someone close to us. The fact that we love someone very much does not necessarily mean that we accept that person's right to think, feel and behave as he does. But if we are to do skilled counseling with those we love, acceptance is as necessary a part of the procedure as it is in counseling anyone else. It is not unusual for a nurse to be placed in a counseling role by friends or members of her family. There are difficulties inherent in attempts to give counseling help to someone with whom, because of a close relationship, we are emotionally involved. In all probability the percentage of failures is higher than the percentage of successes in these instances. However, if we adhere strictly to basic counseling principles it is possible to give help to our friends and relatives.

SISTER KNOWS BEST

When Miss Murray had almost completed her work toward a B.S. in nursing, she was joined at the University by Jane, her younger sister. Miss Murray believed that Jane's entrance into college was largely a decision of her mother, who asked that Miss Murray "look after" Jane. Miss Murray was flattered at first and thought this would be an easy task, but as the year passed she found it more and more difficult. Jane was overwhelmed by the freedom from parental supervision and entered with freshman abandon into an active social life. As a result her grades were very poor. With more pressure from her mother to keep after Jane and get her "straightened out," Miss Murray plunged into a program of counseling her sister. Miss

Murray felt that since she never told Jane what to do she was leaving the decisions up to Jane herself. What she did not realize was that she took the initiative in opening discussions, and did most of the talking and suggesting, giving Jane no opportunity to express her own feelings. In time Miss Murray became discouraged, because there was no improvement in either Jane's grades or behavior.

When her growing feeling of hostility became too uncomfortable for her to ignore, Miss Murray began to evaluate what she was doing to and with her sister. She realized that she was not using the same technics with Jane that she would ordinarily use with a patient. The two things that were missing were acceptance of Jane, including acceptance of her right to feelings and opinions, and an understanding of her own feelings and how they were interfering. Why was she so angry, hostile and disapproving? She had spent a great deal of time and effort, and she felt both were wasted. Jane would accept what Miss Murray told her, agree with what she said, and then would do exactly as she had been doing. Miss Murray felt that she had failed, and was hurt at Jane's lack of response.

As Miss Murray attempted to evaluate her efforts she had to admit that her goal had been to change her sister without considering her sister's desire or motivation to change. Jane had not come to her for advice or help, it was Miss Murray who had gone to Jane. In the light of these facts Miss Murray changed her tactics. Never again did she initiate a discussion about Jane's schoolwork. They saw each other socially and if Jane volunteered something about school her sister listened with interest, giving praise if it seemed indicated. Their relationship became a much more pleasant and relaxed one. At first her new approach was a difficult one for Miss Murray. Many times she was tempted to advise or to suggest something to her younger sister. She felt inadequate with such a passive role when she felt so responsible for helping Jane. However, she discovered that the less she said about Jane's activities—

both scholastic and social— the more Jane volunteered about them in their talks together. This finally culminated in Jane's reaching her own decision about temporarily giving up college. She had found classes uninteresting and her grades were still poor. She reasoned that if she went to work for a while, she could decide if she wished to return to college later. She confided this to her sister expecting the confidence and her decision to be accepted and understood. It was. Admittedly Miss Murray would have liked for Jane to continue at college, but with conscious effort not to interfere she was now able to give her sister the responsibility for making her own decision. For the first time Jane showed some concern about her present work and her own future. She had never had the opportunity to do this before when her overprotective mother and solicitous sister had indicated *their* responsibility for her welfare. Miss Murray reached the conclusion, quite justifiably, that she had contributed to her sister's maturing process at the point where she accepted Jane as an individual with the right and responsibility for determining her own welfare.

People communicate in many ways

A good counselor listens with the ears and listens with all his senses and his mind as well. He listens and observes. Counseling involves an interaction between two people. It may be formal or informal in nature. A patient may say to a nurse, "I have something I would like to talk about with you." The nurse may agree on a specific time and place for the interview. Or the director of nursing may be asked by a student or a staff nurse for an appointment which obviously will be held in the director's office. These are what are referred to here as "formal" interviews, although the atmosphere of the interview may not be formal. By an informal interview is meant the casual, unplanned discussion between two people which may take place wherever they happen to be. In either case, the keynote of the meeting is an interaction between two people, usually in the form of communication between them. We tend to think of communication (when two people are face to face) as verbal. But the alert counselor looks also for the meanings the other person may be trying to communicate in some other way. A person may be saying about some problem "Oh, this doesn't bother me at all," while difficulty in enunciating, or breathlessness, or dryness of the mouth indicate that he is very much upset. Other clues are intonation, the rate of speed with which one speaks, or sudden changes in either of these.

People communicate all kinds of things to us by posture, the way in which they move, muscular rigidity, hyperactivity, facial expression and various physiological symptoms. When the individual talking to you suddenly blushes or begins to perspire profusely, you sense that he is extremely nervous or apprehensive about something. We think of the person who is in constant motion as being nervous, but sometimes the controlled-appearing person is even more nervous. Someone may talk to you as he sits back in a chair, apparently relaxed and comfortable, but the constant motion of a foot or an arm, or continuous smoking may indicate that he is not as relaxed as, superficially, he appears to be. Another may sit, straight and rigid, on the edge of the chair, unconsciously telling you, "This is more than I can stand. I want to get out of here." The words being spoken may indicate that he is glad and relieved to be there. If you accept his words at face value and fail to observe the posture, you may miss a major part of what is potentially being communicated. The messages coming through non-verbal communication channels may be especially meaningful because a person consciously may not intend to send them.

These general considerations apply as much to the nurse in her counseling role as to the counselor who is professionally trained in the counseling field. In the further discussion we will use the terms nurse and counselor interchangeably, with the understanding that we are talking about nurses who are doing counseling as part of their daily nursing routine rather than about the professional counselor.

Recognizing a request for help

From what has been said so far it may seem as though the counselor does very little except sit and listen and watch the other person. In actual fact the good counselor is a busy person, indeed. One thing the counselor must do is to determine that someone actually is seeking help. There are many different ways of asking for help. This is especially true of the informal requests for help a nurse receives. The alert counselor sometimes has to sense that help is being asked. Your co-workers and some patients may make a direct verbal request, "I have something on my mind that I would like to talk over with you. Would you have time . . .", etc. This is simple. The nurse needs no intuition to see what lies behind the words. Someone knows he needs help and he is asking for it. Other requests for help may not be quite so directly worded: "This operation is not a bit serious, is it?" "I used to talk everything over with my mother—but she's gone now." "No one wants anything to do with an old man like me. I wish I would die." "I feel a bit depressed this morning. I don't know what's the matter with me." "Oh—never mind. It isn't important." These and many other seemingly casual comments may be requests for help. Sometimes the individual seeking help through these indirect comments is aware of his need for help though he is not aware of his asking for it. Others may be no more aware of their need for help than they are of their unconscious search for it.

When a troubled patient recognizes what his problem is and shares it with us directly it is relatively easy to begin working on it with him. Unfortunately, all problems are not recognized as such, or if recognized even unconsciously, they cannot be revealed in a direct way to the helping person. When this is true, a nurse must be alert to what the patient is trying to communicate in order to help him recognize, or to face, the problem himself. Even more unfortunate is the situation in which the patient is trying desperately to communicate, and the nurse, because of a mental or emotional block of her own, is unable to interpret or to accept what the patient is saying.

A DISGUISED REQUEST FOR HELP

Shortly after arriving one morning at the Visiting Nurse Society, Miss Cummings received a telephone call from a woman in her district. Although familiar with the patient's neighborhood, Miss Cummins had never met Mrs. Allen, who wanted information in regard to a "health farm" where her sister could go to lose weight. Without attempting to learn more, Miss Cummins explained that there was nothing of this kind in the immediate vicinity. She added that it was possible that there might be such a place in a city not too far distant. However, she urged that Mrs. Allen have her sister see the family doctor who undoubtedly could help her with a diet. The call was immediately forgotten in the pressure of preparing her visits for the day, until, just before leaving the office, she was approached by her supervisor who had just received a second call from Mrs. Allen. To the supervisor Mrs. Allen had said that she, herself, wished to go somewhere where she could be helped with an excessive drinking problem.

With reluctance Miss Cummins returned the call and promised to visit Mrs. Allen that afternoon. Her reluctance may have stemmed from two causes. It was irritating to her that Mrs. Allen had not told her what she really wanted when she spoke to her earlier. Mrs. Allen had been willing to the tell the supervisor her problems but not the staff nurse. Furthermore, the problem of alcoholism, particularly in a woman, was distasteful to her. Thus, when Miss Cummins arrived at the Allen house late that afternoon her observations were affected by her preconceived negative attitude. The door was answered by Mr. Allen, who disappeared after inviting Miss Cummins inside.

In her report the nurse described Mrs. Allen as a middle-aged woman, only slightly overweight, carefully made up, but in a soiled, wrinkled dress, and very nervous. The house, one of the typical development variety, was small, poorly furnished and very untidy.

Apparently unaware of Miss Cummins' negative feeling, Mrs. Allen plunged compulsively into her story. Having lived most of her life in a large eastern city, Mrs. Allen hated the small suburban community to which her husband had moved them upon his recent retirement. There was a great deal of marital friction and she sought some release from her unhappiness by overeating and by drinking a little. On a conscious level, she had carefully figured out her goal in calling the visiting nurse. She wanted to lose weight, thus improving her personal appearance. She felt this would enable her to get a job, to achieve financial independence and to get away from the house part of the time. As logical as all of this may have sounded to Mrs. Allen, it was simply too pat to be realistic. In the first place, there is more to getting a job than personal appearance. Secondly, achieving financial independence is not necessarily the answer to marital friction. Such organized rationalization should immediately have given the nurse a clue to the presence of other problems in the Allen situation.

Here is a summary of Miss Cummins' reaction to the situation Mrs. Allen presented. "I did not feel that I should talk to her about losing weight since she did not really need to do this. I did suggest that her family doctor would give her a diet. I had brought with me a list of resources for patients who need help with alcoholism. However, she did not mention drinking as a problem, and I did not feel I should go over these with her. Another suggestion I made was that she visit Family Service."

One of the basic principles, not only of counseling, but of any helping process, is to begin where the patient is or with the problem the patient recognizes. Miss Cummins may not have felt that Mrs. Allen needed to lose weight, but if the patient herself felt so this should have been accepted and explored. It is probable that Mrs. Allen did not consider this to be a major problem, but it provided one means of finding someone with whom she could share her basic problem. It gave her the opportunity to "feel out" the nurse to see if she was someone with whom Mrs. Allen would be comfortable in sharing her problems. Having met rejection with her overweight problem, Mrs. Allen could hardly risk to discuss the more serious, anxiety-laden and guilt-provoking problem of drinking. In spite of her fear of rejection, Mrs. Allen had attempted once by telephone and once in the interview to bring up drinking, but the nurse would not pursue it. There would have been some merit in the recommendation that Mrs. Allen seek the help of Family Service had this been talked through with the patient and had the reasons for going there been clarified.

On Miss Cummins' return visit to Mrs. Allen a month later, she was discouraged to learn that Mrs. Allen had neither been to Family Service nor sought a diet from her doctor. Mrs. Allen now felt the need of psychiatric help because she sometimes had suicidal urges. In adding this to her other complaints, it was almost as though, having received little response from the nurse so far, she decided to go a step farther in her plea for help. Again she said her marital difficulties were so great that she "drank a little." Even though the nurse had failed to "hear" this previously the patient tried again! Miss Cummins offered to make an appointment for her at the nearest mental health clinic, but Mrs. Allen refused. She said she had already been there, and they would not help her until she did something about her home situation. An astute nurse should have sensed that what Mrs. Allen had been told at the clinic was that they could do nothing to help her until she had decided to do something about the drinking problem. In spite of the fact that the patient's explanation was obviously invalid, Miss Cummins did not explore Mrs. Allen's experience at the clinic. Instead she was silently irritated because all of her efforts to help had been rejected. Her own anxiety at this point made her feel that she must give this woman something concrete, and she brought out the list of resources for alcoholics. She later said she did this "even though Mrs. Allen had not mentioned alcoholism as a problem in any of the visits."

A later interview revealed that Mrs. Allen was still worried about her marriage, concerned about overweight and unhappy in her new neighborhood, with the result that she "drank a little" and overate a great deal. She had not, of course, acted upon any of the nurse's suggestions, but was always cordial when the nurse made her infrequent visits to the home. As for Miss Cummins, she was frustrated because she really wanted to help this "poor woman" but could not get anywhere with her.

What can be done then by a nurse to help this kind of patient? Let us reconstruct part of the interview, looking for the clues Miss Cummins might have picked up, and point out more constructive counseling responses she might have made. Before a helpful interview can be accomplished, the nurse must be aware of her own attitude about the problem, particularly if it is a controversial one or one that has moral or social stigma attached to it. In spite of the generally accepted concept of alcoholism as a disease, there are still professional people who see alcoholism as a kind of irresponsible behavior growing out of moral weakness. In order to give optimum help to any alcoholic, we cannot lump him together with thousands of others as being one of a type. He must be met and accepted as a unique individual with rights and feelings of his own. Since in our complex society alcoholism is increasing, it behooves each member of a helping profession to work through his own feelings about it in order to be able to help the alcoholic sufferer and his family. At best it is difficult for an alcoholic to seek help; when he reaches the point of actually asking for it, the counselor must be ready.

In the beginning of the first interview, Mrs. Allen spoke at length about her marriage and in less detail about her overweight. She casually mentioned the drinking. The nurse should have accepted all of these things and recognized and reflected Mrs. Allen's feelings to motivate her to tell as much as she wished to express at that time. The nurse could have made brief accepting, reflecting comments like these: What is there specifically about her new home that Mrs. Allen does not like? Is it only loneliness? Does she feel any rejection for her new neighbors? What makes her aware of this? What is the cause of the marital friction? Does she feel her husband is controlling her life? How does each of them feel about his retirement? How does she feel that having a job and becoming financially independent can help her? What does she mean when she says "drinking a little?" What kinds of experience has she had with other helping agencies? What kind of help does she expect from the Visiting Nurse Society?

The nurse explores all these things not by asking direct questions but by making Mrs. Allen feel free to express her feelings about them without fear of condemnation or disapproval. For example, instead of asking why Mrs. Allen did not want to leave the city the nurse might say, "It must be very different for you living out here." "It's difficult for anyone to adjust to big moves." "It must have made you angry to have your husband decide to move without consulting you." "I guess a woman has to adjust to an entirely new way of life when her husband retires. That's not easy." Here are some possible responses to other things Mrs. Allen has brought out: "You say you drink a little?" "Perhaps you feel drinking helps to relax you when you're upset about all these things?" "It seems as if these things have been bothering you for some time. I was wondering if you have talked to anyone about them before." "You didn't find the mental health clinic helpful?" "You must have been disappointed to feel they would not help you. It makes you wonder where you can turn, doesn't it?" "Perhaps you are wondering if we are going to be able to help you?"

These are a few of the many possible comments a nurse could make to establish a good relationship with Mrs. Allen, to help her clarify her own problems and to determine what constructive steps are available to her. An important opening that should not have been overlooked was Mrs. Allen's telephone call to the supervisor. For some reason Mrs. Allen at that point had been able to blurt out, albeit briefly, that she had a drinking problem and wanted help with it. If she had not mentioned drinking in her interview with the nurse, the latter could have referred back to this call. "In your telephone call this morning you mentioned a drinking problem; it's hard to talk about it, isn't it?" "I guess these other things are easier to bring up than the problem you mentioned on the phone this morning." To admit a drinking problem on the telephone to a disembodied voice is much easier than to admit it face to face, and the nurse may have to help the patient over this hurdle.

But behind all of the technics a nurse may use lie her own basic feelings. We can assume that Miss Cummins failed to recognize what Mrs. Allen was trying to share with her about a drinking problem because the nurse's own feelings were involved. She may have had unpleasant experiences with alcoholism within her own family or among her friends; she may have been a teetotaler who felt that any consumption of alcohol was morally wrong; or she may have simply felt inadequate to deal with a problem as potentially serious as alcoholism. Hopefully, a nurse can, if she wishes, change her attitude about alcoholism—or about anything else. But if she cannot change her attitude she must at least recognize what her feeling is, in order that it does not blind her to the presence of the problem and interfere with her helping efforts.

Why did he come for help?

In the preceding illustration we saw the difficulty a patient had in requesting a specific kind of help and the problems the nurse had in recognizing the real request. When a request for help is recognized as such there are several things that require the nurse's concentration. She wants, and needs, to know certain facts. Some of them she may learn by direct questioning. More likely, she will attempt to learn them by listening, by sorting them out from the things she is being told. One of the first questions a counselor asks herself is *why* a person turned to her for help. Did the individual seek the counselor's help of his own accord or was he coerced into asking? It makes a tremendous difference. A patient who has no particular desire to talk to a nurse may be urged by someone else to talk to her.

He may be frightened into it instead of being self-motivated. A marriage counseling client may be coerced by his partner to see a marriage counselor, with the threat of divorce proceedings being held over his head if he doesn't. The help a counselor is able to give in such a situation obviously is limited by the poor motivation of the client. Such enforced help, sometimes, is better than none at all, because motivation to continue with counseling may develop after counseling has begun.

The writer recalls the case of a student nurse who was referred to her by the director of a school. The appointment was made by the director.

When the student, whom I already knew slightly through classwork, arrived, she was most cordial and eager to cooperate. She explained that Miss Y. felt she had problems with which she needed help. Then she sat back and waited for me to ask her the questions, give her the advice, and make the suggestions which would lead to a resolution of her problems. When I asked questions she answered them as honestly and cooperatively as possible. But her whole polite attitude seemed to be, "Now just tell me what you want me to do to help you to help me, and I will be glad to do it." At the close of the interview I did not feel that we had progressed very far because the student never had faced the fact that she had a problem. She knew that many things had gone wrong recently in her practical and in her academic work, but these were the result of circumstances. She did not place the blame for her failures on anyone else or anything else. She leaned over backward to accept the blame, and stoutly maintained that she would do better. But at no time did she see the thread of maladjustment that was causing her difficulties. Not recognizing her problem, she could hardly ask help for it. I made no future appointments with her, because I knew that if I asked her to come back she would gladly do so, but that there would be the same results. However, I told her to feel free to call if she ever wished to see me. Several weeks later the student telephoned and asked whether she could, please, see me. We made an appointment and the results were much more satisfactory. She came to me because she wanted to, thus she was motivated to use whatever help I could give her.

Asking for help may be painful

The next thing the counselor needs to consider is *what it has meant* to the person *to ask* for help. A negative attitude about asking for help with personal or emotional problems is widely prevalent.

If a person has a toothache, he ordinarily goes to see the dentist. If he has a pain elsewhere he sees a doctor. If he has a financial problem and needs money he goes to a bank or lending agency. If he needs help in finding a job he goes to an employment agency. In any of these situations he may be uncomfortable about going, but he is not devastated (except in unusual circumstances) by shame or remorse. However, when a person has emotional problems, his attitude frequently seems to be that he should be able to work them out alone. Sometimes they can be, and are, worked out alone. But many times people go on in a kind of half-life, living not as happily or as effectively as they might, laden with problems and worries they are too "proud" to share with anyone else. Even after such a person has recognized that something is bothering him that he cannot handle alone and has sought counseling help, vestiges of the negative attitude remain, "I wish I hadn't said I wanted to talk about this." The person asking for help must necessarily share part of himself with someone else, and this is rarely easy.

What kind of help is he seeking?

The counselor needs to know also *how the person* seeking help *feels the counselor may help*. For instance, if a patient begins to tell a nurse all about her marital difficulties in the hope that the nurse will advise her whether to stay with her husband or not, she would be expecting help the nurse (and anyone else) is not prepared to give. Frustration on the part of both counselor and the person seeking help may be avoided by learning at the outset of the contact that something is expected from the counselor that he is unable to give. Knowing how the person feels the counselor may help, the counselor also gets an idea of how far along the individual is in working through his own problems. A patient may be preoccupied with fear of dying and may talk about it a great deal. If he feels the nurse can do something to make him less afraid, or to remove the reality of the possibility of death, he may have a deep-seated problem or dependency need which will require skilled and careful handling. On the other hand, if he recognizes that the nurse cannot offer any concrete help, but admits to her that it "just makes me feel better to talk about it," the nurse will be able to help him, and he may well become less afraid.

What does he see his problem to be?

One of the most important things a counselor needs to know is what *the person seeking help feels his problem is.* After a few minutes of conversation the counselor may sense that an individual has other problems than the one he is verbalizing, which may seem to the counselor to be more pressing. But the only way these can be reached is through the problem of which the individual is already aware and which *he* feels to be important. For example, in a child health clinic a mother may discuss with the nurse the faulty sleeping and eating habits of her preschool child. As the mother casually mentions the arguments she and her husband have about the child's training, or the fact that mealtimes are always occasions of family rows, the nurse recognizes that the basic problem is not the child but friction in the home. However, if the nurse were to attempt to plunge immediately into a discussion of this, the mother would quickly become resentful and defensive; or else she would withdraw and not try further to receive any help. A skilled nurse, by drawing the mother out, eventually would enable the mother herself to verbalize how the home situation

was affecting the child. Once the mother herself has revealed
the real problem, the nurse can point it out to her.

Discovery of what a troubled patient sees as the real problem is not always simple. The patient may manifest anxiety
and be unable himself to pinpoint it. He may know what
worries him and be unable to verbalize it. The nurse may have
preconceived ideas about what is bothering a patient under
certain circumstances and thereby be blocked from seeing more
than the obvious. An illustrative case is that of a woman re-
covering from a mastectomy.

THE PAIN OF A SCAR

Mrs. Cotta was a forty-year-old widow with one child, a
daughter of eight years. As Miss Gold, the floor nurse, cared
for her each day after the radical mastectomy was performed,
the patient talked freely of the events leading up to her hospitalization. She had discovered the lump in her breast and,
although admitting to being a little frightened, she had called
the doctor. By her own description Mrs. Cotta was a practical,
matter-of-fact person, who was not going to allow her emotions
to get the upper hand in this thing. Two weeks after she had
discovered the lump, the breast was removed and she was making a good recovery from surgery.

An intelligent, well educated woman, Mrs. Cotta plied the
nurse with innumerable questions about cancer. Miss Gold,
a recent graduate was justifiably proud of being able to answer
her questions accurately. This she did with care and at such
length that she failed to notice that the questions were hurled
at her almost compulsively. Mrs. Cotta had accepted her condition so well that the nurse was impressed with her mature
attitude. There was none of the emotional disturbance that
often accompanies a breast amputation. Miss Gold attributed
this to Mrs. Cotta's armament of information about the disease
and to the fact that since she was a widow the cosmetic effects of
the operation did not disturb her.

All seemed well until one day when the doctor was changing the dressing. He asked Mrs. Cotta if she would not like to look at the scar. The patient's eyes filled with tears as she refused and added that it made her physically ill to see it. Tearfully, but emphatically, she said, "I never want to see it, not ever!" The nurse was dumbfounded. After the doctor had left, Miss Gold asked the patient if there was anything she would like to talk about. This question was much too vague to be helpful and the patient responded, "No," as, indeed, most of us would have replied to such a question.

During the next day Mrs. Cotta began talking about her daughter in the same compulsive fashion in which she had questioned the nurse about cancer. She expressed deep concern about the child's anticipated reaction to the scar. How could she conceal it from her? Would it be upsetting to her? Should she tell her about it in advance? If so, what should she tell her? How would an eight-year-old girl react to the knowledge that her mother had only one breast? Obviously Mrs. Cotta had real anxiety about her scar, and *apparently* real concern about its influence on her daughter's feeling toward her. The nurse allowed the patient to raise the questions and to think them through for herself. She did not introject her own opinions or feelings into the discussion. This was good, and Mrs. Cotta undoubtedly found some release in having a sympathetic listener. When she left the hospital, however, she carried with her her strong antipathy toward the scar. She still did not accept it as a condition with which she could learn to live comfortably.

In a later discussion of her counseling efforts, Miss Gold felt that in spite of having established an excellent relationship with the patient, she had not helped Mrs. Cotta to develop insight into her own feelings. Let us look now at how this more difficult goal might have been reached. In the beginning when the patient was bombarding Miss Gold with questions about cancer, instead of answering all of these questions it would have been better to explore the feelings behind the questions and Mrs. Cotta's need to raise them. On the day of the change of dressing episode, a better question than the vague one Miss Gold raised would have been, "An incision like that is not easy to look at, is it?" This would have denoted an understanding on the nurse's part of the patient's feelings. It would also have implied that the nurse accepted Mrs. Cotta's right to feel as she did. Undoubtedly if Miss Gold had encouraged the patient in this way to talk more about how she felt, the discussion would have turned to Mrs. Cotta's feelings about her daughter.

A skilled counselor in this situation would have tried to draw out how Mrs. Cotta felt about cancer, about her operation, the resulting scar, how she felt it would affect her future, how damaging this might be to her self-image and what was behind her concern about her daughter seeing the scar. In all probability her daughter's reaction would be a reflection of Mrs. Cotta's own acceptance or rejection of her scarred self. Therefore, a negative attitude on the part of the little girl could probably be avoided if the nurse would help Mrs. Cotta to come to grips with her own feelings. Because Mrs. Cotta had accepted so "matter-of-factly" her diagnosis, the nurse failed to look beyond to what Mrs. Cotta saw as an important problem.

Who, and what, is he—in his own eyes?

Lastly, the counselor needs to know who and what the person who asks for help is in terms of that *person's self-concept*. How does he see himself? The counselor knows that he is Mr. Jones, that he lives at a particular address and is a mechanic, or a doctor, or a baker, or a teacher, or a lawyer. But this does not tell the counselor very much. Each individual is what he is (and sees himself) in relation to the experiences he has had —joy he has known, sorrow he has suffered, disappointment he has faced, cultural and environmental influences impinging upon his life. Each individual accepts himself, and must be accepted, in the light of these influences and experiences. For example, a person who has been crippled from birth will always see himself in the light of this defect; it can never be forgotten and will always color his expectations, his hopes, his successes and his failures. This does not mean that he will dwell morbidly on his condition; it merely means that the condition is always in the picture he sees of himself. Another example is the person from a minority group, whose life and activities are surrounded and swamped by the lives and activities of the majority. His self-concept will be entirely different from the one he would have if he lived in a place where he represented the majority group. Or think of the prenatal patient who has experienced several miscarriages. She is an entirely different woman from the woman she would be, had the previous pregnancies terminated in full-term healthy babies. These are dramatic examples, but every individual has unique influences in his life which help to determine his self-concept. Although these influences and the ways in which they are operating may not always be readily discernible, the alert counselor is on the lookout for them. The counselor needs to see through the person talking in front of him to see the picture that individual has of himself. The *real* person may not at all be the person who is consciously being presented to the counselor.

In this chapter we have attempted to develop a definition and a philosophy of counseling which can be of value to nurses in their daily work. We hope that the definition and philosophy are broad enough for nurses to believe in their abilities and responsibilities for giving counseling help to people who turn to them. How nurses can use the skills and technics employed in counseling will be considered in the next chapter.

8

The Nurse
and Counseling Technics

It has been evident throughout the preceding chapters that nurses, unless they have had experience and education in counseling, are not going to be professional counselors. Some professional groups trained to do counseling and therapy would object strenuously to the use of the term counselor as applied to nurses. It is not intended that nurses should become or should masquerade as professional counselors, rather it is hoped that nurses will become aware of the opportunities in their own work for helping people with emotional problems. There are people in need of help who never would receive it if it were not for nurses. Some people cannot afford professional help, some are prejudiced against it, some do not know what help is available or how to obtain it. Yet, many of these same people do feel comfortable about discussing their problems with nurses. To protect nurses against the criticisms of those professional people who feel that nurses have no business doing counseling, let us say that what nurses are doing is essentially *nursing*. In order to do the very best nursing of which they are capable they are borrowing some of the tools of the counseling profession. A carpenter may, upon occasion, use some of the tools ordinarily required in the work of the electrician, but it does not make him an electrician. The pharmacist may use equipment usually used by the microbiologist, but he is still a pharmacist at work in his own profession. Similarly, a nurse may use the skills and technics of the counselor without usurping the counselor's place or relinquishing the nursing profession.

Counseling begins with a relationship

Since the core of counseling is the interaction between two people, a relationship must be established before counseling takes place. Sometimes the relationship develops as a result of the contact two people have with each other over a period of time. If a nurse is regularly assigned to the care of one particular patient, she develops an interest in him, and is challenged by the opportunity to do her utmost to promote his well-being. The patient, sensing his nurse's interest in him and becoming acquainted with her work, develops confidence in the nurse. Feeling that he can trust her he does not hesitate to express himself. Occasionally a relationship develops almost instantly. We are all familiar with the experience of meeting someone and immediately feeling that this is someone we would like to know better, or in whom we can have confidence. In professional counseling, the counselor and client are strangers at the first visit, and the relationship begins to develop then. In the kind of counseling nurses are called upon to do, the relationship often develops differently.

While ideally the patient should take the initiative for expressing what is on his mind, the establishing of a good relationship which will enable him to do this is primarily the responsibility of the nurse. Through her warm, friendly, but objective, interest the nurse creates a psychological atmosphere in which the patient feels comfortable and accepted, in which he feels free to talk or not, as he wishes. While occasionally this feeling of comfort and of being accepted is present and apparent at the beginning of the contact between two people, as a rule it is something which needs to develop. In a formal counseling situation the counselor consciously tries to create the atmosphere by introducing herself, asking the client to be seated, seeing that he is made as comfortable as possible, using some of the little courtesies one might extend to a guest. In a physician's practice the situation is similar. Suppose you have a mild pain in your chest, nothing acute, but have had it long enough to wonder about it. You make an appointment with a doctor you have not met before. When your turn comes, you enter the doctor's office and sit down. He may look at you and say, "What is your trouble? Where is your pain? How long have you had it?" and so on. Or the doctor may say, "I see you come from Williamsport. I used to visit there when I was a little boy." After one or two comments of this nature, you relax a little, and the doctor then begins to ask you about your pain. This beginning makes you feel that the doctor is interested in *you*, not only in your pain.

Take another example—you are a nurse in an out-patient department. You are working in a maternity clinic, and the doctor depends on you to interpret his instructions about prenatal care to the patients. A patient comes into your office or the demonstration room; you have never seen her before. You may start immediately by saying, "Now these are the things the doctor wants you to do. I'll explain everything to you first, and then you may ask questions if you do not understand something." You may be very kind and patient in your explanation, but she will not develop the same feeling of ease about returning to the clinic as she would if you approached her differently. A better approach would be to say, "I'm Miss Jones, Mrs. Brown. Won't you sit down? My, it's been a hot day, hasn't it? Do you mind the heat?" The actual words will vary, of course; the important thing is the *feeling* they convey to Mrs. Brown. In the first instance, the feeling that reaches Mrs. Brown is that your talk with her is a routine part of a nurse's job, and that you are going to do the job efficiently and quickly. In the second illustration, the feeling Mrs. Brown receives is, "Here is another person, a fellow human being with a name, who cares how I feel." If Mrs. Brown should have something troubling her she is far more likely to share it with the nurse who uses the second approach than with one who uses the first. Wouldn't you?

The relationship which develops will vary in intensity, and the length of time required to establish it will vary, too.

But it is essential that there be a relationship, an interaction of feeling between two people, before counseling can take place. After a relationship has been established the nurse proceeds with her interview in one of several ways, depending upon the purpose of the interview. In the interview just mentioned the purpose is primarily educational. In this kind of interview the nurse will be much more active than she will be in an interview in which she hopes to help a patient with a personal problem. She will give specific information while the patient listens. The patient will ask questions and the nurse will answer them. Another kind of interview in which the nurse will be active is when she is taking a history or obtaining information from the patient which the hospital or the doctor needs to have. Even then the interview may change and become a counseling interview.

A QUESTIONAIRE REVEALS AN EMOTIONAL PROBLEM

Mrs. D's little boy had been referred to the diabetic clinic by the family service agency. As part of the clinic procedure, a nurse obtained a good part of the family medical history. She greeted Mrs. D. cordially and welcomed the child, attempting to make both of them comfortable in the clinic setting. This was difficult because Mrs. D. was a highly nervous woman and the child was withdrawn and frightened. As the nurse went through the necessary questions she sensed considerable reluctance on the part of Mrs. D. Some of Mrs. D's answers were short and sharply spoken. There were times when she was almost rude. The nurse might have assumed that Mrs. D. was a disagreeable, uncooperative woman and might have hurried to finish with her as quickly as possible. Instead, the nurse stopped in the middle of the questionnaire and commented kindly that these questions seemed to be upsetting to Mrs. D.

At this point the interview changed from being information-receiving to counseling. The mother was frightened, and troubled, and the nurse realized that, if the clinic was to work with the child, now was the time to discover what was troubling Mrs. D. Her cooperation would be needed in caring for the child. Why was she so hostile when all the clinic wanted to do was to help her? In the beginning of the interview the nurse had taken the initiative and asked questions, guiding the interview in the direction in which she wanted it to go. Later, much later, after a diagnosis had been established and a treatment and dietary program worked out, the nurse again would take the initiative in instructing the mother in the use of insulin and in the preparation of the diet. But in this particular instant, when the interview became a counseling interview, Mrs. D. would take the initiative for what was brought out, and the nurse would *listen*. The nurse had used another valuable technic, too. She "recognized verbally" what the woman was feeling. When we previously discussed "encouraging" people to talk, or giving people the opportunity to talk, we did not specifically state how this might be accomplished. *Verbal recognition* of someone's feelings is one of the best methods. The way in which this is done is important too. For instance, a good nurse-counselor would not say, "I see you are scared. Tell me about it. It will do you good." Rather, she might say, as this nurse did, "These questions seem to be upsetting to you." As a general rule this sort of observation will not be met with silence.

Mrs. D. replied quite testily that the questions *were* upsetting. "I've been through all of this before and I'm sick of it." Once again the nurse replied with further recognition of Mrs. D's feelings. She said simply, "I can see that it would get tiring to go over this many times. Not only tiring, but really upsetting." Mrs. D. could not argue about this, she could not be defensive about it, because here was a professional person who was not going to argue back and explain. The unhappy woman replied with more dejection than irritability, "Yes, it is more upsetting than tiring. It gets me all worked up because it always adds up to the same old thing." Mrs. D. stopped, and twisted the strap of her purse around her finger, nervously. The nurse waited, and when Mrs. D. did not continue she said questioningly, "The same old thing?" Without stopping her nervous gestures, and without raising her eyes Mrs. D. replied, "It's my fault my son has diabetes." Mrs. D's eyes filled with tears and she visibly struggled to keep from crying. At this point the youngster, who had been nervously standing by, his eyes shifting from one face to the other, interjected, "My Mom allus says it's her fault I'll never be like other little boys."

Here was opened up by an astute nurse what could be a tremendous emotional problem. It could be a problem with serious repercussions in the life of a child who, because of his mother's guilt feelings, was not being permitted to grow up normally. It is not an exaggeration to say that in those few minutes the emotional life of a little boy was in the hands of a nurse. It would have been possible for the nurse to continue with her questioning of the mother, following the questionnaire item by item, without ever picking up the strong feelings of the mother, feelings which potentially might make an emotional cripple of her son. All that was required to bring this emotionally-charged situation out into the open was the nurse's simple recognition of a mother's feelings.

Technics for encouraging communication

Having reached this point in an interview, the inexperienced counselor wonders how, without talking herself, can she keep the client talking. How can she get Mrs. D., for example, to continue—to explore and to look for an explanation of the feeling she has? Here again, there are certain technics a nurse will find extremely valuable. She can use remarks that are similar in nature to what the patient has said. She may use sounds, or words, or incomplete sentences which may or may not be repetitions of the patient's words. To go back to the D. case, the nurse may respond to Mrs. D's last comment by saying merely, "Your fault?" Or she may make the statement, "You think it's your fault your son has diabetes." Or she may express the same thought in the form of a question. Another technic is the use again of recognition of feeling. "It must be upsetting to feel that it is your fault." Note well that the nurse is saying that it is upsetting to feel (or to think or to believe) that it is her fault. She is by no means implying that it *is* Mrs. D's fault. She is recognizing the fact that Mrs. D. feels this way, and that having this feeling is upsetting to her.

The kind of counselor response suggested here constitutes a large part of the counselor's approach in what has been called non-directive or permissive counseling. The counselor is not telling the person what to do. He is not injecting his own words or opinions or feelings into the interview. He is picking up the other person's words and feelings and is using them to help the troubled person explore and express his feelings further. Let us take a simple sentence and see the various non-directive responses a counselor could make to it.

Mr. A. will go home on Friday after a stay in the hospital of several weeks. A nurse says to him, "I hear you are going to leave us on Friday." The patient replies, "Yes, when I think of going home I don't know whether I am excited or frightened." The nurse might say, "HmHmm." Except for not answering at all, this is probably as non-directive as she can be. And not responding in any way could not be considered counseling in this instance. She might choose to use one single word; she could say, 'Oh?" or "Yes?" Sometimes people are motivated to say more about the subject if the counselor picks up the last word. In this case she would say "Frightened." This illustrates still another possibility. A counselor may pick what seems to be a very significant word from what the person has said and repeat that. "Frightened" happens to be both the last word and a potentially significant one. Sometimes a whole phrase or sentence is repeated. A nurse might respond, "You don't know whether you are excited or frightened." Another technic is to use an unfinished sentence, "You mean that going home is . . . ," and the patient will usually amplify his meaning (and perhaps help clarify his own feeling). Technics of this kind are called reflecting, because you are reflecting what the

patient has said rather than adding anything new to it. Even
in this simple situation recognition of the patient's feelings
may be used. A good response would be, "I guess going home
after so long in the hospital is both exciting and frightening."

In these illustrations of non-directive technics the counselor is primarily inactive, verbally, that is. Mentally she is
probably very active as she tries to see behind the patient's
words what the patient is trying to convey. Even in non-
directive counseling, the counselor may be more active than
in the illustrations. In various ways she may ask a person to tell
her more. "I didn't quite understand what you meant by that.
Could you explain it again?" "That must have been an interesting experience. Can you tell me more about it?" "This particular problem seems to worry you so much. I can't help
wondering why." "That must have been upsetting to you. Do
you feel like talking about it?" "How do you feel about this?"
The counselor may respond to something she senses the patient
is feeling rather than to his words. When the patient indicates
by facial expression, or tone of voice, or gestures or nervous
signs that he has certain feelings which he is not expressing,
the counselor may say, "I have the feeling that you were pretty
much disturbed about that." "Right now you feel angry, don't
you." "It makes you a bit nervous, doesn't it?" "You don't
think you've been treated fairly." Sometimes the counselor
senses these feelings and puts them into words for the patient,
and sometimes she is rewording what a patient has said in an
effort to help him see meaning of which he had been unaware
in his own words. In other words, the counselor helps to clarify
for the person seeking help what the individual himself is
feeling and is trying to say.

To make some of these technics more clear, let us go back
to Mrs. D., the mother of the diabetic child, and continue her
interview with the nurse. We are beginning with Mrs. D's last
comment.

"It's my fault my boy has diabetes."

"You feel it's your fault?"

"Well, my husband always says it came from my side of the family. My mother had diabetes."

"How do you feel when your husband says this?"

"It hurts me. After all it's his child too, and I can't help it if our child is sick any more than he can."

"Perhaps having him say this makes you angry too."

"Yes, I guess it makes me pretty mad. It's so unfair."

"Maybe having us ask you all these questions makes it seem as though we are trying to blame you too."

"Oh no!—Well—Maybe that's why I do mind the questions so much. But I don't *really* mind them. I know you have to ask them. And I do want to cooperate and do everything I can to help my boy."

"We know you do, Mrs. D., and we want to help him too."

Obviously, this interview might have been carried further, because it is apparent that the mother had real problems in her relationship to this boy and with her guilt feelings. But at this point the nurse had the cooperation and the confidence of the mother and was able to complete the history-taking. The larger jobs of helping to alleviate the mother's feelings of guilt, of helping her build a more wholesome relationship with the boy, and of helping the entire family, including the youngster, accept the illness and learn how to live with it would come later.

Sometimes the nurse is over-anxious

There are times when an interview does not proceed as well as this one did, and the nurse tends to become anxious. In some situations the answer to a patient's problems seems so obvious and simple that it would appear to be much easier just to tell the patient the answer. At other times a nurse may herself feel irritable, or depressed or perhaps too hurried to listen constructively to a patient. If the patient is not revealing his feelings easily or is difficult and uncooperative in some way, a nurse is tempted to forget the value of being non-directive and to become too active in an interview. The kind of overactivity the nurse uses depends upon the circumstances.

If the nurse is anxious and worried about the patient's problem, or is anxious about her ability to help him cope with it, her error frequently is in the direction of being reassuring, whether reassurance is indicated or not. Giving reassurance is a common error, and we make it because giving reassurance is so easy to do. In addition, momentarily at least, it may make the person giving it feel a little better. A member of a patient's family may come to a nurse and say, "My mother seems to have so much pain today. I'm afraid she's much worse, isn't she?" A nurse who is anxious herself because the patient does seem to be worse may say, "Don't worry about her, she'll be feeling better tomorrow." It is the old there-there-everything's-going-to-be-all-right routine. To a person who is disturbed or upset about something this is meaningless. It is doubtful whether even a child who is patted on the head and given this kind of childish reassurance is helped by it; a troubled adult certainly is not. In the first place, the person giving the reassurance is not sure that someone will feel better, or will live, or will have a satisfying outcome from an operation. It is hoped that he will, but that is all. Furthermore, the reassurance is belittling to the person who has the problem or the worry. If you say to your roommate that you are terrified of scrubbing for your first operation, what is it you want to hear? She may reply, "For pity's sake! That's nothing to be afraid of. Everybody else goes through it." Does this make you feel better about it? Not usually. More likely it makes you feel that she is belittling your fear. In essence she is saying, "You don't have good judgment or you wouldn't be afraid of a thing like that." An immediate effect of this response is to block the person from expressing further feeling. In the person who is blocked by someone else's reassurance there is a negative feeling stirred up which says, "There's no point in trying to tell her anything because she won't understand; she will ridicule my fear, making me feel foolish."

A nurse's own anxiety may make her move to the core of a problem too quickly, thus arousing anxiety or antagonism or both in the other person. This can be especially upsetting when the situation involves supervising the work of others. In supervision there are occasions when criticism or some kind of disciplinary action is necessary. Sometimes the errors are observed by the supervisor, sometimes they are reported to her by someone else. In the latter case it is wise for the supervisor to be sure of the details before approaching the accused individual.

USING THE LIGHT TOUCH

Mrs. Potts, a nurses' aide in a school for retarded children, was assigned to the unit for babies and very young children. She had been a responsible member of the staff for several years. The professional nursing staff consisted of an educational director, in charge of a training program for non-professional personnel, and Miss Dean, who was in charge of nursing service.

One day the educational director telephoned Miss Dean to say that one of the attendants had reported to her that Mrs. Potts had given all of her babies an ounce of cascara that morning in their breakfast cereal. The educational director expressed her horror as she passed this on, and Miss Dean herself was incredulous. She promised to investigate and to report back. It was time for the day shift to report off duty and Miss Dean called Mrs. Potts to her office.

"Mrs. Potts, did you give an ounce of cascara to your patients this morning, and did you give it to them in their cereal?"

"Miss Dean, what do you mean? What is the matter?"

"Now don't get excited!"

"Don't get excited? About being accused of giving the wrong amount of medication?"

"Mrs. Potts, don't you have a standing order for milk of magnesia to be given in your unit?"

"Yes, I do. But there wasn't enough sent up from the drug room and the doctor wrote an order for cascara. That's what we used to use before we changed to milk of magnesia."

"How much cascara did you give?"

"Why, I gave one dram in a half ounce of mineral oil—just as the doctor ordered, of course."

"Do you always give the laxative in cereal?"

"Yes, I do, Miss Dean. It's the only way I can get the children to take it, and the doctor said that was perfectly all right, as long as they took it. What is the trouble?"

"Oh, nothing to be worried about, I was just checking. Don't worry about it. Everything is fine!"

In spite of Miss Dean's words of comfort, Mrs. Potts left the office with a strained expression. The educational director was satisfied with the explanation, but Miss Dean had an uneasy feeling. Her feeling was not relieved any the next day when she saw Mrs. Potts whose usual morning smile was missing.

"Good morning, Mrs. Potts. Don't you feel well?"

"Oh, Miss Dean! I spent a terrible night! I couldn't believe that you don't trust me when it comes to giving medications." (She burst into angry tears.)

It took a long time to explain to Mrs. Potts what had happened. Even after the explanation it was many weeks before Miss Dean and Mrs. Potts were able to re-establish the good working relationship they had maintained for so long. What went wrong with this interview? Why did Mrs. Potts stay hostile for so long? In retrospect Miss Dean felt that her own resentment about the criticism directed at Mrs. Potts had blinded her. In a hurry to prove that nothing was wrong with Mrs. Potts' work, she had plunged into action without considering how Mrs. Potts would feel. Believing in Mrs. Potts' ability and judgment, Miss Dean could have started her interview in an exploratory way.

"Mrs. Potts, something came up today that I need to ask you about. It seems like a silly thing to bring up with someone I trust as much as I do you. But I had to for your own protection. One of the new attendants had some question about you giving your babies cascara this morning."

"Yes, I gave them cascara. We didn't have enough milk of magnesia."

"I suppose the order was written?"

"Oh yes. The doctor wrote the order for a dram of cascara in a half ounce of mineral oil."

(Laughing.) "Well, that explains that! The new attendant who saw you give it jumped to the conclusion that it was all cascara. I knew better but I had to hear it from you. We'll straighten that out, and perhaps our new staff member will have learned something. How in the world do you give those babies that dose?"

"I have to give it in the cereal, it's the only way they'll take it. The doctor says that's all right."

"Thanks ever so much for clearing this up for me. I'm sorry to have made you late leaving."

There are other ways, of course, in which this situation could have been handled without stirring up Mrs. Potts' animosity. The important thing to remember is not to sound accusing or condemnatory unless you want to make the other person feel hostile and put her on the defensive. When this happens, even though it may be followed by a reasonable explanation, the initial resentment will linger on.

Another error in the direction of talking too much or saying the wrong thing is telling the troubled individual about yourself or others who have had similar experiences. In nursing this is very easy to do because you may have known several patients with similar conditions. When a patient begins to worry about his illness or his operation there may be a tendency on the part of the nurse to say, "Lots of people have this operation and get along very nicely." This does not help the patient, of course. To the patient you are implying that he is not a unique individual but one of many who go through the hospital mill. When you are worried about your own problem, whether big or little, it does not comfort you to know that others are, or have been, in the same boat. It may be true that "misery loves company," but when you are concerned with and focusing on your own misery you are not capable of concern about the misery of others. You are not in a position to profit by sharing someone else's problems. For example, if I bring my baby into your receiving ward and I am panicky because he has swallowed a safety pin, it does not help me at all to have you tell me that other babies have had similar accidents and have recovered from them. This is *not* any other baby, this is *my* baby. This worry is present and real to me. The worries of other mothers, at this moment, are not real to me. I am not the least interested in hearing about them, and I resent your removing the focus of attention from my problem. Telling of other experiences (which is one more form of reassurance) may denote anxiety on the part of the nurse. To the patient, however, it appears to be a total lack of interest, concern and understanding for his worry.

Beware of giving advice!

Because nurses are trained in the area of health education and giving needed information, they frequently err also in the free giving of advice. There is a well-defined difference between giving advice and giving information. If a patient asks you how a particular orthopedic clinic operates, it would be foolish to say, "How do you feel about it?" The patient is asking for concrete information which you may have to give her. However, if the patient asks whether you think she should take her child to Dr. X. or to Dr. Y. it would be equally foolish for you to advise her. When a person asks for advice he may want someone else to shoulder the responsibility for whatever decision he makes. Faced with indecision, an individual consciously or unconsciously is leaning in one direction or another. He asks advice in order to bolster the opinion he already has. The result of advice, obviously, is that the individual takes it or not. If he takes it and his decision turns out well, it was what he had planned to do anyway, and he is satisfied that it was his own decision. If he takes advice and the results are not satisfying, he then blames the person who gave him the advice. In avoiding the giving of advice there is an even more important consideration than these. One of the principles in counseling, indeed in any of the helping professions, is the belief that each individual is responsible for and capable of determining his own welfare. (Obviously, those who are mentally incapacitated by illness or age or the extremely young are excluded from this generalization.) The job of the counselor is merely to aid him help himself when he is blocked in some way. The giving of advice, whether solicited or not, takes away from the responsibility an individual rightly has for himself. Another reason for not giving advice is that the individual, under ordinary circumstances, knows more of his own situation than anyone else can know. What an individual knows may not be present or clear in his conscious thinking, however, and a counselor helps him reach his decision by having him talk it out. The following example illustrates the wise handling of a request for advice.

GIVING HELP WITHOUT ADVICE

A student nurse was struck by a crisis which involved reaching an important decision in her life. She enjoyed nursing, did excellent work, and was well liked by the faculty as well as by her classmates. The eldest of six children of a rural family, she had worked hard during her high school days to make possible her entrance into a nursing school. She had the blessing of her proud parents in her undertaking, even though the family was in too much financial difficulty to give her much help. When she was entering her senior year in the school of nursing her mother died after a sudden and brief illness. This left no one at home except her father to assume responsibility for the housekeeping and the care of the younger children. The student was torn in conflict between her desire to achieve her professional goal and her feelings of responsibility toward her family. Although she talked the situation over with her father, he was of little help because he was caught in the same conflict, feeling he needed her at home but wanting her to finish her training. Fortunately, the student was in a school headed by an understanding director of nursing with whom the student had a series of conferences in an effort to reach a decision. In desperation she almost pleaded with the director to tell her what she should do. But the director was a wise woman and a skilled counselor. Using the technics we have discussed, she drew the student out, helping her express her feelings about the total situation. As the student talked about the possible outcome of either decision and her feelings about it, she was able to clarify what she really wanted most to do. She realized that in the long run she would be better able to contribute to her family if she graduated from nursing school. With the support and acceptance of the director she worked out compromises which would enable her to watch over her family without jeopardizing her education. She worked through her conflict until she was able to see for herself how she could finish training without having feelings of guilt about deserting her family in their time of need. (Her solution was: She asked for and received a two-month leave of absence. During that period she helped her father and her siblings to work out a satisfactory household routine, enlisting the help of a neighbor who could be called in case of emergency. After her return to the hospital she returned home on each of her free weekends, partly to check on how things were going and partly to give emotional support to the younger children.)

In this instance the director might have given advice in either direction, depending upon her own feelings, upon her own emotional needs. If the director were a woman who for some reason had strong guilt feelings about her own family, she might have advised the student to go home and give herself up to the family or she would always regret not making the sacrifice. If she were a woman who felt unrecognized hostility toward her family, or perhaps was envious because she had no family of her own, she might have urged the girl to finish training by all means, impressing her with the fact that she had her own life to think of first. As director of the school she might also have allowed herself to be swayed by the fact that the student was a good one whom the school would not like to lose. Regardless of which way she herself felt, the director had learned that, in counseling others, one's own feelings and opinions must not be allowed to becloud the issue. If the director had given outright advice without allowing the student to work through her own feelings, the student would have felt feelings of guilt if she had not taken the advice and eventual resentment if she had taken advice which did not produce satisfying results. Neither of these things happened because the student, with the help of expert counseling, reached her own decision which was the right one for *her*. It might not have been the right decision for the director or for you or for me.

It is not unusual that a request for advice or information conceals a need to ventilate some emotional disturbance. Less common is the reverse, when someone is emotionally upset over a worry that simple information could eliminate. Again, using sound counseling technics, a nurse may help the individual to recognize his need for information and to motivate him to seek the appropriate help.

BRING IT OUT IN THE OPEN

Mrs. Benz, in her position as operating room supervisor, had developed a well deserved reputation for understanding her personnel and their problems. Always ready to listen, she was frequently approached by her staff with personal problems and job dissatisfactions they were feeling. It came as quite a surprise to her when one of her most competent young nurses became irritable, short-tempered and indifferent in her work. Four months ago Mrs. Mace had been efficient, happy and well liked by her co-workers. At that time, very much in love with a personable young man, Mrs. Mace had taken a month's leave of absence in order to marry and have a honeymoon. Her husband was a graduate student, and Mrs. Mace had returned to her position in the operating room at the end of a month.

Upon her return it was noted that she was fairly quiet which was attributed to her preoccupation with her new wedded status and housekeeping responsibilities. In the three months that followed, however, the quietness gave way first to an emotional withdrawal and gradually to a state of unfriendliness. Since Mrs. Mace would not approach Mrs. Benz to talk about what was bothering her, Mrs. Benz decided she would have to take the initiative before the situation grew any more uncomfortable. Arranging a time when they would be working alone in the preparation of instruments for the next day, Mrs. Benz plunged in very directly.

"You're unhappy, Ann; something must be bothering you. What is it?" This was followed by silence for a few seconds, as Ann looked more unhappy than ever.

"It's just . . . I don't know . . . it's just that Joe wants me to be with him every minute. . . . I don't know how to explain. . . ."

"But surely that hasn't upset you."

"This sounds awful, but I hate to go home at night. I don't like being married. I don't want to get pregnant." Then she began to cry.

After handing her some tissues, Mrs. Benz puzzled over the young bride's answer. Surely a fear of pregnancy could not be her whole problem! As the girl's tears lessened, Mrs. Benz said, "Ann, you must know something about contraceptive measures. Is that the only thing that is bothering you?" After another short period of silence, Mrs. Mace's words rushed out in a torrent.

"I love him! I really do love him! I wanted to be married to him. I want to make him happy, but—I don't know what's wrong with me. I don't like being married. It's awful. But . . .

you know what I mean . . . Oh, no you don't . . . But it hurts so.
. . . Well, now you know . . . What's wrong with me? There
must be something wrong with me for it to be like that!" Again
she began to cry.

"Well," Mrs. Benz thought to herself, "there it is. I asked
for it. I wanted to know what was bothering her and she told
me. Now what? Where do we go from here?" Then, leaning
across the table at which they had been working and looking
Mrs. Mace straight in the eye, Mrs. Benz said, "Ann, I am
certain there is nothing wrong with you. It takes a lot more
time than four months to adjust to marriage and sex relations.
You haven't given yourself a chance. I am certain there is
nothing so wrong that it cannot be worked out."

Now that the problem was out in the open and finally
shared with a wise, understanding person, Ann was more willing
to talk about it. Mrs. Benz learned that this young girl, although a graduate nurse, had had absolutely no preparation
for entering marriage. Extremely romantic and idealistic, but
totally uninformed, Ann had been disillusioned by and unhappy with the sex relations in her marriage. Inhibited and
frightened, she was also unable to share her feelings of disappointment with her husband.

With her own wholesome attitudes toward and knowledge
about sex, Mrs. Benz was able to relieve some of Ann's anxiety,
not with advice, but with information which Ann needed and
did not have. The older woman also gave Ann a marriage
manual and suggested an appointment with a doctor for a be-
lated premarital physical examination.

The result of Mrs. Benz' efforts to help Ann were noticeable in a gradual lessening of the girl's tension and irritability
and increased interest in her work. In two or three months
Ann was like her old relaxed self. A year later when she left
for a maternity leave, instead of coping with a fear of pregnancy, she was happily anticipating the birth of her child.

In looking back at her counseling with Ann, Mrs. Benz,
critical with herself, knew that she had broken several rules of

good counseling by asking questions, taking the initiative, relating personal experiences of her own, and being emphatically reassuring. On the other hand, there were positive elements in her counseling. She had already established good rapport with Ann; she was sincerely interested in Ann's problem, and Ann sensed Mrs. Benz' concern; she was able to discuss a difficult subject without embarrassment and certainly without judgmental overtones. What was most important, of course, was Mrs. Benz' astuteness in recognizing the presence of a problem behind Ann's irritability and professional indifference.

Listening is not harmful

Sometimes a person new to counseling wonders if her attempts may not do more harm than good. This is rarely so because the very fact that a person is sharing his problem with someone else does him some good. If the counselor is listening instead of talking, he probably will never do more harm than good. In spite of knowing this, nurses frequently talk too much. They become over-anxious to be helpful, or they have an emotional need to flaunt their knowledge, to let others see how competent and capable they are. Quite often a nurse starts to explain and interpret to the patient before he is ready to accept an interpretation. For example it may quickly be apparent to a nurse that a mother's difficulty with a problem child lies in the mother's own unconscious rejection of the child. But if the nurse brings this to the mother's attention she will be met with hostility. The counseling opportunity will probably end right there, and justifiably so. There may be occasions when some interpretation or explanation by the nurse of what the patient is revealing is valuable and effective. But on the whole it is more valuable to help the patient find his own explanations.

Probing belongs in surgery, not in counseling

By the same token, "digging" for material which the nurse believes the patient is not bringing out should be avoided. It is possible, figuratively, to back someone into a corner and

force him to talk. Such efforts usually result in counseling failure because of the hostility which is stirred up. The material
a counselor has to use in helping a person solve his problem is
what the person himself reveals without coercion. Some of this
material, as we have noted, may be brought out through non-
verbal means without the person's awareness, but a good counselor does not force things out.

Accept someone's right to his own opinion

Occasionally the problem a patient reveals to a nurse re-
lates to the patient's feelings about some other professional person. Sometimes these are open complaints which may seem to
place the nurse "on the spot." She may feel torn between her
loyalty to other professional people and her need to maintain
a good relationship with her patient. Actually the nurse does
not need to be in conflict. When a patient complains about
another nurse or criticizes the work of his doctor, the competent nurse treats this revelation as she does anything else the
patient tells her. She accepts the patient's right to feel as he
does, without necessarily agreeing with him. Because nurses are
taught to be loyal to the profession, and to respect and be loyal
to members of the medical and allied professions, they sometimes feel called upon to defend these other people against the
criticisms of patients. When we fly to the defense of someone
we are implying that the other person needs to be defended.
Whereas if we really have faith in the person or profession being criticized we should not feel that defense is necessary.
Furthermore, when we defend someone we usually are lining
ourselves up with that person against the person making the
criticism. In our own personal lives there are times when we
feel compelled to do this. In our professional relationships,
particularly with patients, it is advisable to avoid it.

WHAT PRICE LOYALTY?

Mr. M. was a very touchy, sensitive patient inclined to be
easily irritated. In spite of this, Miss Trotter, a student nurse,

with kindness, extreme patience and acceptance had established
good rapport with Mr. M. After Miss Trotter had cared for
him for several days she was off for the weekend. Mr. M. was
given care by another student who happened to be Miss Trotter's closest friend. On Monday morning when Miss Trotter
went in to see Mr. M. he looked up from his bed with a sigh
of relief. He told the nurse it was a good thing it was she who
came in and not that "scatter-brain." He added violently, "If
that other nurse ever dares to come in here again I'm going to
tell her to get out and stay out." Miss Trotter, amazed at his
vehemence, asked him what on earth had happened and what
nurse he was talking about. The patient mentioned the other
student's name in hateful tones and began a series of complaints
about her work and attitude. Before he finished, Miss Trotter
found herself growing more and more tense and angry. Finally,
unable to take more she blurted out, "That's enough, Mr. M.!
You happen to be talking about one of my best friends. I don't
know what happened, but I do know she's a good nurse, and
I am not going to listen to any more of your complaints about
her." If Miss Trotter's purpose was to stop Mr. M's complaints,
she was highly successful. He muttered something to the effect,
"I might have known . . . you're all alike." Then he stopped
complaining. In fact, he stopped talking to Miss Trotter. Miss
Trotter, still bristling from Mr. M's unkind remarks about her
friend, also lapsed into silence. It was a cold, unfriendly atmosphere. Although on succeeding days the nurse and patient became at least mutually polite, the good relationship which
would have enabled Miss Trotter to help Mr. M. was never
recovered.

A nurse's own feelings may be in agreement with the patient, or, as was true of Miss Trotter, she may be in hearty dis-
agreement with him. The wise handling of a patient's criticism
is the same regardless of which way the nurse feels. Here is a
troubled patient, needing to "blow off steam" because of anger
at either a real or an imagined wrong. With Mr. M., a more

constructive way of helping him to handle his anger would have been the use of some of the technics we have discussed. Rather than defending her friend, Miss Trotter might better have recognized Mr. M's feelings, "My, Mr. M., you must have had an upsetting time yesterday." Mr. M. in response undoubtedly would have enlarged on what took place to upset him. In replying to this, Miss Trotter could say, "It isn't easy for a patient to have a change of nurses. We realize that. It's too bad that sometimes it can't be helped." If Mr. M. pursues the issue (which he probably would), with more specific complaints about the substitute nurse's undesirable behavior, Miss Trotter could continue to recognize his feelings and to reflect what he has said until Mr. M. does one of two things. He may talk himself out, or he may talk to the point where he realizes how critical he has been. If the latter happens, he himself will begin to change his feelings and to retract some of the things he has said. In either case his relationship with Miss Trotter will not be impaired. In using these suggested technics Miss Trotter is not agreeing with the patient about what her friend did, nor is she disagreeing. She is not condoning nor condemning Mr. M's opinion. She is merely accepting his right to feel as he does. It is this acceptance which enables Mr. M. to say freely enough how he feels so that his hostility will not be repressed and need to burst out in some other way which may deter his progress toward recovery.

If Mr. M. had happened to be talking about someone whom Miss Trotter did not like, her response to Mr. M. would be just the same. For the sake of the hospital morale and to protect the reputation of the hospital staff, Miss Trotter should not express her own feelings of agreement with Mr. M's criticism. It could do untold damage, even to the nurse herself, if she were to say, "You are so right, that girl is a real stinker." For obvious reasons, this kind of feeling, even though it may be justified, should not be shared with a patient. Disloyalty of this nature can serve only to undermine the reputation of the profession as a whole.

Miss Trotter's response to Mr. M's criticism illustrates another reaction, which, in a nurse-patient relationship, should be avoided like the plague. In fact, it should be avoided in any relationship in which someone is taking a counseling role in an effort to help someone else. Miss Trotter became very angry and she let the patient know that she was angry. If a nurse actually is angry about something a patient has said, it may not really matter whether she deliberately lets him know or not, for he will undoubtedly sense it. The point being made here is that if a nurse really accepts a patient's right to feel as he does even though it may be different from the way the nurse feels, she cannot be angry about it. Sometimes the person being counseled attempts to gain control of the interview by forcing the counselor into an open display of emotion. It may not always be anger; it may be sadness, or dejection, or fear. Once the counselor has allowed himself to be caught in this trap the other person is definitely in control of the situation. At times, every nurse feels angry, or frightened, or sad, or loving, and there are occasions when she may let people know she is feeling these emotions. But if she is carried away by her emotions, as Miss Trotter was, she is not then in a position to help her patient. It is possible, however, to show that what the patient is feeling is being understood and accepted, without being caught and swept away in the patient's own emotional tides.

Looking for hidden clues

Sometimes a conscientious nurse recognizes that a patient seems to be troubled, but in spite of talking together they do not seem to be able to get to the core of the problem. The patient may talk quite freely without bringing out feelings which are significant in his particular problem. Consciously or unconsciously the patient talks around the problem rather than focusing on what is really bothering him. It may be that neither the nurse nor the patient is aware of what the real underlying problem is. When this is true, the nurse may look for certain

clues in what the patient says or in the way in which he behaves which will let her know when they are close to the
emotionally-charged areas. Some of the verbal clues a patient
gives are repeating himself, talking about being nervous or
jittery, expressing strong feelings such as anger or fear, making
very positive, dogmatic statements and emphatically denying
something. An astute nurse can also find clues of a non-verbal
nature, such as changes in physical activity or open displays of
emotion, such as tears or temper outbursts. Sometimes we tend
to forget that the latter are more apt to be the result of deep-
seated anxiety than of actual anger. To illustrate how some of
these clues may appear let us look at a specific situation.

ALL IS NOT AS IT SEEMS

Mr. Q., a young married man, was hopitalized with a gastric ulcer and underwent surgery. Although outwardly polite
and cooperative he gave the impression of being tense, anxious,
and sometimes depressed. Miss Wilson, assigned to give him
care, was aware of his tension and recognized that continual
tension was not conducive to a complete and speedy recovery.
To find out what was troubling him became a real challenge
to the nurse, and she put great effort into her work with him.
After a comfortable, friendly relationship was established, Mr.
Q. began to talk about himself. He had been married two years
and they had a three-month-old boy. As far as Mr. Q. openly
revealed it was a fine baby, and both he and his wife were de-
lighted to have begun a family. On the surface Miss Wilson
could not find anything in Mr. Q's comments which would provide reason for his continuous tension. Then she began listening more carefully and she made some interesting observations.
Over and over again Mr. Q. mentioned how busy his wife was
now. When she did not come in to see him he was not critical,
but spoke repeatedly of how having a baby was tying her down.
He was understanding about this. If any comment he made
could be considered even remotely critical, he qualified and

explained it. Miss Wilson also noticed that whenever she recognized that it must be difficult to adjust to the changes a new
baby brings, Mr. Q. was extremely emphatic about a baby in
their lives being exactly what they had wanted. He strongly
denied the suggestion of any other feeling about it. The nurse
noted too that on two or three occasions when Mr. Q. was
talking about the baby, instead of gesturing freely as he usually
did, Mr. Q. was very still, almost rigid, as though he had to
keep himself under control. Mr. Q. would have been the last
person in the world to think that he was jealous of his infant
son, but in many ways his comments and behavior indicated
this very real possibility. Miss Wilson was convinced that she
was discovering the cause behind Mr. Q's tensions. The amount
of help Miss Wilson could give her patient was necessarily
limited by the short time she had to work with Mr. Q. while
he was in the hospital. Had he been there longer, undoubtedly
she could have helped him further to recognize and express
some of his feelings, and to discover how unrealistic they were.
However, if she had not watched for the clues he was unknowingly giving her, Miss Wilson would never have learned what
was really troubling Mr. Q.

Resistance against help

Sometimes when a troubled person in his conversation
draws painfully close to an emotionally-charged area, he backs
away from it, and this too can provde a clue for the counselor.
A patient, for instance, who has been talking about his fears
may suddenly say that he is no longer afraid. In essence, he is
putting up a sign at the gate of his emotions which says, "Danger! High Voltage! Keep Out!" Or he may suddenly shift the
conversation and attempt to focus it on the nurse rather than
on himself. He may ask her questions about herself, her family,
her experience. He may deliberately avoid talking about topics
or people which might reasonably be included. For example, if
a patient is talking about his childhood and tells about his
brothers and sisters and mother, but fails to mention his father

at all, the nurse would justifiably question in her own mind the kind of relationship this patient had with his father. Sometimes a patient is aware of his efforts to evade a disturbing issue, but usually these are protective tactics of which the patient is totally unaware.

One might wonder why, if a patient is troubled and wants help badly enough to talk about his problems, he would at the same time have a need to protect himself from getting help. Revealing our real selves, even to ourselves, is painful because we are not usually the wonderful people we would like to think we are. Thus, consciously, a person may want the release of tension which comes with verbalizing his feelings, but unconsciously part of him seeks protection against revealing too much of himself. The psychiatrists use the term "resistance" to describe this behavior. Some of the ways of showing resistance have already been discussed. There are others. Have you ever forgotten an appointment with the dentist? For the same reasons that you have forgotten this, people with whom you are working may forget to keep an appointment with you. Many times, people are late for appointments. Perhaps sometimes you are late for class. Usually when we are late we rationalize the reasons. We blame transportation, or being too busy, or the weather for holding us up, when actually what we are doing is showing resistance. We do not want to go, or we do not want to be on time. Another way in which people show resistance to receiving the help for which they have asked is through silence. Even after a patient has "opened up" and has started to talk freely there may be periods of silence which may represent resistance.

While silence may be a form of resistance, it may also be an opportunity for the patient to think about what has been said, to organize further thought. For this reason it is best not to break into his silence immediately, for he may be distracted from some constructive thought. It is better to let the silence persist for a little while. If the counselor accepts the silence without being disturbed by it, the silence will not be disturbing to the patient unless it is a form of resistance. In this case the patient will eventually break the silence himself and then the counselor may help him to see that his silence was a resistance against revealing something.

Nurses, in their informal counseling contacts, may have to contend especially with one form of resistance. Often a patient under great emotional and physical stress will reveal something highly personal to a nurse, and, when seeing the nurse again, will appear to be very distant and cool. A public health nurse had an interesting experience of this kind.

WISE HANDLING OF REMORSE

Miss Robbins was a staff nurse in a generalized public health program. She was making a routine child health supervision visit to a family in her district. Just before she rang the doorbell, she heard angry voices followed by the slamming of what seemed to be the back door. Then there was silence. Although she hesitated at first, Miss Robbins decided to ring the bell. In a few minutes it was reluctantly opened by Mrs. A. Miss Robbins knew immediately that Mrs. A. had been crying, but she made no comment about it. After they had talked for a few minutes about the children, with Mrs. A. reacting in a very distracted, apathetic way, Miss Robbins said kindly, "You don't really feel like talking with me about the children today, do you?" Mrs. A's reaction was an outburst of tears followed by a detailed description of a "fight" she had just had with her husband. In her emotional distress she blurted out a great many things about her marriage, revealing some of their most intimate difficulties. The nurse let her get it all out of her system, doing little more than reflecting what Mrs. A. said and recognizing her feelings. As Mrs. A. calmed down, she apologized for burdening the nurse with this, but added that she did feel much better for talking it out. The nurse was accepting and understanding and suggested that perhaps she could come back next week to see the children. Mrs. A. felt this was a good idea. When Miss Robbins left, Mrs. A. apologized again, but thanked the nurse warmly for her help. Miss Robbins was so sincerely interested in Mrs. A's problems and so glad that she had been able to offer the distraught woman at least the comfort of a good listener, that she was not prepared for the cold reception when she returned a week later. Opening the door only enough to make conversation possible, Mrs. A. politely told the nurse that she would not have time to talk with her that morning. The children were all fine anyway and there was no need for Miss Robbins to make a visit. Although Mrs. A's behavior was unexpected, Miss Robbins realized immediately what was behind it. She realized too that if she were to continue working with the A. family in a constructive way, it would be better to re-establish rapport with Mrs. A. now than to allow the breech between them to widen. Miss Robbins suggested that since she was already there perhaps Mrs. A. could spare just a few minutes, although, Miss Robbins said, she realized that Mrs. A. was busy. Even more reluctantly than on the previous visit Mrs. A. opened the door for the nurse. As the nurse began talking about the children she knew that Mrs. A. was very embarrassed and uncomfortable. She went on for a few minutes and then recognized Mrs. A's feelings of discomfort by saying, "You don't seem to be comfortable about having me here today." At first Mrs. A. denied this, using the excuse again that she was just busy—too busy to talk. The nurse agreed, saying that she certainly knew that having several children kept Mrs. A. busy. "But," she added, "I can't help feeling that there is something more in your not wanting to talk to me." Mrs. A. did not answer. She merely looked more tense. Finally the nurse put into words for Mrs. A. what Mrs. A. was really feeling. She said, "Perhaps you are uncomfortable and embarrassed because of my visit last week. Maybe you even regret a little having told me your troubles." Mrs. A. at first did not know how to answer. She hesitated, and then, as her eyes filled with tears, lowered her head and nodded, saying almost under her breath that she was ashamed. The nurse did not say that it was silly to be ashamed, or that she had never given the matter another thought, or that Mrs. A. did not need to worry about telling her anything. Rather, she replied understandingly, "Yes, I know how you feel." She waited a moment before adding, "Sometimes when we tell a great deal about ourselves we worry later for fear we have said too much. We might even think that the person to whom we've talked won't respect us as much." Mrs. A. looked relieved, and stated that this, indeed, was the way she had felt. Only then did Miss Robbins attempt to reassure her by saying that we all have the need sometimes to blurt things out. She assured her also that she had just as much respect for Mrs. A. now as she had always had. Although this was not the entire conversation of this interview, this was the general theme of it. The result was that mother and nurse then were free again to talk about the children. When they parted, there was an even stronger relationship between them than had existed before.

The nurse-counselor has limitations

One of the responsibilities of any professional person is to recognize his own limitations. Certainly this is true of the nurse who is using the skills of counseling. She may have all the counseling tools at her finger-tips but be faced with someone's problem that requires much more skilled handling of these tools than she is trained to do. One of the elements of good counseling by nurses is the ability to recognize the existence of a potentially serious mental or emotional problem in a patient and, by counseling technics, to motivate him to seek the necessary professional help. Many people in need of psychiatric help would not receive it if a nurse initially were not willing to offer help on her own. The following case illustrates how a school nurse was instrumental in obtaining psychiatric help for a disturbed child.

POINTING THE DIRECTION TO HELP

At registration time for entering first grade pupils, Mrs. Todd, the school nurse, had a routine conference with a young Ukrainian mother of a little girl, an only child. The nurse noticed that Mrs. Yard seemed anxious when asked if Marie had any behavior problems. Although the mother answered in the negative, it was with a hesitance that caused the nurse to make a mental note of her reaction.

Following the beginning of the school term, Mrs. Todd had reason to remember the interview as she observed Marie at play in the school yard and, upon occasion, in the classroom. The child's behavior was hostile and aggressive, bordering on violence. One day when Marie received a mild reprimand from the teacher for her disturbing behavior, she became wild and belligerent and began to scream. Miss Todd came for her and took her to the health office where the child gradually quieted down. After this type of episode had occurred three times, the nurse requested a home visit with the mother.

The evening Mrs. Todd visited the home, Marie was in bed and Mr. Yard was out. The nurse began the interview by expressing disappointment about Mr. Yard's absence, since she had hoped to discuss Marie's behavior with both parents. We begin with Mrs. Yard's reasoning to this.

" I asked you to come now because he is *not* here. He does not think there is anything wrong with Marie."

"He doesn't think there's a problem?"

"No—but I do."

"Is it something you would like to talk over with me?"

"Yes, I would. I *have* to talk to somebody. I don't know anyone. I have no family here. I guess you can tell—I was a war bride. I still don't talk so good. Things were all right until after the baby was born. and then my huband got so mean to us."

"Mean?"

"We can't talk at the table. No spilled food is tolerated,

no noise allowed. Marie can't even have friends in. She doesn't have friends any more. We can't cross him or he strikes us." Mrs. Yard paused, then continued with an almost hysterical quality in her voice: "Are all families in this country like this? Is this normal? I've got to know! I can't go on living like this! Is *your* husband this way?"

"No—I'm happy to say that I don't have that problem. I am . . ."

(Interrupting) "I bought Marie a doll and she pulled all the hair off and smashed it—she does that to all of them."

"Why do you suppose she does that?"

"When I try to stop her she says 'This is Daddy! I hate it! I hate it!' She has bad dreams. She smashes everything she plays with. I'm afraid some day she'll hurt the neighbor's baby or other children."

"When did she first start having nightmares and smashing things?"

"The first time she saw my husband choking me."

"Have you explained this to your husband?"

"Yes, but he says it's all my fault . . . that I irritate him and spoil Marie."

"You and Marie seem to love each other very much."

"She's so good when we're alone. As soon as my husband comes home she starts to misbehave and become destructive."

"You know, Mrs. Yard, I believe you should share this with your family doctor. He might be able to help you. I don't believe Marie is well. Certainly she does need love and understanding."

(Beginning to cry a little) "You're saying she's mentally sick, aren't you? You don't like to hear that about someone you love so much. She's all I have! And we don't even have a doctor. Can you help me find one?"

"I've heard Marie say to the school doctor that she likes him because he doesn't hurt her. His office is in this area. If you would like to see him, I'll call him about Marie and tell him to expect your call." Mrs. Todd gave Mrs. Yard the necessary information about reaching the doctor, promised to keep in touch with her, and the interview was terminated.

Mrs. Yard was fairly well motivated to have help. Nevertheless, she might have been blocked had the nurse not been sensitive to the presence of a problem and to Mrs. Yard's need to share it with someone. Marie was taken to the doctor, who, in turn, recognized the need for psychiatric help and made the necessary referral. The child was found to be in need of psychotherapy, possibly even of hospitalization.

Although all of the details of the mother's story have not been included, it is obvious that the nurse made Mrs. Yard feel comfortable in talking to her. Mrs. Todd let Mrs. Yard speak as freely as she wished. Rather than urging, the nurse merely offered the opportunity. She facilitated Mrs. Yard's continuing by reflecting things Mrs. Yard had said rather than injecting thoughts of her own.

There were, however, several things that might have been handled more effectively in the interview. Because of Mrs. Yard's strong motivation, the nurse's responses had no apparent ill effect. The same responses might have had a deterrent effect with someone whose motivation was weaker. When Mrs. Yard asked Mrs. Todd if her husband were like this, she did not expect an answer and immediately interrupted the nurse's answer. Even if the counselee should expect an answer, it is wiser for the counselor not to be drawn into what may become a personal discussion. Instead of answering Mrs. Yard's personal question it would have been better to rephrase what she was trying to communicate—an anxiety about her marriage being different from typical American marriages, an anxiety intensified by the fact that Mrs. Yard was already somewhat different from her neighbors because of her foreign birth.

Another question Mrs. Todd asked is typical of nurses as well as doctors when they are not sure what to say next: they will ask about time or place. In some instances this may be important. But it was not necessary for Mrs. Todd to ask when Marie's behavior started. The answer would be meaningless

in terms of the total situation. Worse, Mrs. Yard's response
played neatly into her established idea that the child's problem
was entirely the fault of the father. There is little doubt that
Mr. Yard was partly responsible, but with such a close relationship existing between mother and child it is probable that
something within this very relationship is contributing to the
problem. When Mrs. Yard said her husband accused her of
irritating him and of spoiling Marie this should have been explored. Perhaps the nurse's anxiety lest she became involved in
the Yard marital problem caused her to try to boost the
mother's ego rather than to help her look for her part in the
problem.

In some situations, Mrs. Todd's suggestion (without further explanation as to why) that Mrs. Yard share the problem
with her doctor would have been abrupt. Many parents would
not have grasped so easily that the problem might be one of
illness requiring a doctor's help. At least they might not have
been able to accept the idea unless the nurse introduced it more
gradually. In fact, another mother might have interpreted the
nurse's suggestion to ask a doctor's help as rejection of herself
and her child and the problem itself. Being able to motivate
people to seek the help they need and doing it without arousing feelings of rejection is one aspect of good counseling.

There are times when a nurse, because of her own personality or because of the nature of the problem, is uncomfortable when patients reveal personal problems. Because of this,
she may stop a patient immediately from talking about intimate things, saying that she is not trained to help him with his
problems, adding the recommendation that he see his minister
or a psychiatrist or a marriage counselor, or whoever else might
be indicated. What she says may be true. But the way in which
she says it may well discourage the patient from seeking the
help he needs. Many of the people who turn to nurses with
their troubles are not familiar with other "helping" profess-
sions. The way in which the nurse approaches her part of the
helping process may determine the patient's whole attitude

toward receiving help. The patient who has initially been listened to and accepted by a nurse, before being referred by the nurse to someone else, will be far more receptive to the help that psychiatrists, counselors and social workers have to offer.

JUST OBSTINACY?

In the belief that Mrs. Carter could become an active person again, the medical staff at the Rehabilitation Center had set as a reasonable goal for her the ability to walk and to care for herself. Mrs. Carter, a fifty-year-old woman, had had chronic arthritis for fifteen years, with extensive involvement of finger joints and knees. After six weeks of intensive physical and occupational therapy the patient had made no progress. It was at this time that Mrs. Webb joined the nursing staff of the center.

In spite of the fact that Mrs. Carter had been described to Mrs. Webb as an extremely obstinate person who would do nothing for herself, Mrs. Webb's first experiences with the patient were pleasant. Cooperative and obliging, during hydrotherapy Mrs. Carter had extended her knees fully at the request of the therapist. As nurse and patient returned to the ward, the doctors were making rounds. One of them came over to the litter on which Mrs. Carter was still lying and said with a friendly enthusiasm, "Well, Mrs. Carter, let's straighten those knees." With that he pushed down on her knees, and the startled patient let out a shriek, followed by a few expressions of profanity and crying: "You and my husband think I don't want to walk. You are cruel, and I am not going to my treatments any more today." The doctor replied, "We know you can do better than you've been doing," and abruptly left.

As Mrs. Webb wheeled Mrs. Carter to her room, the patient was still crying and talking at the same time. Mrs. Webb listened, making no attempt to interrupt the flow of words. Among other things, Mrs. Carter said angrily, "Don't you think I want to walk and be able to dress like a woman instead of lying around like an old hag?" (Mrs. Webb did not yield to the temptation to point out that if Mrs. Carter really wanted to walk again she must help herself; or that she did not have to lie around looking like an old hag.) "You are married, you know how husbands are. They 'honey' you for a while, but when you get sick they think you want to get sick; they don't care about you any more."

With more of a demand than a request, Mrs. Carter told the nurse she wanted to get into the wheel chair and have a cigarette. After the nurse had moved her and supplied the cigarette, Mrs. Carter told her to leave and close the door because she was not going to any more treatments that day, "I don't care if it *is* costing him twenty-three dollars a day; the old s.o.b.!" Again wisely, the nurse left Mrs. Carter with her thoughts, returning later.

"Hello, Mrs. Carter, did you enjoy your cigarette?"

"Yes, thanks for letting me have one. Most of these people in white think they can run everybody's life. They don't know what it is to be suffering with pain while everybody tells you 'You don't want to get better' and 'you can try harder than this'."

"Of course you get tired of hearing things like that. It must be really discouraging to you sometimes."

With a look of genuine surprise at the nurse's response, Mrs. Carter said quietly, "I know you want me to go to occupational therapy, don't you?"

"Well, if you don't want to go, I'm not going to force you."

With a smile, Mrs. Carter said, "I'd better get there, I'm a half hour late now."

During the days in which Mrs. Webb worked with Mrs. Carter there were many more references made by the patient to her husband. Concerned about her gain in weight she had said several times that "men don't like fat women." Mrs. Webb was beginning to understand that this poor woman was frightened and anxious about the possibility of losing her husband's love. After all, it was at her husband's insistence and through his arrangements that she had come to the hospital. In all her emotional outbursts her hostility seemed to be directed toward her husband and then displaced onto the "people in white." Mrs. Carter's goals for herself did not coincide with those of the staff. Although she said she wanted to walk, she continued to resist treatment. On the other hand, fuel was added to an already burning fire of resentment by members of the staff who were trying to force their objectives on a patient who had not wanted to come into the hospital in the first place.

Because of Mrs. Webb's warm acceptance of Mrs. Carter, the patient was able to express many of the feelings she could not bring out to anyone else. She finally told the nurse that her husband actually was running around with another woman and planned to leave Mrs. Carter as soon as she was well enough to care for herself. The nurse realized what a tremendous emotional conflict Mrs. Carter was experiencing that was motivating her to resist all treatment. From the patient's point of view her only security lay in the disability which would enable her to keep her husband.

In this instance there was not much more that a nurse could do on her own. She listened kindly and with acceptance and reported her concern about the patient to the staff psychiatrist. Unfortunately, it was a staff decision that Mrs. Carter be returned to the care of her husband at home. It can only be hoped that at some future time (because of the interest Mrs. Webb had shown) Mrs. Carter will be motivated to seek further help, both emotional and physical.

A patient may feel rejected by the nurse who is afraid to allow him to express his feelings and to reveal his problems to her. He may then avoid trying to find the professional help he needs rather than run the risk of further rejection. Some nurses say that helping to find solutions for the marital, emotional, social and other non-physical problems of their patients should not be part of nursing. This may be true. (It is *not* always true.) But no nurse can dispute the fact that helping a patient find relief for any problem which may be affecting his physical well-being is a vital part of nursing.

The nurse-counselor justifiably, and with real benefit to the patient (or whoever is involved), uses the counseling skills of listening to, accepting, reflecting and clarifying whatever the troubled person expresses. She neither praises nor blames, carefully avoiding any statement, behavior or reaction which may arouse or increase guilt feeling in the patient. Above all, she maintains in strictest confidence whatever someone tells her confidentially. The only exception to this is where it is to be repeated in a professionally ethical way to help the patient. One of the arguments occasionally heard against the counseling function of the nurse is that nurses are busy and giving counseling help is time-consuming. Nothing could be farther from the truth. In the first place, the necessary counseling is done as the nurse pursues her routine duties. And in the second place, a counseling approach to human relations in the long run saves precious time because of the improved cooperative attitudes it develops within the people who are helped by the nurse-counselor.

Two counseling situations from the field of school nursing illustrate the time-saving potential of skilled counseling as compared to the time-wasting effort of more active and quicker methods. School nursing experience, as are all areas of nursing, is filled with counseling opportunities. Sometimes the school nurse is identified with school authority and is resented. It takes skill to convert this resentment against authority into an accepting feeling that the school nurse wants to help. It also takes time. School nurses, like the rest of us, frequently feel the pressure of work to the extent that they believe they cannot afford to devote precious time to counseling. In reality the counseling often takes less time than experimenting with other ways of motivating parents to care for their children's health needs. Two situations that follow illustrate how time-consuming methods other than counseling can be, and how effective skilled counseling can be even against the obstacles of prejudice.

THANK YOU, NURSE!

When Mrs. Peck asked permission of her school principal to make a home visit to the Blairs, he replied, "Go to it! If you want to—but you'll never get *that* family to accomplish anything!" He further explained that all of the suggestions made in the past to the Blair family had met with violent reactions and no cooperation. In spite of his discouraging response, Mrs. Peck proceeded with her plan to visit the home. Her goal was to get medical help for Betty's hearing loss. In advance of her visit, Mrs. Peck gathered as much information about the Blair family as possible and learned that it was a family of many problems. An older boy had been placed in a special class for slow learners. This had been done over the fierce objections of the mother who accused the school of belittling her child and making a "jackass" of him. One sister of Betty had a speech defect, too. Intelligence, achievement and readiness tests indicated that all of the children were low average or below.

When Mrs. Peck visited, the mother was not at home. According to neighbors, she was spending most of her days closing up the tenant farm where the family worked during the summer. Since the Blairs had no telephone Mrs. Peck resorted to writing. Explaining Betty's hearing loss as simply as she could, Mrs. Peck asked Mrs. Blair if she would get in touch with her at the school. After waiting a reasonable length of time with no answer, Mrs. Peck called Betty to her office.

Even though the nurse had difficulty understanding Betty, there was good communication between them. This was undoutedly because the nurse was interested in Betty, and the child was aware of this interest. Being careful to cast no reflection on the mother, Mrs. Peck explained to Betty that she had written Mrs. Blair, but the letter must have been lost in the mail because there was no answer. She then asked Betty to take a note home to her mother, and to have her mother come to school to see Mrs. Peck. The nurse explained to the child what was in the note and why it was important. The results were a child thrilled with a sense of an important mission and a note from the mother agreeing to come to school.

Thinking of what she knew about Mrs. Blair that would be helpful in talking to her, Mrs. Peck attempted to prepare for the interview. She knew that Mrs. Blair had had unpleasant experiences involving the school and therefore would need much patience and understanding; that Mrs. Blair had great feeling for the children; that the family was in a very low income bracket; and that Mrs. Blair was easily upset emotionally. When Mrs. Blair arrived the nurse saw an untidy, obese woman in her late thirties. Her clothes were soiled and she wore no stockings. Like two of her children, she had a noticeable speech defect. In her arms she had an eight-month-old baby who seemed dull and listless when she was placed in a chair. After introducing herself and asking Mrs. Blair to sit down, Mrs. Peck began with the interview.

"I'm so glad you were able to come. It must be hard for you to get away when you're so busy."

"I just came because Betty says she can't hear right, and I want to know what it's all about. "

"Of course, you do. You see, Mrs. Blair, we do hearing tests on all the first grade children, and according to Betty's test she isn't hearing as well as she should. There may be something causing this that can be corrected. That's why I was so anxious to talk with you."

(As the nurse spoke, Mrs. Blair indicated her resistance by looking over Mrs. Peck's head or out of the window, and by buttoning and unbuttoning her coat repeatedly. When the nurse finished her explanation there was a moment of silence.)

"I suppose what *you're* tellin' me I can believe . . . but most of the time all the people in *this* place want is to make monkeys out of my kids."

"And you're afraid that I might be doing that too?"

"Maybe you wouldn't, but those damned teachers would!"

(At this point the nurse realized that she was identified in the woman's mind with the teachers. That is why the woman made no reference to Mrs. Peck's letters, giving credit for her being there entirely to Betty.) " Your feelings are pretty strong about the school, aren't they? And I'm sure you must have reasons for the way you feel. But really all I want to do is to help Betty as much as I can. That's why *I* wanted to talk to you. There isn't any other reason."

(Still defensive) "Well, what do you want me to do? How serious is it, anyway?"

"Well, when a child does not hear well, she may not hear the instructions the teacher is giving, then she can't follow directions and makes unnecessary mistakes—mistakes she wouldn't make if she could hear what the teacher was saying."

(The key word stirring Mrs. Blair's anxiety and hostility seemed to be "teacher," for here she flushed and almost jumped out of her chair in her anger.) "Why are all the kids in this school so smart? Why do the teachers let them laugh at other kids all the time?"

(Taken aback by Mrs. Blair's sudden explosion, and not knowing to what she was referring) "I wonder why, too, sometimes. Have you any ideas?"

"No, but I'm sick and tired of kids laughing at Betty all day."

"I don't blame you a bit because Betty's a sweet little girl." (Pause) "You know, the thought just occurred to me— little children are very cruel to one another, sometimes without meaning to be. They laugh when children do something different or look different or sound different. Sometimes people laugh because they're uncomfortable. Do you suppose if Betty doesn't hear the teacher's directions and does the opposite of what the others are doing, it might strike some of the children funny? And, of course, when Betty talks her speech *is* different. It doesn't take much to get children started, you know. Do you suppose that could have anything to do with it?"

(Grudgingly) "I guess it could, but it still isn't very nice. How can I stop them?"

(Here the nurse and mother talked together about possible causes for Betty's hearing loss, when the mother suddenly changed the subject.) "What do you mean by saying that Betty talks different?"

"Why, she doesn't pronounce sounds as she should; she uses a kind of baby talk."

"Well, she talks like all the Blairs, don't she?"

"Yes—Yes, I guess she does." (Waited to see what Mrs. Blair's reaction would be.)

(Slowly, looking puzzled) "Gee, I knew that I sometimes talk funny, but I never thought it could hurt anyone else. I wouldn't knowingly hurt my kids for nothin'."

"I know you wouldn't, Mrs. Blair. It's because I know that you want to help them that I asked if you would come to talk with me."

The balance of the interview was devoted to plans and and arrangements for medical help for Betty. When the interview ended, Mrs. Blair thanked Mrs. Peck, then began to pick up the baby from the chair. Then, with deliberation, she turned from the baby and faced Mrs. Peck. "Thank you for treating me like I had some sense."

In thinking through the success of this interview and the reasons for it, Mrs. Peck came to some sound conclusions. In other instances in which school personnel had tried to motivate Mrs. Blair, in all probability they neglected to give her the opportunity to voice her own opinions. Therefore any decisions that were reached she felt were reached without taking her, the parent, into consideration at all. Parents are hurt by this sort of treatment; they feel thrust aside. It is almost as though they are being told, "You are only the parent; we are the experts." This attitude is enough to make any parent want to fight instead of "cooperate." In terms of time spent with Mrs. Blair, the results of this *one* interview are: All of the youngsters are in speech therapy; Betty's hearing defect has been corrected with a tonsillectomy; and the nurse has the complete cooperation of the family.

As a contrast to this situation, let us look at another school nursing situation.

LET ME ALONE, NURSE!

Miss Lyon had her first contact with Mrs. Peltz when the first grade child fell and cut her head. The nurse telephoned the mother, asking her to come to school because Miss Lyon felt that Jane's cut should have a couple of stitches. The mother was very upset and said that someone must have pushed Jane to make her fall. Miss Lyon assured her that it was an accident. Mrs. Peltz came to school, said the child did not need stitches, and took her home. A couple of months later, Jane was sent to the health office by the teacher because of marks that resembled chicken pox. Miss Lyon took Jane there and then took her home. The mother did not ask Miss Lyon to come in, and Miss Lyon left.

Throughout that first year of school the teacher complained that Jane was not clean and had a bad odor. She was sent to the nurse occasionally to be cleaned up, and the nurse on one occasion gave her a change of clothing, with the comment "Why doesn't your mother see that you are washed and have clean clothes?"

When Jane began her second year of school she was not promoted but continued in first grade. She had a different teacher, and the complaints about the child's lack of cleanliness were even more frequent and intense. Again the child would come to the nurse's office to be cleaned up. Miss Lyon learned from the youngster that her sister in third grade got her ready for school. By October the other children did not want to sit anywhere near Jane, the smell was so bad. Miss Lyon telephoned Mrs. Peltz and asked if Jane had a bedwetting problem. Mrs. Peltz said she had a terrible problem, not only with Jane, but with the child in third grade as well. Over the phone, Miss Lyon talked with Mrs. Peltz about possible causes and treatment for enuresis, and Mrs. Peltz promised to "see what she could do." The situation improved for a few days, and then regressed to what it had been. By November the child was beginning to suffer embarrassment from the complaints of the teacher and the rejection by her classmates. The odor and general unkempt condition of the child remained. Once again Miss Lyon telephoned the mother and asked if she would please see that Jane was bathed and had clean clothes on when she came to school. The mother explained that she was working from four o'clock until midnight now, in order to help out financially, and she did not always feel like getting up to get the children ready for school. Again, she promised to "see what she could do." For less than a week the child was clean. Then it started all over—dirty socks, soiled dresses, soiled underwear, uncombed hair and that frightful odor.

This time Miss Lyon took the situation to the principal, and together they drafted a letter to Mrs. Peltz stating that the condition must improve or more drastic measures would be taken. Soon after the letter was sent, the teacher called Miss Lyons to come and see the child. Her lack of cleanliness was as usual, but in addition, in the middle of winter, all the youngster had on was her dirty dress, soiled pants, socks and shoes. On this occasion the principal and the nurse took Jane home. The mother was not dressed and was obviously very unhappy to see her guests as well as to see Jane home from school again. The outcome of the interview was not surprising. Mrs. Peltz became very angry. Shouting and cursing she accused the nurse of picking on her child. She screamed at the principal, "You make that nurse let me alone!" The child was terrified. The principal finally had to step in and cut short Mrs. Peltz' tirade against the nurse.

Now that the damage has been done it is probably too late for Miss Lyon to try to establish a good relationship with this mother. Miss Lyon cannot understand why, with all the time and effort she has put forth in the interest of Jane, she has been unable to gain the cooperation of the child's mother.

When one considers all of the time spent on phone calls, non-productive visits to the home, letters, cleaning up the child, conferences with the teachers and principal, a counseling interview in the very beginning, based on the principles illustrated in the preceding case would indeed have been a time-saver.

Admittedly, there are some nursing situations which appear to be so hopeless, so frustrating, that it is difficult to conceive of counseling technics as being time-saving or of any other value. Such a case follows. In spite of the feeling of frustration the public health nurse experienced, the case serves to illustrate the nurse's use of counseling technics and how her own feelings and the feelings of the patient are involved in counseling.

DEFEAT OR CHALLENGE?

Miss Watson, a public health nurse newly appointed to the agency staff, had been introduced by her predecessor to Mrs. Ager, an elderly woman requiring nursing care three times a week. The previous nurse had described the care given as uncomplicated, but she had added that the patient was difficult because nothing was ever done to her satisfaction. During the ensuing weeks Miss Watson found this to be true. Mrs. Ager complained that she was not washed hard enough, or that the nurse was too rough. When her hair was pinned up it was too tight or too loose. Although able to wash her own face, the patient refused to do it because it was the nurse's job, but she frequently criticized the nurse because she did not get her face and ears clean.

Soon after she took over, Miss Watson brought in some embroidery work for her patient, believing that doing this work Mrs. Ager would feel less useless. Observantly, the nurse had noted that in the past Mrs. Ager had embroidered a great deal. Mrs. Ager's reaction was outrage. Huffily, she snapped, "I can't do this anymore, I'm much too weak!" The nurse took the handiwork back with her and did not mention it further, but she felt discouraged at the patient's lack of cooperation and lack of appreciation for the interest the nurse had shown. The patient, in becoming angry, was reacting to what she had interpreted as the nurse's lack of sensitivity to her illness. Had the nurse waited until she had established a comfortable relationship with the patient the results might have been different. Even then an indirect approach would have been better, one which would let the patient take the initiative herself. Implicit in an indirect approach would be the nurse's understanding of why the patient is not motivated to do something at this moment.

On another occasion, concerned about Mrs. Ager's obvious loneliness, Miss Watson suggested the possibility of the patient's entering the County Home. This was in answer to Mrs. Ager's frequent question about what was going to become of her. Instead of recognizing this as a patient's need to talk about her anxiety as she faced the future, the nurse jumped in with a solution. Mrs. Ager was furious at such a suggestion. As lonely as she was she did not perceive herself as a candidate for the "poor house," which was her idea of a county home. Once again the nurse had moved too rapidly and too directly.

Any effort to help someone like Mrs. Ager must be based on some understanding of her feelings. Here is an elderly woman, partially incapacitated, whose husband died after Mrs. Ager had become ill enough to need care. She had no children, and, probably because of her habitual complaints and self-pity, she had no friends with the exception of one woman who paid her a brief visit every two weeks. At her age, to what could Mrs. Ager look forward?

One morning when Mrs. Watson was giving care to Mrs. Ager everything was wrong. After the usual complaints, Mrs. Ager began a tirade. She belittled visiting nurses in general, avowed that she would never contribute a dime to the United Fund because the Visiting Nurse Society would get some of it, and then turned her attention to Miss Watson—that she was an incompetent nurse and simply did not care about her. That was too much for Miss Watson. As she expressed it: "This was a great blow to my pride, for I thought I had been showing her that I did care, by all the little extra things I had been doing for her—polishing her nails, putting up her hair, listening to her, agreeing with her. This time I just looked at her and said, 'All right, if you think I don't care you can finish your bath yourself!' With that I threw down the washcloth and left the room. Of course, I came back and the rest of the care was completed in silence." This incident was never referred to again. And never again did Mrs. Ager ridicule nurses, although she continued to complain and criticize minor things.

In exploring the feelings of the nurse, we can assume that Miss Watson had some preconceived ideas about Mrs. Ager, based on what she had been told by the nurse who preceded her. Information given in advance about a patient's undesirable behavior may arouse various feelings within a nurse. If she has a great deal of confidence in, and respect for, the informing nurse, the information may set up a barrier within the nurse. She will then approach the patient with her defenses up in anticipation of the patient's attacks. On the other hand, an advance warning given about a patient may act as a challenge to a nurse, as it was to Miss Watson. She had entered Mrs. Ager's home with almost grim determination to establish a successful relationship with this patient who had been described as difficult. Because of her newness to the agency it was important to her that she do a more than creditable job. This accounted for her unusually vehement reaction to the accusation that she didn't care about the patient.

In caring for an elderly, lonely invalid, the nurse must reckon with environmental factors which set narrow limits on what she can expect from counseling technics. Mrs. Ager has little realistic hope that her condition will improve. She looks forward for the balance of her life to being at least partially dependent on others, in her case, dependent on the public health nurse. She knows, too, that the nurse comes because it is part of her job. With these situational limitations, why should Mrs. Ager change her whining self-pity into pleasant acceptance? Realistically she might be helped to accept her circumstances in a way that would bring more pleasure and gratification to her and that would make her more acceptable to others, including the nurse.

The most effective place to begin is with Mrs. Ager's constant complaints. Instead of arguing, or explaining, or apologizing, or, worst of all, ignoring them, the nurse should verbally recognize the *feelings* behind what Mrs. Ager is saying. Let us consider some of Mrs. Ager's daily complaints and two possible sets of answers to them, one set using the technic of recognition of feeling.

Complaint: You're late again. I thought you'd never get here!

1. I came as soon as I could but we've really been busy.

2. It must seem very late to you when you've been looking forward so much to having someone come.

Complaint: Can't you rub a little harder? You're just pushing the washcloth over me.

1. I guess I was afraid of hurting you by rubbing too hard.

2. It's no fun to have someone else do this for you, is it?

Complaint: You didn't get my ears dry again. You always leave them moist and it's so annoying!

1. I'm sorry. Here—I'll dry them again. Is that better?

2. Yes, that must be very uncomfortable for you. I'll try again.

Complaint: There hasn't been a soul to see me this whole blessed week! People are so selfish, never thinking of others—of me here in this apartment all alone.

1. Don't worry. Mrs. B. usually comes in once a week or so, doesn't she? She'll probably be dropping in soon.	2. You're feeling pretty lonely this morning, aren't you? It's not easy to feel that people don't care about us.

On the basis of experience with the use of simple recognition of someone's feelings, we can surmise the course the conversation would take, depending upon the nurse's comments. With the first set of responses, a patient, feeling irritable, depressed and full of self-pity, could (and usually would) argue in each instance. The second set of responses, using recognition of feeling, opens the door to additional complaints, which in turn should receive the same kind of response. The outcome usually is that the complaints, anxieties and other negative feelings are released with their acceptance by the nurse. After that, it is not unusual for the patient himself to begin to hear how he sounds and to take the first step toward behaving differently. Using the episode in which Miss Watson lost her temper, we will illustrate how a different attitude on Mrs. Ager's part might have been achieved.

Mrs. Ager: It's a terrible thing to have to be dependent on visiting nurses. You never know what time they'll turn up, and when they do get here they only half do the job.

Miss Watson: Right now you feel pretty angry with visiting nurses, don't you, Mrs. Ager?

Mrs. Ager: I certainly do! And believe me, I won't give one dime to the United Fund this year, because you nurses get part of that too. If I weren't helpless I'd never let one inside this house again!

Miss Watson: Having to depend on us makes you feel like fighting back at us, I guess. I can understand that.

Mrs. Ager: You! Humph! A lot you understand!

Miss Watson: Sometimes it must seem to you that I don't understand very much. You're pretty angry with me especially, aren't you?

Mrs. Ager: You're the worst of the lot. You go on doing your work and all the time I know that you don't care about me at all!

Miss Watson: You feel that I don't care?

Mrs. Ager: Well, you certainly act that way. You've got a job to do and you do it. You want to get out as quickly as possible! You don't care about me, I'm just part of your work.

Miss Watson: I can see how you'd feel if you really believe I don't care.

Mrs. Ager: But you are always in a hurry.

Miss Watson: It must seem that way to you. You'd like my visits to be longer, wouldn't you? I can understand that. Maybe that's what you mean by my not caring.

Mrs. Ager: Maybe it is. I just get so lonely, and then I blame you, even though I know it's not your fault.

This dialogue in a real situation would continue, and the tension and antagonism would dissipate as the patient found an acceptable release for her feelings.

Before leaving this situation we should consider further what actually did happen when the patient accused Miss Watson of not caring. Because of the special efforts she had made on behalf of Mrs. Ager, Miss Watson was hurt by the patient's accusation and she reacted with immediate anger, part of which was a defense against letting Mrs. Ager know how hurt she felt. Though nurses have the need to react emotionally just as have other human beings, as professional people they also have the responsibility for controlling their own emotions in certain situations. Sometimes such control may seem hard or impossible. About the incident, Miss Watson tells that Mrs. Ager never again ridiculed or derided nurses. This may seem to be a desirable outcome of Miss Watson's anger, but it fails to account for the patient's *need* to express her negative feelings about nurses. Miss Watson's outburst indicates also that she was taking personally feelings that the patient was displaying. To Mrs. Ager, nurses were a symbol of her unbearable dependence on others, and Miss Watson was the logical object of her hostility. This interpretation is born out by Miss Watson's later comments that when she was occasionally relieved by other nurses the patient compared them unfavorably with Miss Watson.

If it does happen that a nurse gives vent to her anger in working with a patient it is possible for the destructive influence to be corrected. A gracious and sincere apology can restore a good balance to the relationship, and sometimes can improve a relationship that was not comfortable at first.

Miss Watson's closing comments on the report of this case reveal that she feels she is doing little to help this patient and does not feel any closer to her. Perhaps if Miss Watson would allow Mrs. Ager the opportunity to express all her negative feelings, even those about nurses, with warm acceptance, she will have a greater feeling of accomplishment.

There is no question that the counseling of the lonely aged can be a disheartening process. An equally trying experience is answering the questions a child has about death in an effort to allay the fears of death. As difficult as this may be, the careful use of counseling technics may replace possible panic reactions with a serene acceptance. The following case in which a student nurse did a skilled job in her handling of this situation is presented in her own words.

THE PRETTY PINK DAWN

Bethann was a lovely eight-year-old girl. Hers was a terminal illness. She was afraid and wanted someone with her much of the time. One morning she called me. I went into the familiar toy-surrounded cubicle and put my hand over her tiny, chubby, clenched fist.

"Nurse, what is that noise?"

"You hear the birds the doctors use for experiments."

"What kind of experiments?"

"Well, they test drugs and do operations on the birds to be sure they are safe for people." I had found that it is best to be truthful with children and not to talk down to them. I also remembered my own childhood and how I felt closest to adults who talked to me on their own level, thereby helping me to feel like an intelligent individual being.

She sighed, "Oh . . ." and closed her eyes, appearing to fall asleep. I waited, sensing that she still had some question and needed me near her.

"Do the birds ever die?" Her eyes were open again and full upon my face.

I know that a dying child needs words and serene, emotional support from an adult who recognizes fear and is able to help her meet the unknown with security. At this time, Bethann needed a composed and serene me with a truthful answer, for she had learned to trust and depend upon me.

"Yes, sometimes the birds die." I replied.

"Why?" (I knew she would ask this question.)

"Sometimes the drugs cannot stop the diseases the birds have; or sometimes the birds get too much of one of the drugs."

"Am I going to die?" Her question was straightforward, asked as only a candid, trusting child could ask it.

"I don't know." I hesitated for only a second and then went on, "We will all die at some time; it is only God's guidance of our world that determines when. No one can determine when it will be or how it will be; we must just live and try to see what is good in each moment we do have."

"Like that beautiful pink color that is filling the sky now, or a dish of ice cream, or the feeling I get just before I go to sleep? I'm happy then." She was smiling now. I realized that a weight had been lifted from her tired little body and that her mind was to some extent more free.

That morning at eleven o'clock, Bethann closed her eyes. "I'm tired, and I want to remember the pretty pink dawn of today . . ." She sighed and was gone.

9

The Nurse's Relationship with Drug-Dependent Patients

Although it may seem unusual for a book on human relationships to devote an entire chapter to the various drug dependencies, this subject is included here for four reasons. First, the problem is a growing one, resulting in tremendous social, economic, and medical difficulties. Second, it constitutes an area about which many nurses know little. Third, the lives of most addicts, including alcoholics, are characterized by interpersonal relationship problems with which the nurse is necessarily concerned. Fourth, with few exceptions, the contributions nurses can make in this area are of a counseling nature, utilizing the counseling skills we have already discussed. (The few exceptions are those situations, such as acute withdrawal, when counseling only cannot be effective and when other nursing skills may be necessary.)

It is difficult to determine the scope of the drug abuse problem. Most of the figures that even approximate reliability are related to hard-core narcotic addicts. These figures have come largely from the records of narcotic agents, the police, and our relatively few treatment facilities. According to the statistics available, it is estimated that approximately 80 percent of the nation's narcotic addicts are concentrated in four states. A great many of them are in New York because of the high incidence of narcotic addiction in New York City. Of course, more addicts are to be found in urban than rural areas because the dealers and pushers who serve as the source of supplies can more easily remain anonymous there. It has been said that eight large cities contain approximately 75 percent of the country's narcotics addicts, although no one really knows for sure the extent of the narcotics addiction problem.

Accurate figures on the number of abusers of other danger-ous but nonnarcotic drugs are even more difficult to obtain. We do know that this population is growing, but we do not have even an approximate idea of the number of those who are dependent upon marihuana, barbiturates, amphetamines, LSD, and other dependency-producing substances. Statistics are un-reliable, partly because of the different ways of interpreting the term "drug abuser"; some people use this term to describe both the experimenter who uses a drug once or twice and the fre-quent user.

It is not the purpose of this chapter to go into detailed descriptions of drug dependencies and their effects, but some information about them is necessary for all nurses. The recom-mended reading list at the end of the book contains excellent source material for those who wish to study the problem further.

In the past, drugs that were misused were considered to be either habituating or addictive, and four factors determined the category to which they were assigned: *tolerance, psychological dependence, physical dependence,* and *deterioration.* Those sub-stances producing all four of these conditions were considered to be addictive in nature. Those not resulting in physical de-pendence were considered to be habit-forming but not neces-sarily addictive.

The term *tolerance* means that more and more of a sub-stance is gradually required to achieve a "high." *Psychological dependence* implies that although the individual needs the drug emotionally, he does not undergo physical withdrawal symp-toms when deprived of it. When *physical dependence* is pres-ent, the person who has used the drug consistently over a period of time and who is then deprived of it undergoes a withdrawal syndrome, sometimes mild (depending on the substance itself and how much of it and for how long it has been used), some-times extremely severe, and occasionally fatal. *Deterioration* (physical, economic, and/or social) frequently accompanies prolonged, excessive use of an addictive substance and some-times accompanies excessive use of a habit-forming substance.

Although the terms addict, addictive, and addiction are still in common use, medical and other professional workers in the field of drug abuse now use the terms dependent, dependency, drug dependence, and drug dependent. The term dependence was developed by a World Health Organization (WHO) committee that met in 1964 for the purpose of clarifying the confusion created by the terms addiction and habituation. The WHO definition, in part, is as follows: "Drug dependence is a state of psychic or physical dependence, or both, on a drug arising in a person following administration of that drug on a periodic or continuous basis. The characteristics of such a state will vary with the agent involved, and these characteristics must always be made clear by designating the particular type of drug dependence in each specific case. . ."

Types of drug dependence

According to the WHO definition, the dependence must be related to a particular drug or chemical agent. For instance, dependence on the morphine-type drugs includes dependence not only on heroin and other opium derivatives, but also on the synthetic morphine-like drugs. There is also dependence on the cocaine-type drugs, on the barbiturates, on alcohol-containing substances, on the cannabis-type drugs including marihuana, on the hallucinogens including LSD and several other chemical substances that are less well known and less frequently used but which also result in altered states of consciousness.

Every nurse should know which of the previously mentioned drug dependencies are addictive, i.e., have the potential for developing physical dependence in the user. Even more essential, every nurse should understand that whether a drug is addictive is not as important as a knowledge of the total effect that dependence on it has upon the individual and society. Many of the abused drugs, even those not addictive, produce an alteration in the abuser's relationships to his total life environment. Substances that cause physical dependence, if used long enough and in large enough doses, are: all of the opium derivatives (morphine, heroin, codeine, paregoric), the synthetic drugs of the morphine type (meperidine, methadone), all of the barbiturates, and alcohol. All of these drugs are depressants and if used regularly will result in physical dependence; the one exception is alcohol, for which only certain people (alcoholics) develop a physical dependence. The amphetamine drugs and cocaine, all stimulants, do not foster physical dependence nor do the hallucinogens (marihuana, LSD, etc.). With two exceptions, cocaine and the hallucinogens, users develop tolerance for all of these drugs, which means that they must have larger and larger doses in order to develop the desired euphoric state. All of the drugs listed in this paragraph have the *potential* for developing psychological dependence.

Of course, many other substances are subject to abuse—glue and various other inhalants, and other hallucinogens. Not included in the WHO classification is a large number of drugs that today constitute a major part of the drug problem. These are known primarily as tranquilizers, antidepressants, and mood elevators. Once again, reliable statistics on the incidence of abuse of such drugs are difficult to obtain. There is some indication, however, that the number of abusers of the drugs in these three groups is probably higher than for other drugs, with the exception of alcohol. Dependence upon them is usually psychological. Their abuse frequently has its roots in a perfectly legitimate use, when the drugs are prescribed by a physician for the alleviation of "nervousness," depression, or anxiety. While this type of dependence affects primarily adults, many youngsters now are "popping" almost any medication they can get their hands on in their search for "kicks." It is not unusual for them to help themselves to the prescription drugs prescribed for their parents.

Marihuana, pro and con

It is not our purpose here to describe the effects of, or the treatment required for, any of the currently used drugs, but marihuana should be considered in some detail because it is in such common use. For a long time it was legally classified as a narcotic, although it is not a narcotic but a hallucinogen. It is believed that most teenagers smoke "pot" at one time or another and many are thought to be regular users without necessarily becoming heavy users. Inasmuch as there are no withdrawal symptoms, marihuana is not addictive. Probably many of the young people who try it do not continue using it.

Although a large majority of marihuana users do not become heroin addicts, LSD users, or "pill poppers," it has been estimated that as high as 90 percent of heroin addicts were first introduced to drug use with marihuana. It may be assumed that at least some of the LSD users also began with the use of this allegedly benign, mood-changing drug. Thus, youngsters looking for a more intense high may eventually move beyond the relatively harmless marihuana and turn to stronger, more harmful substances. The term "relatively harmless" is used deliberately because marihuana is not believed to be totally harmless; experts in the field recognize that at present we do not know all the potential dangers of its use. Some argue for legalizing it without restriction. Others, probably the majority, feel that total legalization is not feasible, but that laws governing its use should be less stringent and punitive.

HARMLESS OR DEVASTATING?

I once observed a 16-year-old girl having a "bad" LSD trip. We who were with her could not know the actual experience she was having as we tried to calm her until she could be taken to a hospital. All we saw were the outward signs, the screaming, writhing, and crying. Although presumably conscious, she seemed to recognize neither her surroundings nor the people with her. How could such an experience possibly be justified as a search for increased awareness, a heightened state of consciousness? A talk with the overwhelmed mother revealed that this youngster had been on drugs, beginning with marihuana, since she was *twelve years old*. On what basis, then, can it be said that marihuana is not dangerous?

A way of life

Many articles have been written about the life of the drug-dependent person. The heroin addict becomes a dropout from society by virtue of the habit itself. His entire life is devoted to his drug routine: obtaining the necessary money, contacting the pusher, using the drug, enjoying the high he obtains, and then starting the rounds again lest he be caught short and undergo the agonies of withdrawal. To a much lesser degree this total involvement is another danger of marihuana. Although not faced with the withdrawal syndrome, some of these youngsters devote their lives to obtaining and using marihuana.

Another effect of drug abuse on the addict's life style is that often he forgets about life goals that are considered acceptable; he develops a lethargy that undermines any activity related to constructive living. Thus, great physical, mental, and social potential may be lost to society.

One major danger in drug abuse that cannot be overlooked is its relationship to crime. This is particularly relevant when use of the drug results in physical dependence. A drug-dependent person, especially one dependent on heroin, will go to almost any lengths to obtain money to support his habit. Since the habit may cost him much more than he can earn, it is usually impossible for him to obtain the needed money without resorting to stealing or selling drugs himself. Women dependents frequently obtain their funds by prostitution, although they too may steal. As a general rule, the drug-dependent person is not vicious or aggressive, but he will usually run any risk to avoid the torture of withdrawal. Thus, drug-taking actually becomes a way of life. How can we know whether this was the cause or the effect of taking the drug?

We can not assume that the middle-class boy or girl who

experiments with LSD or uses marihuana on a regular basis has the same reason for turning to drugs as has the ghetto dweller (who is likely to be a hard-core heroin user). In both cases, using any of the drugs we have mentioned provides an *escape* but the environments being escaped are quite different. It is difficult for those who accept the mores of our middle-class society to understand people who choose to run from the security of such a value system, but it is not so difficult to understand the ghetto-dweller's desire to escape what frequently appear to be socially, culturally, and economically hopeless living conditions. Although a desire to escape from various social problems undoubtedly leads to much drug abuse, our society must take some of the blame for making this abuse possible. Doctors frequently prescribe dangerous drugs, hoping, but not knowing for sure, that they will be used according to directions and not abused. Today, the mass media bombard us with advertisements for drugs to cure one condition or another. We are medication-oriented, and frequently we overlook the fact that even the most familiar drugs may be dangerous. Another reason why drug abuse has become such a problem, especially among middle- and upper-class people, is that never before has a society been as affluent as ours. Whereas previous generations have had to work hard for what they obtained or achieved, many of our young people today have things handed to them. As a result, they are not as goal-directed as previous generations were.

Who are the drug addicts?

Drug abusers cannot be identified by race, nationality, socioeconomic level, or educational or cultural background. They run the gamut from the ghetto-dweller turned criminal to the respected physician who, using narcotics initially to relieve his own pain, has become "hooked." They are youngsters who become involved in glue-sniffing or marihuana use because they want to be a part of a peer group already indoctrinated into these forms of escape. They are suburban housewives who have sleeping problems and who are "helped" by prescriptions for barbiturates from family physicians. They are simply people, people of all kinds, searching for escape, looking for relief from physical or psychic pain, people in conflict with society's standards for them, people frustrated in their search for their own identity in today's mixed-up, violent world.

Treatment potential

The word "potential" is used advisedly here because whether the various treatment facilities that are now available live up to their titles is a moot point. In the first place, the rate of recidivism among drug dependents is very high. What little follow-up there is seems to be inadequate. Some facilities do claim certain degrees of success but their statistics, when studied closely, are rarely found to be scientifically accurate.

Three major approaches to the handling of drug dependents are: medical, penal, and, the newest one, the "concept" approach. Our consideration will be limited to the first and the last of these approaches.

Medical treatment facilities may be divided into two categories: inpatient and outpatient (or clinic) facilities. Among the inpatient facilities, the federally operated hospitals for addicts at Lexington, Kentucky, and at Fort Worth, Texas, are the best known. Some of our state hospitals now accept drug patients, as do some private psychiatric institutions. A few general hospitals, municipal, state, or private, accept some drug dependents for hospitalization during withdrawal. In the past few years some hospitals and rehabilitation centers for alcoholics have accepted nonalcoholic drug patients. It is difficult to evaluate the effectiveness of such treatment programs, and how objective the people responsible for such programs can be is open to question.

Another medical treatment that may be conducted on an outpatient basis is the use of methadone. Physicians who object to this type of treatment do so largely because they view it as a transferring of the patient's dependence from one addictive drug to another. Advocates of the method point out the following advantages: Methadone is cheaper and its regular use can obviate the criminal and underworld activities involved in obtaining morphine and heroin. Also, while a patient is on methadone, taking heroin or one of the other opiates does not usually create the desired "high." The ultimate objective in this treatment is total withdrawal, with the maintenance dose being gradually decreased. When withdrawal does not seem possible, a secondary objective is the legal use of the drug in maintenance dosage, which is felt by the advocates of the method to be preferable to the illegal use of the opium derivatives.

Scattered throughout the country are a few clinics that attempt medical and psychological treatment of drug-dependence victims. The term "attempt" is chosen deliberately because it is questionable how much can be accomplished on an outpatient (possibly once a week) basis with drug abusers. An occasional user may be helped in this way to "kick the habit." However, the major and most effective uses of such a clinic are, first, to refer the patient to an inpatient facility appropriate to his needs, and, second, when indicated, to give him continued supportive counseling and medical treatment following his discharge from an inpatient facility.

A type of treatment facility that has been growing in terms of both reputation and increasing numbers embodies the Synanon, Daytop, and Concept philosophies. Offshoots of all these organizations are scattered around the country. They actually developed years ago out of the Alcoholics Anonymous (AA) program, but their philosophies and directions have changed markedly from those of AA.

Three unique factors characterize these treatment facilities. Perhaps the most important one is that the staff is composed almost exclusively of former drug dependents. Another factor is the long period of residency required; those who are really motivated toward total rehabilitation remain in residence for at least 18 months and quite often for two years. The third unique factor in these facilities is that no medications or chemicals of any kind are used, and there is an absolute taboo on physical violence. As a way of expressing anger and hostility, verbal violence is encouraged at specified meetings, sometimes called encounters.

The major theory behind these treatments is that drug abusers have never grown up and learned to accept adult responsibility. Incoming residents are treated like irresponsible children who must gradually earn whatever privileges are available. Everyone is required to assume increasing responsibility for the operation of the residence, with the newest or most recalcitrant residents being given the most distasteful tasks. However, they have the opportunity to work up to responsible administrative positions.

Many professional people in the drug-abuse field question whether these ex-drug-dependent residents are able to continue functioning without drugs out in the larger community, away from the protectiveness and limitations established by the therapeutic community to which they have adjusted for so long. Those who have completed the Concept type of program successfully are considered "confirmed," and statistics from the therapeutic communities seem to indicate that the majority of confirmees have not returned to drug use.

However, in spite of progress that has been made, we still have a long way to go in discovering how to cure drug dependency of any type. Treatment facilities are relatively scarce, and, in many instances the drug problem is handled by penal personnel. The dependents themselves also create obstacles to treatment through their lack of motivation. Although some want desperately to get off drugs, others who say they want to be free of the habit only want to withdraw temporarily in order to lower their tolerance level so that when they begin taking the drug again they will need less of it to obtain a "high." They will thus, for a while (until the tolerance builds up again), need less money to support the habit.

TO JAIL OR ELSE

One young methedrine abuser, an attractive, intelligent boy from a fairly stable, but not wealthy, family background, came to a clinic (as many do) through the courts. Part of his probation requirement was that he must go to the clinic, undergo individual counseling, receive psychotherapy with a psychiatrist, and have group counseling. (The individual counseling was finally eliminated as unnecessary.) The boy has been extremely faithful to these commitments. He does not want to go back to drugs. Without much assurance, he says he believes he is thinking less about how wonderful it would be to "shoot" again. But actually, after all these weeks, he says emphatically that the real thing that is keeping him "clean" is a fear of going to jail. Perhaps even this motivation is better than none.

Counseling with drug dependents

Because so little is conclusively known about drug dependents, their personalities, their needs, their interpersonal relations, and their family backgrounds, it is difficult to spell out specific counseling techniques that may be effective with them. One problem is that drug dependents are often skilled "con" artists. Unless we can see the physiological results of the use of drugs (e.g., in the pupil of the eye), it is frequently true that we cannot be sure whether they are on a drug. (Incidentally, many of them come to clinic wearing dark glasses!)

A BREAKDOWN IN PROGRESS

For well over a year I worked with a 30-year-old, unmarried, homosexual woman who had been attending a psychiatric clinic for years. Her clinic involvement was interspersed with various hospitalizations of relatively brief periods. Her drug dependence was of the barbiturate type. We had established what I thought was a good therapeutic relationship. She made much of her willingness to share with me things she had never shared with anyone else. After about six months she had a "slip," and went back on the drug, although not to the degree that she had maintained before. With the help of one of the physicians on the staff, she was gradually withdrawn again, and weekly counseling continued for several months. Then it so happened that I had to be away for four weeks. The patient was prepared for this well in advance and seemed to accept it. After my return she frequently broke appointments, always with what appeared to be a good reason. It was several weeks before I learned that she was on barbiturates. In all probability, the real reason for breaking her appointments was that she was unable to face telling me of her latest slip. It is also probable that her return to drugs was an expression of her hostility toward me for being gone so long.

In both of these case illustrations it is possible to pick out personality traits which *may* characterize drug abusers. Dependence upon other people was a characteristic of both of these people. However, the young man was an extremely passive person, while the young woman tended, at times, to be quite aggressive. Although they were of average intelligence and both were high-school graduates, they were extremely immature in their reasoning and every other way.

Many drug dependents brought to a drug-abuse treatment clinic are quite young; frequently they are brought in by their parents. In one study it was found that narcotic dependency begins at age 19 or younger in 45 percent of the cases; 89 percent were addicted by age 29 or younger. Thus, dependents are not likely to be chronologically mature or stable community residents, or to be married. In those instances in which they are married there are manifold problems, producing great hardship for the spouse and children as well as for the drug dependent himself. Economic problems, especially, are overwhelming. It is not uncommon for both spouses in young marriages to be drug-dependent.

Summarizing what many of the experts believe about drug abusers, we come up with the following facts which are usually accepted by the members of the medical profession: (1) There is no known relationship between drug abuse and intelligence. (2) Drug abusers tend, on the whole, to feel inadequate and to suffer from both anxiety and depression. Whether this personality characteristic is due to the use of dangerous drugs, or whether it was a reason for starting to take them, has not been determined, and may vary with the individual. (3) Many experts believe that drug abusers often have special difficulties in developing and maintaining meaningful relationships with other people. Many begin their use of drugs in the teens because the special trials and conflicts of this period make coping with life difficult. Teen-age dependents attempt to find their way out of the adolescent maze through the comfort afforded by various drugs. For some of them, especially the college-age group, the use of drugs provides an adventure—something new, different, exciting, and rebellious. This is not to imply that rebellion per se is necessarily undesirable, but it should have as a goal something better than escape from reality.

What meaning does the foregoing information about drug abusers have for nurses who will be in counseling or nursing relationship to them? The counseling skills already discussed can be used, although there may be some qualifications. If we can accept that many drug dependents are extremely immature, we recognize that considerable directiveness in counseling may be indicated. When the counselor knows she is being "conned," she should make this known to the patient. In such a situation it is important to differentiate between the patient and his behavior. Because of the patient's feelings of inadequacy, guilt, unworthiness, and rebelliousness, it is necessary that *he* feel accepted as a person by the counselor, but she should *not* accept his undesirable behavior. If she is to help him, he must not think that he is getting away with "conning" her.

Most important in working with any drug dependent is the counselor's attitude about him and what he is doing. While she may not know the reasons for his behavior—whether it is caused by feelings of inadequacy, a search for meaning in life, greater conscious awareness, revolt against the establishment, a desire to escape—what she must always remember is that he is a human being, frequently pained and in conflict, and in need of all the supportive counseling help she can give, but particularly in need of being accepted as a human being.

Alcoholism

While alcoholism is a drug dependence of the same type as barbiturate dependence, it is considered separately here because it presents different social, cultural, medical, and therapeutic problems. In the first place, the use of alcohol in our society is generally accepted. This cannot be said so far of any of the other dependence-creating drugs. In terms of numbers, the alcoholic problem is considerably more extensive. An estimated 100 million of the people in our country 15 years of age and over, are users of alcohol. Of these, probably ten million are alcoholics, problem drinkers, abusers of the drug—it matters little what they are called. Each year about 100,000 people cross the line from social drinking to alcoholism. Our extensive alcoholism causes an economic loss to the country of more than two billion dollars a year. Also, for each victim of alcoholism there are considered to be four or five other people who are suffering as a result of the alcoholic's drinking; these are family members, friends, co-workers, and employers.

For many people the term "alcoholic" conjures up the picture of the skid-row bum. But as a matter of fact, a large majority of the country's alcoholics are people like us: husbands going to work on a fairly regular basis, housewives carrying on their household responsibilities to some degree, professional people of various disciplines, members of our families, relatives, friends, neighbors, and co-workers.

What is alcoholism?

The definitions of alcoholism are many and varied. Most of them mention one or more of the following characteristics:

an inability to control one's drinking, both when and how much to drink; and interference with one or more important areas of one's life, family functioning, financial responsibilities, social obligations, or employment status. The term implies a dependence upon alcohol with deleterious effects upon both the alcoholic and the society, particularly the members of that society who are closest to the alcoholic himself. Because the use of alcohol varies with different social milieus, another criterion is whether the drinker consumes more than is customary among his own social group. With extremely rare exceptions, *alcoholics* begin their drinking as *social drinkers*. Given a group of ten social drinkers, nine of them will continue to drink normally, according to accepted usage, for the rest of their lives. One of these ten will develop an increased tolerance for alcohol and will then become dependent on it.

This is a preaddictive dependence, a psychological dependence, and control of drinking is still possible. Even in this period the drinker becomes preoccupied with alcohol, gulps drinks down, sneaks drinks, and may have his first blackout. A blackout is not the same as "passing out." Blackout is a form of alcoholic amnesia in which an individual may be functioning apparently normally as he drinks, but later has no recollection of some or all of what he has done or said while drinking. This condition is difficult for the nonalcoholic, particularly the nonalcoholic spouse of the alcoholic, to understand and accept. Frequently a spouse accuses the alcoholic of lying about his behavior when he actually cannot remember what he had said or done.

The addictive phase of alcoholism is reached when the drinking gets out of control because the drinker, although he may have some limited recognition of his problem, does not really accept it. He always has reasons for drinking and often blames other people or circumstances. He may make some efforts, always unsuccessfully, to cut down; he feels remorseful about his behavior and makes further promises to cut down which he never keeps. This stage progresses and he finally enters an acute phase of alcohol dependence which he is helpless to reverse. All aspects of his life undergo deterioration; he may lose his job, his family may leave him, he begins to drink in the morning, and he loses all control over his drinking. Actually, his tolerance for alcohol *decreases*; thus the emotional and physical effects of his drinking become much worse with smaller amounts. If he does not receive help he begins to deteriorate socially, emotionally, and physiologically—a process that terminates in liver, brain, or other physical damage. The ultimate end is death or institutionalization. This process of becoming an alcoholic may move very fast or take as long as 15 or more years.

Alcoholism, like the other drug dependencies, is not a respecter of persons; it cuts across the whole of society, reaching the rich and the poor, the educated and the uneducated, the highest and lowest on the social ladder. Possibly because alcoholism frequently takes many years to develop, the alcoholic seeking help tends to be older than those seeking help for other addictions. However, there is now a noticeable downward trend in the age of alcoholics who call for help from treatment facilities and AA groups. This could mean that alcoholics are turning for help at earlier stages of their illness but, unfortunately, it also reflects the fact that the incidence of alcoholism among young people is increasing very rapidly. For many of them alcohol has become the drug of choice to replace other mood-altering drugs. In some communities children are known to have started using alcohol at the age of ten or eleven. Among the teen-age group, the upward trend has reached alarming proportions.

Although, in terms of numbers and the devastation it creates, alcoholism is a greater problem at present than the other addictions, there is one advantage: more is known about alcoholism and alcoholics than is known about other drug dependencies. It is true that behavioral science research has not delineated an alcoholic personality any more than it can describe the personalities of the other drug dependents, but there are certain facts about alcoholics, their backgrounds, and their current lives which can be of value to those trying to help them.

The family of the alcoholic

It is well known that the presence of an alcoholic affects the personalities of family members and undermines the functioning of the family as a unit, but it is also believed, although the means are less well understood, that family members contribute either to the alleviation or to the persistence of problem drinking. Any treatment or preventive approach to alcoholism should, therefore, include others in the alcoholic's life, particularly those whose relationship is very close.

Marriages in which the husband is an alcoholic are apt to be characterized by a high degree of conflict. The wife's complaint is usually her husband's drinking. The husband's complaints vary, but almost always include undesirable attitudes and behavior on the part of the wife, with nagging taking first place. These conflicts usually are of long duration, sometimes going back to the premarital days.

One of the functions of the counselor in working with these unhappy marriages is to help the couple work out a differentiation of their sex roles. These two people are completely unclear about what to expect from each other. A battle of the sexes is going on in which neither knows where he stands. Is the woman primarily a wife, a companion, or a mother to her husband? And what is he? Is he a husband, or is he a little boy to be taken care of? Because of cultural pressure, the alcoholic is constantly reminded that he is not the virile, adequate male society expects him to be, a man in control of his environment and able to care for himself. His wife's nagging and expectations only reinforce the feelings of inadequacy he already has. Her demands upon him also destroy his hope for, and fantasy about, being cared for and mothered. She may take care of him, but she exacts a big price for her ministrations, because she really makes him suffer.

One of the most common conflicts in these marriages is the struggle for control. I remember particularly a couple in group counseling: when we attempted to find out what it was that the wife really wanted, she said, "I guess I want him to *do* what I want him to do, and to *stop* doing the things I don't want him to do!" The husband in this situation actually did the controlling, but in a much more passive way. He withdrew, removing himself from his wife in every way possible, including a refusal to argue. This was infuriating to her; she would have given almost anything to get him to argue. He could always win, too, by simply going out and getting drunk, over which she had no control.

The children in such marriages are, of course, likely to suffer greatly. In our society children learn at an early age what is expected of them as males or females. When alcoholism is a problem for one of the parents, the sexual roles of the parents are distorted. The alcoholic, whether husband or wife, feels inadequate as a parent. The nonalcoholic parent then attempts to fill the roles of both father and mother, and is usually unable to do a satisfactory job at either. When the father is the alcoholic, the child frequently is caught in a struggle between a rigid, moralistic mother and an unpredictable father upon whom he cannot depend. Also, alcoholics are not *always* drinking; thus, the child has to learn to adjust his behavior to a constantly changing situation. He doesn't know what is expected of him, nor does he know what he can reasonably expect from others. A fact of major significance for everyone concerned with prevention is the higher rate of alcoholism among those who have had an alcoholic parent. Interestingly, also, the rate of alcoholism is higher than average among the parents of the spouses of alcoholics, particularly wives.

Studies have indicated that the wives of alcoholics often had emotional problems prior to marriage. Sometimes their own neurotic needs led them to select an inadequate, alcoholic husband whom they thought they could control; thus the woman's need to dominate would be satisfied: It is recognized that the most commonly used defense mechanisms of alcoholics are denial, projection, and rationalization. Studies have found these same mechanisms used by their wives. The wives have been found to be more than usually prone to depression, anxiety, various overt signs of nervousness, basic feelings of insecurity, and tremendous hostility which is frequently unrecognized, suppressed, or expressed indirectly. When it is unrecognized and repressed, the hostility is often converted into a physical symptom of some kind. The inadequacy of the alcoholic male, of course, plays into these neurotic needs of the wife. The spouses complement each other.

When we talk about the wives of alcoholics, we cannot accept this description as definitive, because it comes from studies of wives who stayed with their alcoholic husbands. Perhaps these wives are more neurotic than the many wives who divorce such husbands. It is true, however, that those who stay seem to need the opportunity to suffer, to be martyrs. One of the questions which should be raised about the personalities and neurotic needs of the wives of alcoholics is whether their problems existed prior to the marriage or whether they are the result of harrowing years of experience with alcoholic husbands. It is possible also that the male alcoholic gravitates toward the woman who is controlling and domineering in order to satisfy some of his own dependency needs.

While no specific pattern is followed by all of the families in which alcoholism is present, there is a general trend. As drinking and conflict in the home increase, the resultant shame and embarrassment lead to withdrawal of family members into the narrow confines of the home. In the absence of outside activity the family becomes preoccupied with the drinking problem: how to stop it, how to hide it, how to cope with it. Soon all of the conflict between the parents, between the parents and the children, even the ordinary conflicts that exist in a family where alcoholism is not present, are seen as having derived from the drinking. For instance, most of us recognize that during adolescence children naturally show a certain amount of rebellion against parental authority. Most families ride along with this. They handle it; they are perhaps upset temporarily, but not thrown by it. It is accepted as a relatively normal part of growing up. In the alcoholic family, this is often not true. Adolescent rebellion is magnified and blamed on the drinking. "If you hadn't been drinking, if you had been a better father, this never would have happened, he wouldn't have done these things!" And, of course, we know this is not necessarily true.

Eventually the nonalcoholic partner begins to feel less sure of himself or herself. He has been blamed for so long for being the cause of the drinking that he actually begins to feel guilty about it. The children are already shaken and insecure, and the alcoholic, feeling more and more guilty and anxious, needs more and more of the tension-reducing alcohol. Now, if no steps are taken to help the situation at this time, family disorganization is inevitable. The family members give up in their efforts to understand or to stop the alcoholic. The children finally are faced openly with the fact that the parent is a "drunk." No more efforts are made to keep the neighbors from knowing. The family ceases to care about being self-sufficient and turns to the court or to some community agency for help. At this stage the alcoholic father is usually totally excluded from the family. Many who work with alcoholics have found that this is one of the father's major complaints—the fact that he feels shut out —and he has been, literally.

It would be heartening to believe that relief from alcoholism would resolve all of the problems. It is not unusual at all for wives of alcoholics to say that this is all that is necessary. But after sobriety is achieved, and it is usually believed today that this *must* come before treatment for the underlying problems can be effective, there is an unsettling shift again in the family roles. The sober man, who wants to take what he feels is his rightful place as head of the family, runs squarely into conflict with the children, who have become accustomed to ignoring him and his opinions. Frequently he puts pressure on them, which they rebel against. The wife is afraid to relinquish the responsibility she had necessarily accepted; she feels uncomfortable discussing problems with her husband, because she has become so accustomed to avoiding issues. If he makes a major decision about something affecting the family and it does not turn out well, her feelings of superiority come again to the fore, and his own feeling of inadequacy is reactivated. Sometimes, in the wife's enthusiasm to have things done right, she attempts to manage her husband's life for him. She wants to make decisions for him and overprotect him. If he is already on the road to sobriety or is having some kind of treatment, her efforts can only interfere. Frequently, relinquishing her role as family head becomes so upsetting to the wife of an alcoholic that her own emotional symptoms become more apparent, or she may develop various physical symptoms.

An additional problem in marriages in which alcohol abuse has been present is the sudden realization that, with sobriety, the partners are strangers to each other. A very young couple for whom the use of alcohol has been a way of life since they met, may find that the achievement of sobriety completely upsets, possibly even reverses their perceptions of each other. Many such couples describe the frustrating, walking-on-eggs feeling that has damaged their ability to communicate with each other. Frequently both partners complain that anything they say is misconstrued and leads to an argument that results in a total breakdown in communication. They have never had the opportunity of knowing each other in an alcohol-free state.

The woman alcoholic

Although many of the problems of alcoholism are the same for both men and women, some workers in the field believe that for women alcoholics there are differences in the extent of the problem, in society's and the family's acceptance of the problem, and in the alcoholic's feelings about herself. An estimated 40 percent of all alcoholics in this country are women. This means that four million American women are alcoholics. The rate of alcoholism among women has been steadily increasing, which is quite natural since the number of women who drink has increased. We cannot be sure of the statistical accuracy of the preceding figures because many women problem drinkers who recognize that their drinking is out of control are reluctant to seek help. Sometimes the family of a woman alcoholic, even knowing about the problem, is terribly ashamed and afraid of having others know about it. Instead of seeking help, the family shields and protects her in the erroneous belief that they are protecting their own reputations. This reaction is, at least partly, a reflection of our society's misconception that it is more disgraceful for a woman to be an alcoholic than it is for a man. Her feeling of guilt is proportionately greater, which, in turn, interferes with a healthy life adjustment for her. Many women alcoholics begin drinking later in life than do the men. However, on the whole, their movement from controlled social drinking to the phase of alcohol dependence takes place much more quickly than for the male alcoholic. Also, many more women than men become problem drinkers because of some specific emotional or physical crisis or trauma. This accounts in part for their later start toward alcoholism.

When the husband is the alcoholic, his wife, possibly because of the neurotic needs we have discussed, wants to protect her husband as well as the family reputation. The husband of the alcoholic wife is much less tolerant and gives the impression of being far more interested in the family's good name than in his sick wife. This may be due partly to his inability to accept alcoholism as an illness, an attitude the nonalcoholic wife seems more ready to accept.

The role of the nurse

In working with alcoholics the nurse has a twofold role. She may have to care for the terminally ill alcoholic who has developed one or more of the acute pathological conditions resulting from excessive use of alcohol. Or she might be required to give nursing care during the withdrawal syndrome of alcoholism, which may result in convulsions, delirium tremens, or even death; nurses usually carry major responsibility on the staffs of detoxification centers. In both these instances the nurse's skillful care will be under the medical direction of a physician; therefore it will not be considered further here. While counseling may not be involved in these nursing situations, the nurse's attitude toward the patient and his family, even under these circumstances, may influence the situation for better or worse.

The second part of her role is directly involved with attitudes and counseling. Any nurse, including the nurse in the hospital, in public health, in a school, or in industry, is likely to be placed in a counseling role affecting the alcoholic. Every nurse may have some responsibility for counseling the alcoholic's family and possibly for early recognition of the illness. Because of this, all nurses should be familiar with the ravages of alcoholism upon the patient and his family, and when intervention may be indicated, they should know how to help these families resolve some of their problems.

A new dimension in the care and treatment of alcoholics with which the nurse should be familiar is the use of recovered alcoholics as nonprofessional personnel in treatment facilities. Unlike other nonprofessional personnel who look up to the professional status of nurses, recovered alcoholics look down upon professional people working in this field. In two alcoholic rehabilitation centers known to the author, the only professionally trained people are nurses and physicians, and it is inconceivable to the ex-alcoholic staff members that nurses have anything to offer, except such routine nursing activities as giving medication or care during convulsions, or taking blood pressures or temperatures. After several years of operation, only recently has one of these institutions included nurses in staff meetings! Part of this stems from the belief of many alcohol dependents that the only ones who can help them are other alcoholics who have gone through similar experiences. This is ridiculous, of course. All adults have had the kinds of feelings alcoholics have—feelings of inadequacy, pain, degradation, guilt, hostility, and many others. The origins of these feelings in non-alcoholics may have been different, but the feelings themselves are similar. Many obstetricians, for example, are phenomenally successful in giving pregnant women emotional support, yet these doctors never have had and never will have the experience of pregnancy themselves.

The use of counseling

I do not wish to leave the reader with the feeling that alcoholics, or other drug dependents, are unique in their need for, or reactions to, having help. The characteristics of a troubled alcoholic turning to a professional source of help are not different from the characteristics of any troubled person seeking professional help. However, the alcoholic and his spouse may feel more intensely about both their problem and their need for help. If the average person is anxious or frightened or resentful or bitter about needing help and asking for it, the alcoholic and members of his family tend to be more so. As with the other drug dependents, during the early part of counseling the alcoholic is desperately in need of some real direction. The classic nondirective therapeutic approach tends to be anxiety provoking and confusing. Another point to be brought out is the real value of joint counseling with the alcoholic and the spouse or another member of his family. The alcoholic is not living in a social vacuum and he needs to be treated in terms of, and in conjunction with, his relationships with the significant others in his life.

Often the wife of an alcoholic needs help to understand that nagging can be of no possible use against this problem, and that the husband should not be protected from the consequences of his drinking. The person helping the family must understand the intense frustrations, suffering, and deprivation the nonalcoholic spouse is experiencing. Sympathy with the alcoholic spouse can be carried to such an extreme that the nonalcoholic spouse begins to feel guilty and defensive and is inclined to want to take the blame for everything. If there is to be a change within the family, however, the spouse must see that there cannot be a continuation of the old ways of reacting, of relating to each other, and of behaving generally.

One way in which counseling with alcoholics and drug dependents may differ from counseling with nondependents is that the average person who turns to you for help is usually willing and able to reach out at least part of the way. This frequently is not true of alcohol or drug dependents. They tend to be distrustful, suspicious, and withholding of themselves, and the nurse counselor must reach out farther toward the patient, must actually give more of herself.

In an earlier chapter we pointed out that a counseling situation may be spontaneous and brief. The following case history describes such counseling with an alcoholic.

WHO? ME?

Some time ago my co-worker, John, and I were interviewed on a radio "talk" show. Our subject was alcoholism and marriage. There was a live audience, also. In the middle of the program the announcer was interrupted by a loud, irate voice from the back of the room. Although what the person said has been forgotten—if it ever was clear—he did sound inebriated. One of the employees quieted him, and it was all over in the flash of a second.

When our part of the program was over, we left the stage and walked through the audience to the door at the rear of the room. John had been right behind me, but I lost him when I reached the outside door of the building. I waited a few minutes and then left. When I saw John the next morning, I asked what had happened to him. He said, "Do you remember that drunk sitting in the back of the room? He grabbed me on the way out." John repeated their conversation. The man was very belligerent, and he said to John, "I bet you think I'm drunk, don't you?" John is a very casual, easygoing person, not easily ruffled, and slow. He said, "Well, I hadn't really thought about it. Do you think you are?" And the man said, "Oh, you professional know-it-alls are all alike! Everybody who takes a little drink now and then has to be an alcoholic according to you. That's what you said up there, isn't it? Well, isn't it?" John replied, "Not exactly. We don't have anything against drinking. Some people have problems with it and some people don't." The man said, "Well, I haven't a problem with it." And John said, "Well, you're one of the lucky ones." The man continued, "Do you know how much I drink a day? I drink a fifth of whiskey every day. It doesn't bother me a bit. What do you think of that?" John replied, "I'd say, you're pretty lucky. Most of us couldn't even afford to buy a fifth a day, let alone drink it." The man said, "I can afford it all right. I've got a job, and I'll tell you something else, I've never missed a day at work." John replied, "Boy, that's wonderful." "Well, nobody's going to call *me* an alcoholic!" John said, "No, I'm not going to. If you don't have a drinking problem, I don't think anyone ought to call you an alcoholic." The conversation continued like this for quite a few minutes. John listened and replied until the man gradually began to lose some of his belligerence and to slow down. As John started to make a move toward leaving, the man said, very hesitantly, "You wouldn't happen to have one of your cards on you with a phone number, would you? You know, I think maybe I do have a problem."

It may be difficult to accept that this is counseling an alcoholic. But if this man had been seen for the first time in an alcoholism clinic, the counselor's goal might have been similar. The counselor would hope to help the man recognize his problem and to motivate him to do something about it. In this case, John had achieved this goal by: *accepting* the man where and how he was at that moment; *listening* without condemnation;

and showing an *interest* in him. This is an oversimplified picture of counseling, of course, but it includes fundamental ingredients.

Training to do the job

The average nurse probably does not receive much education about alcoholism and the other drug dependencies. What nursing education in these fields does provide is a limited knowledge about the condition and care of the acutely ill drug dependent (alcoholism is now included in this term). As we become more aware of the problems and how to help these patients, nurses will have to learn more about how to work with drug dependents and their families.

Two points of view about counseling of drug dependents need to be considered. One is that a drug dependent is a person, and therefore you treat him—taking cognizance of individual differences, of course—as you treat any other person. The other is that the drug dependent is very special, requiring specialized handling and specific knowledge of his condition. Actually, both of these things are true. With all due respect to diagnosis, we counsel the individual not according to his diagnosis but according to his unique needs and his own particular ability to use help. However, we must know something about the condition itself in order to anticipate what the patient's needs will be.

The learning required lies in two major areas. One is knowledge about drug dependencies, their treatment and prognoses, about community resources available to dependents, and about ongoing research in the field. The other, possibly more important area is concerned with attitudes. Hopefully, negative attitudes about drug dependence, as about other stigmatizing conditions, have been counteracted to a degree by nursing education and experience. Nonetheless, some nurses retain a judgmental attitude about drug dependence. The possibility of modifying attitudes by education is an open question. Attitudes are "caught" rather than "taught." It is doubtful that existing attitudes about drug abuse can be influenced by the lecture method of teaching. However, individual conferences with staff members will undoubtedly be helpful and should constitute an important part of inservice training in drug abuse.

An institution or agency can approach training for work in the field of drug dependence in two ways. One is to have an inservice training program for the entire nursing staff; the other is to provide intensive training about drug dependencies for a few staff members who will have the responsibility for work with these patients. In general terms, either training program should cover the following areas of information: definitions; etiology; medical, psychological, and social ramifications of the illnesses; principles of counseling, including counseling of the dependent's family; current medical treatment; community resources; knowledge of the available literature and its source; and, if possible, field trips to agencies or institutions already working with drug abusers. It may be necessary for a nurse to acquire her education in this field on her own, particularly if she has been selected by her institution to become involved in one of the new developments in the field. This kind of training will become more and more common as the problems and concomitant interest in the field grow.

The basic elements of the nurse's training will be similar to those already outlined, but she will have to take the initiative for locating and using these elements. Here there is no substitute for people. Most of those already working with drug dependents in any setting welcome the neophyte and are happy to offer opportunities to observe, to listen, to question. Of course, there is a tremendous amount of resource material available for the individual who is training herself just as it is for the training of a whole or part of a staff. In many large communities there are frequent meetings on various aspects of drug abuse as well as meetings of Alcoholics Anonymous groups which an individual can utilize for self-education. The help of the latter for those who work with alcoholics cannot be underestimated. Less well known and less widespread is the group called Narcotics Anonymous (NA). When this group is available, it is as important a follow-up for the drug abuser as AA is for the alcoholic. In addition, both groups provide invaluable learning experiences for the nurse.

Finally, two points are worthy of reiteration. Drug dependents—whether they be heroin dependents, LSD users, barbiturate dependents, or alcoholics—are human beings. They are human beings with acute problems needing all the professional help available to them. The nurse's ability to make her contribution to any of these troubled people will depend upon two things: first, and probably of greatest importance, an attitude of understanding and acceptance; second, a great deal of knowledge and accurate information about these conditions.

10

Communication: Art or Necessity?

Although people have always been aware of the importance of being able to communicate with each other, probably no word in the last decade has grasped the attention of society more than "communication." This more intense awareness of its importance has led to the development of new and expanded ways of interpreting communications.

Occasionally we hear the term "the art of communication." In one sense, this term is valid, for communication at its highest level of productivity may be interpreted as an art. Certainly many art forms are recognized avenues of communication—painting, sculpture, music, literature, and drama, for example.

But communication is also a necessity. Indeed, it is the cement that holds all of our interpersonal relationships together. Without the ability to communicate, an individual cannot develop relationships with other people. Even the tiny infant communicates his feelings, but if he is to survive and enjoy some degree of satisfaction in life, he must learn to communicate in ways that will be understood by other members of the society in which he lives. Our focus in this chapter will be on the communication that takes place in the nursing situation.

The usual definition of communication is limited to "the conveyance of thoughts, words, letters, symbols, and messages to another." As most of us use the word today, its meaning is much broader than this. For instance, psychiatric literature adds to the above definition "the transmission of feelings and attitudes," and includes not only verbal communication, but the many nonverbal forms of communicating feelings.

Ideally, communication is a completed cycle. To illustrate: John verbally expresses to Mary an opinion on a conscious level, possibly tinged by his unconscious with emotion; Mary's sensory receptors pick up the words and the accompanying emotions. In turn, her conscious mind responds with words, while both her conscious and her unconscious minds sometimes involuntarily send a nonverbal emotional response to what John revealed. Thus, a communication cycle is completed. One might ask if communication actually would take place if there is no response from Mary. Probably so, assuming that Mary is mentally and physically capable of expressing herself verbally and of showing emotion. If she angrily chooses not to respond, this in itself could represent a response, thus completing the cycle.

While there may be many variations in her choice of words, depending upon the cultural background and educational level of the person with whom the nurse is communicating, certain basic principles apply to all communicative efforts if they are to be successful. Some of these principles are similar to those discussed in Chapters 7 and 8 as being an important part of good counseling. The person on the sending end of the communication should be clear, honest, and nonjudgmental, and avoid talking down to people. On the receiving end of the communication, one should be open-minded, listen attentively, accept the right of someone else to be different, and be alert to the emotional accompaniment of what is being communicated. As in counseling, the nurse must always remember that a mentally healthy individual must basically be responsible for himself, and our communication should not tend to take this responsibility away from him. These elements will be considered in more detail as we illustrate some of the communication problems nurses meet.

The communication about which we are concerned in this chapter, however, involves not only a response, but interpretation of both the original message and the response. It is in the interpretation of what has been communicated that many interpersonal problems develop. Some years ago a co-worker gave me a card with the following words typed on it: "I know that you believe you understand what you think I said, but I am not sure you realize that what you heard is not what I mean." This statement is an excellent illustration of what too often occurs in our attempts to communicate.

Types of communication

Many of the circumstances in mutually responsive communication involve both verbal and nonverbal methods of communicating. The two most important settings for mutually responsive communication are the one-to-one situations and small group meetings. Others, in which only a small share of our communication activities occur, also deserve mention, however.

One of these settings may involve one-to-many communication, that is, teaching and lecturing to large groups of people. The response from a large group is felt rather than heard. With experience, a good speaker should be able to sense whether his ideas or opinions are being understood and either accepted or rejected. He can then modify his presentation accordingly. In the teaching situation, responses to what we say are usually verbal as well as nonverbal, and the communication cycle is more easily completed than with a lecture audience. Some of our one-to-many communications take place through the mass media, such as radio or television. Here we may have responses from those around us, but not from the great unseen audience, at least not at that specific time.

Another major form of communication that does not provide for responses is the written word. In the last few decades, the number of nurses who have published books and articles has grown phenomenally—a very gratifying fact—but until fairly recently most of the textbooks used by student nurses were written by nonnurses. The written communication provided by notes in case records represents another communicative experience for nurses, and a valuable one. The importance of accurate, clear recording cannot be overemphasized. It should be factual and objective in order to lessen the possibility of being either misunderstood or misinterpreted, and, above all, legible.

Participants in communication

In today's nursing world the nurse must communicate with a wide variety of persons. In first place among all these people are patients and their families. The people in this group differ enormously in ability to communicate, in cultural and socioeconomic background, in personality, in age, and in many other ways. The nurse's communication with this group is important not only in terms of the welfare of the patient, but because these people are probably the most influential in determining how society as a whole views the registered nurse.

Physicians constitute another important group with whom nurses usually have a mutually interdependent relationship, and this may, in itself, foster communication difficulties. Other co-workers run the gamut from persons much like nurses themselves, in training, opinions, standards, and ability, to people who are so different from them in every way that nurses have difficulty in accepting them at all, let alone communicating effectively with them. Other professional people with whom nurses need to communicate include teachers, social workers, nutritionists, and the staffs of various community health and social agencies. There are enough differences in the professional backgrounds of all these people to create communication difficulties even though all are professionally trained. Another group that is gradually becoming more involved with nurses' activities is the growing number of so-called paraprofessionals. Whether or not nurses have negative feelings about paraprofessionals' increasing involvement in professional areas, these people are assuming more and more responsibility in the delivery of health services. Many nurses work extensively with volunteers and in this group, too, backgrounds, educational preparation, interests, and abilities are varied enough to contribute to communication problems.

Communication problems

Differences in professional background and abilities among all these groups is a major factor in communication problems. Having even more effect on the development of problems are differences in emotional level which influence communication and understanding. Awareness of this will facilitate the nurse's communicating with some assurance that her message will be accurately understood and interpreted.

While there may be many variations in her choice of words, depending upon the cultural background and educational level of the person with whom the nurse is communicating, certain basic principles apply to all communicative efforts if they are to be successful. Some of these principles are similar to those discussed in Chapters 7 and 8 as being an important part of good counseling. The person on the sending end of the communication should be clear, honest, and nonjudgmental, and avoid talking down to people. On the receiving end of the communication, one should be open-minded, listen attentively, accept the right of someone else to be different, and be alert to the emotional accompaniment of what is being communicated. As in counseling, the nurse must always remember that a mentally healthy individual must basically be responsible for himself, and our communication should not tend to take this responsibility away from him. These elements will be considered in more detail as we illustrate some of the communication problems nurses meet.

COMMUNICATION WITH PATIENTS AND FAMILIES

Of first importance are nurses' communications with patients and their families. Usually, but not always, this involves attempting to communicate with someone whose orientation is quite different from that of the nurse. She must be sure that what she says is clear enough to be received as she means it and not misinterpreted. It is fallacious to expect that nonprofessional patients and families will understand nurses' messages from the nurses' frame of reference. On the contrary, as professional people, nurses have the obligation to perceive the patient's or family's frame of reference and to try to reach this in their communication. For the patient or family member to express what he really feels, an emotional atmosphere that will induce spontaneity must be created. Frequently a nurse is perceived as an authority figure, and a person communicating with her will tend to say what he thinks the nurse wants to hear, rather than what he really thinks and feels, perhaps because he is afraid of ridicule or criticism. The nurse should counteract this by encouraging him to express any feelings he may have even though they may seem hostile or inappropriate to her. This kind of acceptance necessarily includes understanding and sometimes requires a tremendous amount of patience.

SHE ASKS ME OVER AND OVER

The following conversation, overheard in an official public health nursing agency, illustrates the need for patience in verbal interaction. Mrs. Smith, a young, competent, public health nurse, was told by the receptionist that Mrs. Brown was on the phone and wanted to talk to her. "Tell her I've left for the day!" snapped Mrs. Smith angrily. Then turning to those in the office she said, emphatically, "I know what she is going to ask me. She has asked me over and over again. I have explained and explained, but she keeps right on asking!" Obviously, an evaluation of Mrs. Smith's relationships with other patients would not be accurate if it were based on this single episode. After all, we all have our off days. The obvious breakdown in communication between her and Mrs. Brown should be explored, however. If the patient has the need to keep on asking, the nurse's explanations are not really being communicated. She may be giving too much explanation and not allowing Mrs. Brown enough opportunity to express her own feelings or opinions.

Communication involving the nurse, the patient, and his family generally pertains to two major categories of equal importance. One category is the illness itself; what caused it, what can be done about it, and what kind of physical and medical care is required. If hospitalization is a possibility, what will that experience be like? What about the prognosis? Whether in a hospital or community setting, the nurse will be expected to share her knowledge about the illness with both the patient and his family. Depending on the condition and the seriousness of it, the nurse may not be able to communicate along these lines to the recipient's satisfaction. The responses to some of the questions asked will be the prerogative of the doctor. Nevertheless, the nurse can dispel much frustration by encouraging the patient and his family to express their fears and doubts. The other category of importance in communication among nurse, patient, and family is the emotional or adjustmental difficulties growing out of the illness. These may run the gamut of potential family problems: economic worries, especially if the patient is the major breadwinner; meeting the patient's emotional needs; keeping the rest of the family as stable as possible; adjusting to changing relationships, possibly including changes in sexual activity; and, finally, fear of death. Actually, no segment of family life or the interfamily relationships is left untouched by the development of a serious illness of one of the members.

NURSES EASED PAIN WHEN WE LOST OUR CHILD

The literature contains innumerable instances of supportive nurses giving help to troubled families in times of overwhelming illness. One in particular is worth repeating; it involved the cooperation between a hospital nurse in pediatrics and a city public health nurse. Of all the tragedies nurses meet, none is more devastating than the youngster with a type of leukemia that does not respond to any kind of therapy.

One of these was Mimi, a beautiful five-year-old girl, youngest in a family of four, happy, lively, loving, and beloved by all the family, especially the maternal grandmother. The history of her illness was not unique. There was the initial diagnosis, the chemotherapy, and brief periods of remission at home alternating with hospitalizations. Eventually she went home to die. The child's suffering could not be eliminated, of course, but, as told by the family members, some of their pain was alleviated by the concern of the two nurses. Both always had time to answer questions or to listen when there were no answers. Both made the family feel special and cared about.

Frequently a child's illness creates destructive feelings in parents—anger and the "Why our child?" reaction. Almost always there are unjustified feelings of guilt which often lead to overprotection and the development of dependence. When a grandparent is involved, friction may result from that person's need to indulge the sick child, and any efforts by the parents to discipline or to foster independence in the child are resented. It is not unusual for a grandparent to blame one or the other of the parents for the child's condition, thus setting the stage for additional family conflict.

COMMUNICATION WITH COWORKERS

The second important group with whom the nurse must communicate effectively includes all of her co-workers—physicians, social workers, voluntary agency staffs, paraprofessionals, and volunteers.

A teacher of our acquaintance once asked a group of students to describe their communication with members of other professions who were involved with patients' care. Their responses backed up her own belief that unsuccessful efforts to communicate with co-workers are partly the result of the nurses' own feelings, not only about other professional people, but about themselves. About communication with members of the medical profession the students said, among other things:

"Medical personnel, even interns, feel they have more knowledge and experience than nurses." "They talk down to us." "Doctors don't always cooperate with nurses in carrying out hospital routines." "Doctors do not give credit to nurses for their knowledge about the physical and emotional welfare of patients." "Doctors generally do not treat nurses with the respect they show toward professional equals."

About their communication with social workers the students said: "Social workers make no effort to communicate with us personally. They use only the telephone." "They do not seem to trust the judgment of nurses in regard to patient welfare." "Often inquiries about the patient's home situation are interpreted as interference." It should be noted that occasionally there is an overlapping of social work into nursing that can lead to strained communications between the two groups. On the other hand, nurses are also sometimes guilty of not trying to understand social workers' responsibilities.

One observation that emerges from this study is that the nurses frequently felt they were being looked down upon. However, many of their comments reflected defensive behavior, the tendency to criticize other professionals, lack of understanding of other professionals' goals, unwillingness to accept the contributions others have to make, even a lack of trust of other health workers. None of these feelings are conducive to effective communications among co-workers. When nurses feel the lack of acceptance or lack of recognition by co-workers they are probably reflecting lack of acceptance of themselves as competent professional people on a par with other professionals. A more mature attitude and one more conducive to improved communication is genuine satisfaction when progress has been made because several people of different professional backgrounds have pooled their knowledge and skills in a cooperative effort. One public health nursing student expressed this attitude in a term paper in which she analyzed her relationship with a patient who was receiving help from several professional sources. She wrote, "I had to decide whether it was more important that I help the patient, or that he be helped." She matured considerably when she chose the second alternative.

The nurse's self-image plays a different role when she communicates with paraprofessionals. Members of this fast-growing group of health workers carry many titles, including nurses' aide, mental health aide, health technician, and alcohol or drug counselor. Many times the nurse sees herself as superior in training, education, and experience to the nonprofessional members of the health team. Not only does she perceive herself in this way, she actually is superior in these areas. In spite of this, or perhaps because of it, effective communication is extremely important if nurses and their patients are to receive optimum benefits from the work of nonprofessional personnel. The establishment of good communications with members of this group will enhance personal and professional growth for them and for nurses too.

Specific problems in communication

Having looked at some of the types of communication and some of the groups with whom nurses must communicate, let us now look at a few specific problems of communication. All people perceive things uniquely as a result of their own personality development and their unique experiences, both of which are different from those of anyone else. It is these differences that cause interpretative difficulties.

One important problem is created by the careless use of terminology. Nurses should avoid the imprecise and ambiguous use of words and be aware of the possibility that the other person may be using words incorrectly. In recent years many of us have been "sick" over the increasing use of the word "sick" to denote some form of mental or emotional aberration which the user is unable to define, or does not bother to define. The word has been used so loosely that it actually has lost its definitive meaning in everyday use. Other inaccurately and loosely used words are "neurotic," "hostility," "aggressive," "assertive," "inferiority complex," "uptight," "normal," and so on. Calling someone an introvert, a sissy, a bully, or using any label, will arouse different feelings in different people, and will elicit different responses depending on the person's particular background and experience.

Differences in social and cultural backgrounds are partially responsible for these varying reactions. Words or terms are sometimes used differently in different cultures; there may even be an actual language barrier. Even so, communication is frequently possible with gestures and signs, and certain facial expressions are universally recognized and interpreted. At the beginning of World War II a young nurse working in a defense area in the rural South discovered that cultural differences between herself and her clients had a real impact on her communication ability. Much of her work involved venereal disease interviewing, and some of it was unsuccessful until she asked a young doctor from the South to discuss the problem with her. Then she learned that between her "correct" choice of words and her Yankee accent, her patients were not comprehending much, if anything, of what she said. She did not do much better in understanding them, not so much because of accent, but because of their choice of words for familiar sexual activities. Their speech was like a foreign language to her, just as hers was to them.

Nurses need to be aware of such problems in understanding. If you were a patient being spoken to by a public health nurse in a language not your own, how would you feel as the volume of her voice increased and she became excited in her efforts to make you understand? We are often guilty of speaking more and more loudly to the person who does not understand our language. The only thing we communicate when our efforts become frantic is a putdown of the other person. Too often the message is received as "if you were more intelligent, you would understand me."

In addition to the difficulties arising from the simple use of language, other differences in social or cultural background create problems. Attitudes and behavior acceptable in one ethnic, national, social, or even religious group may not be acceptable in other groups. In communication the nurse must be aware of what constitutes acceptable thought, verbal expression, and activity in any specific subgroup of society. It is also necessary to avoid stereotyping, because in any specific group there are going to be great differences among individuals.

Another problem arises from differences in perception by people in different generations. Neither the elderly nor children enjoy being spoken to in a patronizing way. Sometimes the very old and the very young are able to communicate with each other better than with people in the middle stages of life. This may be because both are victims of having their perceptions ignored. It may also be that the elderly and very young perceive many things similarly. For instance, they are both accused of being forgetful, careless, demanding, or in the way. For nurses to have satisfying communication with individuals in either of these age groups, they must make the effort to get behind the words to their perceptions of people, situations, and circumstances. What are the perceptions of this small human being surrounded by a world of giants who have complete control over him and his activities? Sometimes we lose sight of the peopled world as the child sees it. And that irascible, opinionated old woman—what are her perceptions? How must it feel to be watching life hustle by through the activities of others rather than your own? It must be like a rushing river, carrying away everything in its flow while one badly bent tree limb is wedged between rocks, left behind as it were. For most of us, the frustrating, helpless feeling characteristic of many of the elderly is still ahead of us. It will be better than implied here, or worse, depending in part upon the communication skills of those who care for or about us.

Communication efforts with children include answering or in some way responding to hundreds of questions, many of which seem meaningless to the average busy nurse. Too often a child's questions are brushed off completely, communicating the message that the question is too unimportant to be answered. Or it may be answered fully and satisfactorily, completely ignoring the child's perception of the topic and the limits of his understanding. A most distressing and poignant memory recalled by a student nurse involved a nonverbal communication she received as a child from a public health nurse. The student's childhood had been one of material and emotional deprivation. On one occasion when her mother was ill enough to require the care of a visiting nurse, the house was dirty and untidy. Any help the nurse gave has been forgotten. What the student remembers is the nurse looking around critically, then saying, "Do you have any clean newspapers? I can't put my things down here" thus communicating to the child the inadequacies of her home, family, and life style.

Probably all communication problems have their roots in perceptive and interpretative difficulties. Sometimes a family member or one of a married couple will grow emotionally and intellectually leaving the other, or others, far behind. When this happens, as it often does, communication may be impeded or broken down entirely. This may be partly due to a universal focus on individual growth, including continuing education, with special emphasis on the needs of women. In fact, in many of the instances where this phenomenon has developed, it has been the woman of the family who has made tremendous strides in her efforts to develop as a person in her own right. This is to be expected, of course, as a natural outgrowth of the current emphasis on women's rights. Often when a wife feels she has grown and her partner has not, there have been unhappy results, beginning with the breakdown in communication. "We don't have anything to talk about any more!" Some women students taking courses beyond high school admit to finding other male interests at school, particularly when they do not have the backing of both husband and children in their educational efforts. Some marriages have ended in divorce because of this. It would seem that the person who has had the desire and opportunity for self-growth may also have an obligation to sharpen her sensitivity to the perceptions of the others around her and to make an effort to reestablish communications. Sadly, some women have used their families and husbands in fulfilling their growth needs, but have forgotten this after achieving their goals.

In many instances the wife has devoted the early years of marriage to caring for husband, children, and home. The husband, as a result of contacts in the working world, has developed broader, diversified interests outside the home and has become increasingly successful in business. The higher education that contributed to his success was frequently made possible by his young wife's willingness to work and support the family while he was in school. In a "good" marriage, the husband will try to enhance his wife's growth so that they may move ahead together. Unfortunately, some marriages fail because the husband feels his wife has not kept pace with his intellectual and social growth. Probably both partners are partially responsible for this failure.

SALLY AND JIM WORK THINGS OUT

A public health nurse recently struggled over such a situation with a family in her district. Over a period of many months, Mrs. King established a comfortable, friendly relationship with all three family members, Sally and Jim and their only child. While Sally was not unhappy, she had become restless and dissatisfied with her life. Just caring for the child, her husband, and the home was not enough to fulfill her. (How often we hear this!) She talked about going back to school and, with Mrs. King's encouragement, she did so. She made new friends, developed new interests, and became active in a women's self-help group. This turned out to be a serious threat to Jim, and all meaningful communication came to a halt. "What's the use of trying to talk to her? I don't even know her any more. She certainly is not the girl I married!" His attitude toward Mrs. King also changed for, unwittingly, she was squarely in the middle of the conflict. It appeared that she might have to move out of the case, but before doing so she asked for a three-way conference with them. Fortunately, the conference was successful in helping the couple to begin resolving their difficulties and reestablishing communication.

Some growth-inspired women are not actually aware of what is happening to them or to their relationships. One professional woman of our acquaintance continues to grow intellectually and has moved far beyond her high-school-graduate husband. When they are together in a group this woman constantly focuses on her professional interests to the total exclusion of her husband, and this bothers their friends. In response to a comment about her intense devotion to her own interests, she smiled comfortably and said, "We have our way of relating." The unspoken thought of the questioner was, "I wonder?" since there is not much evidence of communication between them.

Special kinds of communication

One of the most popular current topics and activities in the area of communication is small group relationships. Communication is the basis for all of the many groups that have sprung up in the past few decades. The names chosen by these groups reveal their similarities and their differences: sensitivity, self-awareness, assertiveness training, Gestalt, consciousness-raising, attack, encounter, confrontation, marathon, EST, recovery, family therapy, sex therapy, transactional analysis, psychodrama and so on. The names suggest the stated goals and the methods used in groups—increasing self-awareness, improving communication skills, enriching personal relationships, changing one's self-image, heightening consciousness, or developing greater capacity to feel and to share feelings with others. Perhaps all of these goals are expressed in the modern phrase, "getting in touch with your feelings." Some of the groups utilize exercises involving physical contact and a few of them use nudity.

The purpose of some of the groups is strictly self-help, and for these no regular leadership is provided. Most groups have some form of leadership—sometimes a professionally trained person, but often one with no training whatever except having been through the experience himself.

As with any activity that seems almost to explode into popularity, accurate knowledge about the potential value or harm of experience in these groups is difficult to obtain and even more difficult to evaluate.

The mass media have disseminated a vast amount of information on groups through television, magazines, newspapers, and books, some of which has been prepared by individuals who feel they have undergone a valuable growth experience and some by professional people, often psychiatrists or psychologists.

A few years ago a psychiatrist wrote an article for a daily newspaper outlining the dangers of some of the current groups. He included illustrations of emotional injuries sustained in the group process. The following quotation is from my letter-to-the-editor response which was also published:

> One of the appalling factors in the use of these allegedly "therapeutic" groups . . . is that they are frequently conducted by professionally untrained persons. . . . Apparently anyone who wishes to advertise himself as a group leader may do so. Presumably, the people in the case illustration (cited) returned to mental health. Others, as a result of such "therapeutic" group experiences, are beyond psychiatric help; some are dead. A responsible surgeon, when he makes a large abdominal incision, knows for what he is looking, removes the offensive part, and has the skill to heal the wound he has made. If a group leader is going to rip someone open emotionally, he should know what he is trying to do and why, and he should have the necessary professional skill to close up the emotional wounds he has produced.

Having noted some of the negative aspects and abuses of small groups, let us now consider some of their positive features. By participating in various groups, many people who have never had the opportunity to develop a genuine love relationship, whether with a parent, friend, spouse, or sibling, or who have never been able to recognize or accept their feelings or share them with anyone, may have a wonderful, growth-inducing experience. Among their gratifications in the group experience are the recognition that they are not alone, the knowledge that others are having similar problems and feelings, and learning that health, help, and hope all exist. Many of the current leaderless self-help groups have been careful not to probe too deeply with the result that they are doing a phenomenal amount of good. Among these are Alcoholics Anonymous, Alanon, Narcotics Anonymous, Overeaters Anonymous, and Recovery, Inc.

Basically two factors will determine the outcome of the "encounter group" experience for any individual; one is the degree of his emotional stability at the time; the other is the training, experience, and sensitivity of the person leading the group. There are many invaluable sources in the literature which should be explored by any professional person working with others to help them resolve emotional or adjustmental problems. The nurse especially should be alert to the variety of group experiences available, their potential for good, and the risks involved. Certainly these groups represent a powerful form of communication.

11

The Nurse in the Community

Early in this century a newly graduated nurse had very few options open to her in the practice of her profession. Admittedly, nursing had come a long way since it was first described by Florence Nightingale in her *Notes on Nursing: What It Is and What It Is Not,* but the employment opportunities for nurse graduates in the early nineteen-hundreds were limited to staff nursing, teaching, or supervision in the hospital, and to private duty, occasionally in the hospital but more often in the home where the nurse usually worked a 24-hour day. Today, nursing offers many varieties of opportunity. Various nurse specialists practice within the hospital setting and increasingly are being employed by the hospitals to provide a liaison between hospital and community health services in order to ensure continuity of patient care.

Expanding horizons

The greatest expansion in nursing has taken place in the community itself. As one reads of the newly developing positions for nurses outside the hospital, one has a feeling that the potential for nursing opportunities will stretch as far as the imaginations of nurses themselves. For many, the challenges in the community are greater than those in the hospital. The demand for specialized nursing skills per se is probably no more important, since the majority of the critically ill who require such skills are still cared for in institutional settings. There are other equally compelling demands, however, upon the ingenuity of the nurse in the community. She is away from the protection of the hospital hierarchy which will, and in some instances must, accept responsibility for her actions. At times, membership in the hospital hierarchy becomes irritating, especially when the focus seems to be upon trivia. On the other hand, hospital employment provides a sponsoring, protective umbrella which can lend comfort in the sometimes stormy weather that results from ineptitude in patient care. Help, advice, and established controls are always available in a matter of seconds. The nurse in the community does not usually have these supports. While they may sometimes be available, they are not always immediately obtained, thus making it necessary for a nurse to make her own decisions and accept responsibility for them. In some cases, it is only after the nurse checks back with her employer that she learns whether her decision was acceptable or wise.

Community nursing activities

Titles for community nursing positions vary depending upon whether the nurse has an employer, that is, a sponsoring agency, or whether she is an independent practitioner. Among the community nursing positions that have existed for years are public health nursing, in which the nurse works with an official agency; visiting nursing, in which the nurse works for a visiting nurse society or some similar volunteer health agency; industrial nursing; school nursing, in which the employer may be a board of education or a public health agency that contracts for nursing services to the school district; working as a nurse receptionist in a physician's office; or practicing as a nurse-midwife under agency sponsorship. Recently added nursing opportunities include such positions as psychiatric nurse-clinican who is employed by a community mental health agency, clinic, or crisis center; nurse-administrator of a nursing home or rehabilitation facility; county health nurse working on a rural mobile health unit. The role of the nurse-midwife has expanded; she is now sometimes sponsored by a private obstetrician, family planning program, or public health agency. Finally, we have the nurse practitioner, whose recent appearance on the nursing scene seems as exciting today as the beginning of industrial nursing or public health nursing did years ago.

These new nursing opportunities brought with them concomitant obligations. The nurse in the community today must be prepared to practice with greater independence and increasing responsibility. This requires a large measure of self-reliance. In the recent past, well-meaning instructors and administrators spoke so often about the "challenges in nursing" that the term became a cliché. Today, the term seems especially appropriate when applied to the expanded and still expanding horizons for nursing.

OVERCOMING REJECTION BY PATIENTS

Occasionally the hospital nurse is faced with rejection by a patient. Depending on her position, she may discuss it with her immediate superior in the hospital hierarchy. For a supervisor this could be the director of nursing or the patient's physician. If the patient's feelings are strong enough, there may be no further communication between the patient and the particular nurse. Should the same situation occur in the community, however, the developments would be quite different. For example, Miss Thomas had acquired the necessary advanced education and clinical experience to become a qualified nurse practitioner. With mixed feelings, Dr. Davis, a general practitioner with a very active practice, who knew Miss Thomas and had confidence in her, hired her to do physical examinations, take medical histories, treat minor illnesses and injuries, and act as a health educator to both his patients and their families. Both nurse and physician were somewhat apprehensive about how their partnership would work out, and both were eager for it be successful. Miss Thomas was gradually introduced to Dr. Davis's patients and to his methods of work.

One particularly busy day, three months after their partnership began, the doctor received a request for a house call which he turned over to Miss Thomas. The patient, Mrs. Batz, who was in her sixties, had made a good recovery from a coronary attack several years before. Dr. Davis's present goal was to prevent her from becoming a cardiac invalid. Mrs. Batz had few interests outside herself and her health. She frequently became apprehensive about some symptom and frantically asked for a house call when what she really wanted was attention and reassurance. She assumed that the assistant Dr. Davis promised to send would be a physician. Her surprise and disappointment on seeing the nurse were expressed in overt hostility and rejection. Attempting to create a new professional niche for herself in the community's health service delivery system, Miss Thomas could hardly explain to Dr. Davis that Mrs. Batz wouldn't have her. A nurse in such a situation certainly is faced with a challenge requiring special skills in communication, counseling, and interpersonal relationships generally.

The community health team

In community nursing the variety and number of productive interpersonal relations the nurse must maintain are almost unlimited. The concept of teamwork in the hospital is quite familiar. Because of the differences in preparation and experiential background of the various health professionals in the community, teamwork there becomes more complex. In spite of its inherent difficulties, the need for interdisciplinary teamwork in the community is imperative. An infinite number of community problems can be handled best by a team of professionals working together, but one problem that has grown to frightening proportions is child abuse.

TO BREAK THE CHAIN OF CHILD ABUSE

The Curtis family, consisting of Jack and Alice, two emotionally unstable parents in their early twenties, five-year-old Jill and three-year-old John, was referred to the Visiting Nurse

Society by the social worker in a family-planning agency. The public health nurse soon discovered a whole constellation of family and health problems. The collage of her findings was a classic picture of child abuse with its many physical and emotional ramifications. First, Jack and Alice were immature parents, both of whom had emotionally deprived backgrounds in which there had been a pattern of brutality. Second, there was also an acute economic problem, although this is by no means always a part of the child-abuse picture. In fact, it had initially been the caseworker in the department of welfare who had referred Alice and Jack for family planning when Alice became pregnant for the third time.

Jill was destructive, hostile, and physically violent toward John. John was timid, frightened, and withdrawn. Prior to the visiting nurse's first visit he had been briefly hospitalized for injuries sustained in a "bad fall." The nurse's suspicions were aroused when she learned that less than two months later he had had another "accident" that required attention in the emergency ward. A visit to the local hospital and a talk with one of the emergency room nurses confirmed what the nurse already believed. Both children appeared frightened of their parents, especially of Jack. Jill's fear was angry and aggressive; John's fear was timid, cowering. There was little evidence that these children had much contact with others; they seemed confined to the home most of the time. Some or all of the familial and individual characteristics of this situation are present in most child-abuse cases.

The Visiting Nurse Society's contacts with this family continued for five years, and, largely as a result of team efforts, some progress was made in the family's health and welfare status. Alice and Jack were given family planning information in the belief that these two troubled people were not emotionally equipped to be "good" parents. Jack was referred to a vocational guidance center for counseling that might help equip him for more reliable employment. The entire family was referred to a family service agency for help with their conglomerate emotional problems. Jill was referred to a kindergarten, and, after she entered elementary school, contact was maintained among the team members—teachers, family service personnel, the school nurse, and the nurse from the Visiting Nurse Society. John was placed in a nursery school which gave him opportunity to associate with other children as well as adults who were different from his parents. The Curtises were urged to become involved in a recently formed community agency for child-abusing parents. Jack was reluctant to participate and did not follow through after a couple of token visits to "get everyone off his back." Alice did pursue it and profited by her experience. The courts were not directly involved in this case, although the family had a history of being reported by neighbors for child neglect. In other cases court personnel might well be a part of the community team.

The remarkable aspect of this situation and others like it was the teamwork among representatives of the different agencies, with the public health nurse taking a leading role in pooling all these resources. No one of the health and welfare agency representatives could have accomplished as much working alone. This much community effort deserves a happy or successful ending. Here we need to ask, "what should be the criteria of success in such a complex situation?" One limitation we have to accept is that success does not necessarily mean a lived-happy-ever-after ending. In this instance, largely because of Jack's overwhelming emotional instability, the Curtis marriage eventually terminated. Alice, with tremendous difficulty, pulled together a life for herself and the children. The new baby girl was given a good chance not only for survival but for healthy development. John slowly moved out of his shell. Jill had some residual problems with aggression and hostility, but was functioning at a much better level. Most importantly, the terrifying chain of child abuse was broken. This problem appears to be self-perpetuating; it is often said that the little victims of child abuse today become the child-abusing parents of tomorrow.

Success? I believe so. It was the direct result of public

health nurses working in their own community as part of a
team and utilizing all of the community resources known to
them to be applicable in such situations. This kind of cooperative effort takes as much skill as working in a hospital intensive
care unit. Coordination like this also reemphasizes the potential
of the nurse in the community.

The preceding case report illustrates only a few of the
family problems a community nurse may meet in today's complex society. Inherent in every major social change are potential difficulties that may result from society's efforts to adjust
to the new, the different, the innovative. The changing status
of women is a perfect illustration. Originally developed primarily to attack economic discrepancies, the women's movement has now extended into almost every facet of our society's
individual, as well as collective, lives. Every nurse working in
the community has felt the impact of these changes in her patients and their families. Many social problems are related to
the changing status of women. Increased sexual activity before
or outside of marriage may lead to either abortion or unwanted
pregnancy. Lack of maternal supervision in the home sometimes contributes to the absence of self-discipline in adolescents,
and consequently to a large variety of emotional and social
problems. It is possible that the extremely high divorce rate is
related to, if not the direct result of, the desire of women for
greater economic and social freedom. Conflicts are arising
within the members of certain religious groups because women
feel they should have the right to determine the size of their
families. The force of these internal conflicts is felt throughout
our societal structure.

It is not the responsibility of the community nurse to
determine or to judge the effects of all these sociological changes.
But she needs to be aware of them and of their influence on
her professional efforts.

Another social change that touches the lives of all of us is
the shifting age of our population. Advances in medical science

have made it possible for people to live much longer than our forebears ever believed possible. For some fortunate individuals this means increased usefulness and capability into very old age. For others it means manifold problems of rejection by busy families, physical incapacities frequently accompanied by pain, and, perhaps the most painful development of all, loneliness. There can be no single solution to the problems inherent in the aging process. Many senior citizens give up while they still have potential for achieving more, for making additional contributions to society. A perceptive nurse in the community is frequently in a position to give the encouragement needed, not just to keep going and doing, but to find satisfaction in the process. Her awareness of her own feelings and attitudes about the aged and about growing old is a vital element in her ability to work successfully with these people. Furthermore, her awareness must include self-knowledge, that is, a consciousness of her own attitudes about all sociological change.

This is particularly true in the broader concept of community nursing. Counseling opportunities and responsibilities within the context of nursing care have already been discussed in detail. Today many of the community nursing positions are actually counseling positions. Some of them involve individual counseling. Many more involve counseling with specialized groups, for instance, groups of parents of mentally retarded children, groups of pregnant teenage girls, or groups of the elderly. The problems dealt with are not medical or nursing problems, but difficulties in adjustment and emotional problems. Some community nurses are part of a team in the private practice of counseling for any kind of emotional problem.

In many ways the community nurse has something unique to offer the counseling process that neither the psychiatrist, the psychologist, nor the social worker have. It is the very special kind of relationship that has developed over the years between nurse and patient or nurse and patient's family, a relationship involving mutual comfort and professional flexibility. In no other field of nursing is this as valuable as in community health nursing.

RECOMMENDED
READING

ALCOHOLISM

Alateen—Hope for Children of Alcoholics. New York: Al-Anon
Family Group Headquarters, Inc., 1973.

Demone, H. W., et al. *Alcoholism: An Evaluation of Intervention
Strategy in Family Agencies.* Final Report. Boston: United Community Planning Corp., 1974.

Hoff, Ebbe C. *Alcoholism: The Hidden Addiction.* New York: Sea-
bury Press, 1974.

Tracy, D. *What You Should Know About Alcoholism.* New York:
Dodd, Mead & Co., 1975.

Sources of available publication lists:

National Council on Alcoholism, 2 Park Ave., New York, N.Y.
10016.

AA General Headquarters, Box 459, Grand Central P.O., New York,
N.Y. 10017.

Al-Anon Family Group Publications, 182 Madison Square Garden
Station, New York, N.Y. 10017.

Publications Division, Rutgers Center of Alcohol Studies, New
Brunswick, N.J. 08903.

DRUG DEPENDENCE

Bourne, Peter G., ed. *Addiction.* New York: Academic Press, 1974.

Burkhalter, P. K. *Nursing Care of the Alcoholic and Drug Abuser.*
New York: McGraw-Hill Book Co., 1975.

Consumers Union Report. *Licit and Illicit Drugs.* Mount Vernon,
N.Y.: Consumers Union, 1972.

Glatt, M. M. *A Guide to Addiction and its Treatment.* New York:
John Wiley & Sons, 1974.

Weisman, Thomas. *Drug Abuse and Drug Counseling.* New York:
Jason Aronson, 1974.

Winick, C., ed. *Sociological Aspects of Drug Dependence.* Cleveland: Chemical Rubber Co., 1974.

EMOTIONAL DEVELOPMENT

Mezer, Robert R. *Dynamic Psychiatry in Simple Terms.* New York: Springer Publishing Co., Inc., 1970.

Starr, Bernard D., and Goldstein, Harris S. *Human Development and Behavior: Psychology in Nursing.* New York: Springer Publishing Co., Inc., 1975.

RELATING TO PATIENTS

Johnson, Margaret Anne. *Developing the Art of Understanding.* New York: Springer Publishing Co., Inc., 1972.

Lipkin, Gladys B., and Cohen, Roberta G. *Effective Approaches to Patients' Behavior.* New York: Springer Publishing Co., Inc., 1973.

Peitchinis, Jacquelyn A. *Staff-Patient Communication in the Health Services.* New York: Springer Publishing Co., Inc., 1976.

Ujhely, Gertrud. *Determinants of the Nurse Patient Relationship.* New York: Springer Publishing Co., Inc., 1968.

THE FAMILY, COUNSELING, AND PSYCHOTHERAPY

Bockar, Joyce A. *Primer for the Nonmedical Psychotherapist.* New York: Spectrum Publications, Inc., 1976.

Goldberg, Martin. *Psychiatric Diagnosis and Understanding for the Helping Professions.* Chicago: Nelson-Hall Publishers, 1973.

Harper, Robert A. *Psychoanalysis and Psychotherapy: 36 Systems.* New York: Jason Aronson, 1974.

Lieberman, Morton A., et al. *Encounter Groups: First Facts.* New York: Basic Books, Inc., 1973.

Satir, Virginia, et al. *Helping Families to Change.* New York: Jason Aronson, Inc., 1975.

INDEX

A

Acceptance
  by parents, 59–61
  degrees of, 59–60
  effects of, 12–13
  guilt feelings, 89
  of patient, 25, 88, 200–204
  self, 58–59, 91, 110
Accidents, 89
Adaptation, 8, 77–100
Addictive drugs, 234–236
Adjustment, *See* Adaptation
Adolescence
  emotional development in, 30, 39–41
  regression to, 41–42
Advice, 196–199
  significance of request for, 199
Aged
  communications with, 273, 281, 286
  and family crises, 110–117
Aggression, 40, 84–85
Alcoholism, 119, 121, 246–259
  age of alcoholic, 248
  blackout, 247
  definition, 246–247
  family problems in, 249–253, 254, 255, 256
  nurse education about, 259–261
  personality factors in, 249–252
  phases of development, 247–248
  requests for help, 168–173
  social drinking and, 247
  statistics, 246
  in women, 253–254
Anger
  defeating counseling, 204
  nurse's, 227, 230–231
  physical signs of, 83
  significance, 205
  See also hostility
Anxiety
  signs of, 166

  universality of, 160
  unrealistic, 153–154
Apprehension, *See fear*

B

Birth stress, 79
Blushing, 166

C

Cancer
  breast, 102–104, 177–179
  fear of, 149–152
  in child, 268–269
Charity, acceptance of, 110
Child
  abuse, 282–284
  communicating with, 273–274
  development, 9, 26–30, 34, 66–67, 75, 79
  family and, 58–63, 66–70, 88, 110–115
  fear manifestations, 14
  feeding, 64–65
  handicapped, 52–53, 61–62, 109
  needs, 50–56
  nurse and, 49, 57
  parents and, 62–65, 110
  rejected, 107
  self-acceptance, 58–59
  sexual development, 70–71
  siblings and, 71–73
  society's responsibility, 56
Cleanliness, compulsive, 36
Communication
  definition, 262
  encouragement of, 186–189
  in groups, 276–278
  interpretation of, 263, 274
  non-verbal, 166
  problems in, 266, 271–274
  types of, 264